Passages From The Past, Volume 2

John Douglas Sutherland Campbell
Argyll (Duke of), Hamish MacCunn

Nabu Public Domain Reprints:

You are holding a reproduction of an original work published before 1923 that is in the public domain in the United States of America, and possibly other countries. You may freely copy and distribute this work as no entity (individual or corporate) has a copyright on the body of the work. This book may contain prior copyright references, and library stamps (as most of these works were scanned from library copies). These have been scanned and retained as part of the historical artifact.

This book may have occasional imperfections such as missing or blurred pages, poor pictures, errant marks, etc. that were either part of the original artifact, or were introduced by the scanning process. We believe this work is culturally important, and despite the imperfections, have elected to bring it back into print as part of our continuing commitment to the preservation of printed works worldwide. We appreciate your understanding of the imperfections in the preservation process, and hope you enjoy this valuable book.

PASSAGES FROM THE PAST . .
VOL. II

H.R.H. The Princess Louise
(Duchess of Argyll)

PASSAGES FROM THE PAST

By His Grace
THE DUKE OF ARGYLL
Author of "Life of Queen Victoria," etc., etc.

WITH TWO PHOTOGRAVURE PLATES
AND OTHER ILLUSTRATIONS

VOL. II

London: HUTCHINSON & CO.
Paternoster Row   1907

Argyll, John George Edward Henry Douglas Sutherland Campbell

PASSAGES FROM THE PAST

By His Grace
THE DUKE OF ARGYLL
Author of "Life of Queen Victoria," etc., etc.

WITH TWO PHOTOGRAVURE PLATES
AND OTHER ILLUSTRATIONS

VOL. II

London: HUTCHINSON & CO.
Paternoster Row   1907

CONTENTS

VOL. II

CHAPTER XXI

Christmas Day, 1868, at Argyll Lodge—Mr. Gladstone—Politics—The India Office—Society dinners and parties—Curious trial in the Court of Queen's Bench—Lord Elcho—Fishmongers' dinner—Sister Scholastica—The Foreign Office and Persia—Party at Highclere—Lord Mayo's emus—Scots Education Bill—Bill for the Repression of Crime—Decision of the Convent Case—Mr. Fawcett—Parliamentary debates: Election expenses, the Ballot—Lord Lawrence—Tom Taylor's play, *Won by a Head*—Irish Church Committee—Marlborough Club—Agrarian murders—Newab Nazim of Moorshedabad—Visit to Germany—Berlin and Sans Souci—Berlin society—Land banks—Rent banks—Educational difficulties—The Fatherland—London—The Kriegschule . pp. 343-367

CHAPTER XXII

Ireland—Duke of Leinster—The Bishop of Down and Archbishop Whately—Nearly arrested as a Fenian—Irish police—" My race "—Assassination of Lord Mayo—Fenian murders—Provincial Home Rule—The Gaels—Protection—Dual ownership—Land purchase—Tenant right—Irish stories—The five old provinces . pp. 368-384

CHAPTER XXIII

France—The Emperor Louis Napoleon—The Tuileries—Visits of ceremony—Napoleon at Camden House . . . pp. 385-389

CHAPTER XXIV

Letters of congratulation on marriage—Lord Dufferin—Disraeli—Dean of Westminster—Lines by Principal Shairp—Offer of Canadian Governor-Generalship—Coburg—Lieutenant Campbell pp. 390-397

CHAPTER XXV

The Churches—Common forms of worship—Toleration—Girls' public day-schools—Poor Clergy Fund—Letter to Archbishop

pp. 398–406

CHAPTER XXVI

Nova Scotia—On the s.s. *Sarmatian*—Halifax harbour—Admiralty House, Halifax—Ottawa—Ontario—G.-G.'s Office at the Houses of Parliament—Prologue for dramatic performance—New Brunswick—Government House, N.B.—St. John, N.B.—Prince Edward Island—Toronto—Labrador dogs—Ottawa—Quebec—Poem by Louis Frechetti—Montreal—The River Cascapedia—The camp—Sport—The bear-trap—Labrador coast—Evangeline's country—Highlanders at Cape Breton—Ottawa—Dr. Macgregor—Westward Ho !—Lake Superior—Qu'appelle River—Fort Qu'appelle—On the Saskatchewan—Fort McLeod, N.W. Territories—Buffalo—The Rockies—The Cascapedia again—California—San Francisco—British Columbia—Victoria, N.B.—Santa Barbara—Monterey—The White House, Washington—Cascapedia Cottage—Middle Camp, Cascapedia River—Citadel, Quebec—Long Point, Lake Erie—Californian birds—New Mexican Indians—Scots in Canada

pp. 407–506

CHAPTER XXVII

The prairie—The Mormons—English and Scots emigrants—"Gone to Canada"—Calgary—Alberta—Need of railways—Lines on Alberta—Canadian prairies—Mounted Police—Marching records—Fort Shaw, Montana—Address to Mounted Police . pp. 507–517

CHAPTER XXVIII

Notes on Imperial Federation—Imperial Council suggested—Greater attention given to Colonial questions—Disadvantages of public discussion—Influence of sentiment in fiscal matters—Britain's interest to foster that principle—Necessity of encouraging Colonial manufactures—Moderation required in fiscal policy . pp. 518–524

CHAPTER XXIX

Dunrobin—The "Kraken"—The Gulf Stream—The *Dædalus* and the sea-serpent—Abundance of fish on the Sutherland shore—Harriet, Duchess of Sutherland, and her improvements—Benevolence of the family in estate management—Origin of the name Dunrobin—Mimic warfare—Old forts . . . pp. 525–532

Contents

CHAPTER XXX

Iona—Poem—Columba's grave—An enterprising snake—Beauty of the coast—Columba and Columbanus—Iona's cathedral—Discoveries on the island—Columba's hymn . . pp. 533-541

CHAPTER XXXI

The Isle of Mull—Loch "Baa," a water Paradise—Letter from Lord Ellesmere—Knock House—Maria Blachford—Seals and sea-fishing—The hind and her fawn—Inchkenneth—Visited by Dr. Johnson—Iona—Colouring of the coast—Mackinnon's Cave and Dr. Johnson—Ancient sepulture—Oak woods—Sport in the isle—Cul-ri-Erin and Cul-ri-Alban—Highland stories—An authentic ghost—Golden eagles . . . . . . pp. 542-559

CHAPTER XXXII

Kintyre, or Head of the Land—The Stone of Destiny—Southend, Kintyre—Golf-links—The MacDonalds at Dun—Improvements—Scenery—Antiquities and local industries . . . pp. 560-566

CHAPTER XXXIII

An Armada wreck—Bruce's charter—"Admiralty rights"—The diving-bell in the seventeenth century—The *Florencia*—Captain Pereira's escutcheon—Metal-finder and divining-rod
pp. 567-572

CHAPTER XXXIV

Changes in means of locomotion—Mid-Victorian coaches and coachmen—Old travelling carriage described . . pp. 573-574

CHAPTER XXXV

The founding of British East Africa—Enlargements and developments—Cape to Cairo railway—Importance of Nubia—The Mau plateau—Letters to Mr. Goschen, Harcourt, and Sir William Mackinnon—Progress of the work of development . . pp. 575-597

CHAPTER XXXVI

Uganda—Wealth of the country—Imports and Exports—Suppression of the slave trade—Progress of missions—The sleeping fever—Opposition of "Small Englanders"—Successful results achieved . . . . pp. 598–601

CHAPTER XXXVII

Country-house acting—*The Coach and Six*—*Diarmid*—Opera in English . . . . pp. 602–674

INDEX 675

LIST OF ILLUSTRATIONS

VOL. II

H.R.H. PRINCESS LOUISE, DUCHESS OF ARGYLL (*Photogravure*) *Frontispiece*

	FACING PAGE
A DOG'S DEVOTIONS	380
H.R.H. PRINCESS LOUISE	390
THE ST. LAWRENCE AND BATTLE-FIELD OF QUEBEC	414
WOLFE'S CREEK	414
QUEBEC	448
MIDDLE CAMP, CASCAPEDIA	450
LUNCH HOUR ON THE CASCAPEDIA	450
THE CASCAPEDIA	452
QUEBEC	452
"TRAKADY" ON THE CASCAPEDIA	454
CHELSEA, OTTAWA RIVER	454
THE CASCAPEDIA	456
RED INDIANS	466
ELBOW RIVER	470
RIVER SASKATCHEWAN	470
FRASER RIVER	478
INDIAN TORCHLIGHT PROCESSION	478
GOVERNMENT HOUSE, BRITISH COLUMBIA	480
THE CASCAPEDIA	480
THE FOUR SISTERS	482
SHUSWAP LAKE	484
THE FOUR SISTERS AND MOUNT HOPE	484

List of Illustrations

	FACING PAGE
MOUNT BAKER	486
SEAL SHOOTING, EGG ISLAND	492
FROM OUR SCOW	492
DUNROBIN CASTLE	525
IONA	534
IONA, FROM THE CATHEDRAL	536
DUNSTAFFNAGE	538

PASSAGES FROM THE PAST

CHAPTER XXI

Argyll Lodge, *Christmas Day,* 1868.—Mr. Gladstone dined with us yesterday. He is in good spirits, although obliged to become, as people say, "a Greenwich pensioner" (as M.P. for Greenwich) after his defeat in Lancashire. He expresses surprise at the number of his followers who have lately become Ballot advocates, and in his re-election speech said that freedom of voting must be secured above all things, but that he himself would still rather see an open exercise of the Franchise. Expectations seem to have been raised high that considerable reductions in army and navy expenditure may be made, and he thinks that at last "we shall be able to strike a blow at" the practice of allowing captains on detached service at distant stations to exercise their own discretion as to whether this or that may be considered an insult to the British flag. This can only be prevented by having no captains with ships at stations where insults may be given to us!

The cry of a "free breakfast table" set up by John Bright, in one of his latest speeches, is being much taken up. Cardwell deplores that so much is promised, making what can actually be done in the way of reduction of expenditure afterwards seem small. Gladstone repeated a good improvement for the church classification, "low," "broad," and "high," the new names being Platitudinarian, Latitudinarian, and Attitudinarian.

Things are looking more ugly in the East. France wants a conference (European), and will probably get it, the other powers not having much choice in the matter now that the Greeks have regularly set the magazine on fire. The assertion of their Minister for Foreign Affairs that it was not against any law that armed and organised bands should be formed at Athens, and march to Piræus to take part in helping the Cretan insurrection, although Greece is at peace with Turkey, must be looked upon as simply showing that a Government in Greece does not exist strong enough to oppose any obstacle to popular passion for aggrandisement.

I am busy every day at the India Office. Interesting questions about Salt Duties, Irrigations, Army Armament, and promotion of officers, are coming on.

Feb. 1, 1869.—London has been very dull. Weather warm and often wet, and few people in town. People are more comfortable about the East; for although Greece threatens to be troublesome there is a general opinion that she must be sat on if too bumptious, and Russia is not violently taking her part. India work of course heavy. A great lowering of salt duties in Bengal. A partial armament of the Sepoy army with the breech-loader—say a contingent in each Presidency. Keeping all the artillery in our own hands. The strengthening of the Bengal Government either by again dividing the Presidency or by giving new secretaries to the Lieut.-Governor, but with no decrease of the responsibility of the Governor-General. Nothing to be done yet, actively, to counteract Russia in Central Asia. Shere Ali, supported in Afghanistan with money and arms, has beaten Raman, and is *de facto* Ruler of Cabool. No Cabinet Councils except at long intervals.

Dined with Captain Horner. He is much against the notion of disassociating Indian and home army, with very short enlistments, from the past.

Two days ago a party at H. Reeves', of *The Edinburgh Review*. The Compte de Paris was expected, but was kept at home, owing to his wife having to take to bed. The De Greys, who were also to have been present, were prevented by the news of a sad hunting accident in Yorkshire, where a ferry boat full of men and horses was upset in the Ure, and several gentlemen, Sir C. Slingsby, etc., drowned. Some of Lady de Grey's relatives had been there, and she had not heard whether they had escaped. Later accounts said they had, and had done good service in saving life.

Courtenay was there, who was private secretary to Lord Dalhousie during his viceroyship, and seemed more annexationist than his great chief, who according to my father, always drifted rather than went into that policy.

Dined with Merrivale, who calls the India Office "Nova Scotia" because Grant Duff, my father, and I are all at work there.

Dined with the Gladstones. Lord de Tabley there. Talk much of election politics. Gladstone said he had stood ten contests, and never had an election petition go against him, and thought he could not stand it if he had, but "would shoot himself." A Cabinet to-day; outline of what is to be done with disendowment funds in Ireland pretty well sketched out. Gladstone said if the Tories were wise they would bring in a Bill for Household Franchise in Counties. In Ireland at least, we are nearly all pledged to vote for this equalisation.

Went to Queen's Bench Court, where Chief Justice Cockburn is having a curious trial, arising out of squabbles in a convent near Hull. One of the nuns, on account of various faults, was made to retire, as she says, through persecution of all sorts. She claims damages. Defence for convent people is that the Mother Superior only enforced rules sworn to by recalcitrant nun. A great crowd in Westminster Hall and Palace Yard, who receive the nuns on their appearance with no cordiality.

A pleasant letter from Mayo, from Calcutta. He declares himself to be as anxious for the success of my father's administration of India as if he were one of his (Mayo's) political friends. Mayo has already had a touch of fever.

Dined with Elcho, Lord Bury, and Lord Rosslyn. Elcho says Lamont of Knockdhu, late M.P. for Bute, is going to make an expedition to the North Pole, "where all Gladstone's enemies are now obliged to go."

Elcho spoke triumphantly of his election, though he had a narrow squeak for it. His coolness is amazing. One day, when canvassing, he met his opponent, Lord Wm. Hay, engaged in the same way, and going up to him, took him by the arm and offered to introduce him to some electors whose acquaintance Lord Elcho believed he had not yet made.

There is to be a request presented to Government, to order an inquiry as to how volunteer forces had best be reorganised. Rawlinson very anxious to show how easy it will be in a few years for Russia to bring down troops by steam transport to regions round Bokhara. Steamers to the Caspian, thence by railway (a new concession—or Government undertaking) to the sea of Aral, whence again by steamers up the two great rivers. Southward A. had lately found a mountainous range, easily flankable, and behind it, a fruitful valley, where an army might comfortably subsist. All this does not frighten most of us, for the distance still to be covered before reaching our northern frontier is very great, and the country difficult, and we are confident of being able to oppose any force debouching through the mountains if it ever got near the " iron ranks " of our army.

Dined with the Fishmongers, at their great City Hall. The entertainment was one to the Ministry. The head man, the Prime Warden as he is called, was very nervous, and read all his speeches from big foolscap sheets held in his hand before him. There were endless toasts, the dinner beginning at six, and lasting till midnight—six mortal hours ! All the Minister's names were coupled with some toast involving subjects on which they were particularly anxious, so soon before the meeting of Parliament, not to speak. Gladstone managed to fold good generalities in beautiful and earnest language. Granville, in replying for the Lords, very good, and reminded the Commons that the amount of business done in the two Houses must not be judged entirely by the amount of talk. He chaffed the Bishops, who had dined with the Fishmongers in the same Hall two nights before, with having been so jolly on the eve of such grave church events.

Feb. 14.—Went to Convent Trial. The Mother Superior under cross-examination, and excusing her petty bullyings of the Sister Scholastica, whose evidence has not yet in any way been shaken. It is thought the jury will give the lady (who did not want to leave the convent, and attributes all her annoyances to the Superior's wish to make her do so) damages, though the counsel for the defence says they are too poor to pay. The Roman Catholics take much interest in the trial, afraid of course of convents getting into bad repute.

Saw Hammond at Foreign Office, on the proposal to give the Persians some of our officers to drill their army. He has no objection, and thinks we are already pledged to give them some. Lowe and others of the Cabinet do not like the notion, afraid that Persia may only become a tool in the hands of Russia against us.

Sun., Feb. 21.—Highclere. The Carnarvons asked me some time ago, and I find a pleasant little party, consisting of Sir Wm. and Lady Heathcote, Lord Salisbury, the Mintos, and Lord Hardinge. Lord Salisbury's ease of mind about the Russians in Central Asia is very comfortable for the Russians and himself.

He would even allow them, unmolested, to take Herat. Lady C. tells a good story of Mayo and his gardener. It seems that Mayo, shortly after starting for India, bought a pair of emus and was very anxious that the birds should breed. He gave directions that he should be informed how they got on, and on his arrival at Bombay received this letter from the gardener: "My Lord,—one of the emus you left with me has laid an egg. We are doing our best to hatch it, and, in your lordship's absence, we have taken the biggest goose we could find to put it under."

Feb. 25.—A very good speech in the Lords from my father on introducing the Scotch Education Bill. There is to be a strong Central Board, with great powers for local compulsory assessment where necessary. We hope to get the Privy Council grant, without complying with the English necessary conditions for obtaining such grants of a classification of scholars. In England this is done that the richer ones may be obliged to help themselves. We, wishing to keep up the system by which many different classes attend the same school, detest classification. The Lords have had this Bill introduced in consequence of a complaint from Lord Salisbury that Government were giving everything to the Commons, and the consequence was that nobody could properly attend to or debate Bills that only came up to the Upper House during the dog days.

A Bill for the Repression of Crime, which Bruce was to have brought in in the Commons, is also to be given as a sop to the Lords to-morrow, and Kimberley is to bring the plan of the Government forward. Granville and Lowe are rather impatient with the Scotch wish to get the Privy Council grant without classification, and do not much like the principle of the Repression of Crime Bill.

Dined with Mr. and Mrs. Pereira. She was a Stonor, sister of the Monsignore, and liked much in Rome last year.

Feb. 27.—There is much excitement about the verdict given by the jury of £1,500 damages against the convent at Hull in favour of Miss Sawin, who has had to wait seventeen days till the trial was over. I have been to the court three times during the seventeen days, and have always found it crowded to suffocation. The priests were of course very anxious that the convent should escape, and all the Roman Catholics are loud in their condemnation of Miss Sawin, the recalcitrant nun.

March 17.—Dined with men who were with me at the Edinburgh academy. A good deal of speechifying, but the dinner was otherwise pleasant.

March 21.—The season is beginning, and the heavy work of the session has opened. There have been several interesting Parliamentary debates, the House being always so full that unless one comes for prayers, or indeed for half an hour before prayers, one finds every seat on the floor taken; an uncomfortable place in the Gallery is one's only recourse. The first division of interest took place on Fawcett's reiterated attempt to get the necessary expenses of election put upon the ratepayers. He talked his usual amount of nonsense about this enabling poor men to get into Parliament, when it is obvious that unless a constituency subscribes voluntarily to pay for a member's very heavy expenses, not only at an election, but during his residence in town, he cannot possibly afford to be a member. The necessary expense of hustings, polling booths, etc., are only a very small item in the long bill of costs.

One man after another in this debate proclaimed in the coolest manner that the constituency ought not to look upon him in any other light than as a man who had conferred a signal favour on them, and that therefore his burden should be made as light as possible. By putting the necessary expenses on the rates, we should educate the constituencies into taking a proper view of the transaction, and show them that they must no longer think that they were conferring a favour upon a man by choosing him, when in choosing a member they were only doing their "solemn duty." And all this after these gentlemen had, only a month ago, been going round hat in hand to voters, begging, cajoling, and hoping that electors would send them, and them only, to St. Stephen's. Of course the elector thinks that if he elects a man that man ought to be grateful. Certainly, if there are two of the same politics to choose from, it is a favour to return one of them, and I cannot see how you can make people think they ought to pay a man's expenses so long as he solicits votes. The only considerations that seems to me to weigh in the matter are the following:

That it is desirable that all election expenses should not be so heavy as at present.

That the most effective check had best be applied, whether by putting pressure on the candidates or constituencies.

That the candidate has in this instance no power of curtailing the expense, or that at least it is extremely difficult for him to do so.

That this is easier for the constituency, or ratepayers, who for this item of expense would be most competent watchers and cutters down of expense (on hustings, etc.).

Therefore they had best have the management and payment of it.

Then we had a ballot debate. This is a subject to be referred to a select committee. There is the moral objection against secrecy, which I do not think much of. The objection that it is un-English; yet no Englishman ever hesitates to influence public opinion if he can do it best that way—by writing anonymously to the Press. The objection that it is unmanly. Well, we may learn a lesson or two in manliness from Americans, and others.

Many holes may be picked in the present rather imperfect systems in other countries, but I believe that for every hole you can pick in a system of voluntary secret voting you can pick twenty in a system of open voting.

In order, economy, and increase of numbers of votes given, the advantage is with the ballot. There is of course one obvious danger, that men in a time of bad feeling would often give votes to a man who promised them anything they thought would most hurt the man opposed to them—that, in short, they would give votes in secret that they would be ashamed to avow openly.

There is the great question of machinery. It has been tried in almost all the States in Europe. In none has the experience been quite satisfactory. Neither is it in America. Yet I do not believe the American people would go back to open voting. G. Bunsen writes to me to say that in his constituency of Sollingen, his and his opponent's committee came to an understanding to try really secret voting, by having the tickets of each candidate printed on identical paper. The result was a really secret ballot. No one knew till the box was opened who had got the majority.

Better machinery exists in Australia. In some of the colonies there, there is only one ticket with the names of the candidates printed on it, and this is given to the voter by the Government office, in the polling booth. Each voter strikes out the name of the man he dislikes, and drops the ticket in the box. This system has been evaded by the man giving a false ticket, and not the Government officer's.

Then there has been the renewal of the Irish Church Debates. We are in the middle of the second reading. Nothing could be finer than the speeches delivered by Gladstone and Bright.

Sir John Lawrence has come back, and we have seen a good deal of the great and simple man; he is to have a peerage, and would like to retain his own title. There is, I believe, a Lord St. Lawrence already, but when Sir John was told of this he said, "Well yes, but he's a saint, and I'm a sinner."

April 8, 1869.—The wrangling over the Scotch Education Bill still continues. The clergy, with delightful disregard of each other's feelings, all pulling different ways. Many deputations came yesterday. The United Presbyterians are in favour of combined secular and separate religious " education," and oppose any religious teaching in schools, even if it be authorised by a majority of resident rate-payers.

The Lawrences went with my parents to Windsor, some days ago. Lord L. stayed talking with them till near dinner-time and then went off hurriedly to dress, and found that he had taken two coats with him, a pair of buckle shoes, but no tights or stockings. The company assembled in the corridor below. J. Lawrence sent one servant after another all over the house above, entreating for a pair of trousers. The Queen wanted to wait for him, and remarked that it was a very important part of the dress, she heard, that he had left behind him. My father suggested that it would only make him more shy if she waited for him, so they sat down, and after a while he appeared to make apologies, in ordinary evening trousers, with the bright buckles on his shoes below them.

A new play by Tom Taylor—*Won by a Head*, a story of modern life between 1840 and 1847—is a failure. A Yorkshire jockey rises from the post of valet to that of Prime Minister. Sensation is discarded, and the dialogue, which is good but not entertaining, plays round Italian Court intrigue, which an English audience is much too dense to appreciate.

May 2.—The Irish Church Committee has been slowly and wearily dragging itself along, and the night's discussions rarely close before one o'clock. On one occasion only has our majority gone down below ninety, while the quiet advance of the party shows good discipline.

The new Marlborough Club is a great success. I play bowls there, and sup on late nights, till three in the morning, and I find the exercise the alleys give one very pleasant exercise in town, where one can get so little.

May 14.—An old butterman, who was some time since promoted by the townsmen of Cork to the position of Mayor, has nearly succeeded in depriving us of our Whitsuntide holidays. At a dinner given in honour of some celebrated Fenians, about to leave for America, the butterman said that O'Farrell, who fired at the Duke of Edinburgh in Australia last year, was a man possessed with noble feelings. Of course it became necessary to prevent a man who was so liberal of his admiration from holding any official position, and a Bill of Pains and Penalties, depriving him of his office, was to be brought in. He was to appear at the bar of the house, and plead his cause. O'Donoghue and Maguire managed, however, to persuade him to send in his resignation, which he did, and then changed his mind and withdrew it. But then he started for London, and the popular applause that in Ireland had encouraged him being in England no longer audible, his courage oozed out, and a final resignation appeared. This allows us fourteen days of holiday, and I take advantage of it by starting this evening, or to-morrow morning, for Berlin. There have been some more agrarian murders, and a grim joke is going about apropos of a new Bill to provide a close time for the shooting of sea-gulls, that some independent member should bring in a similar Bill to provide a close time for the shooting of Irish landlords.

We have had an immense party at the India Office, in honour of a Newab Nazim of Moorshedabad, who wants a large sum of money, in addition to the £150,000 a year he already has, to provide for contingent wants. He has left nineteen sons and twenty daughters behind him and is melancholy about forty other children who have been born to him, but who have died.

Berlin, *May* 22.—The King and Queen are away. The Crown Prince is to go and see the new works at Jahde, and we are to send the *Warrior* from England to do him honour. The French Ambassador, Benedetti, was very jealous on hearing of the *Warrior's* intended visit, and asked Loftus why she was to be sent, and was told that it was only natural, Heligoland being "one of our naval stations" and so near, and the family relations so close. Not satisfied, he applied to the King to let a French man-of-war come to do him honour at the newly fortified harbour; but the King said he did not want any French vessels there, and is altogether inclined to be not polite, as no politeness was shown him when last in Paris—the Emperor, curiously enough, not making him a return visit.

Visited Sans Souci, which was looking lovely, with many flowers out, and the lilacs and laburnums round the fountains contrasting well with deep green of the orange-trees, and fine white-blossomed horse-chestnuts. Another time I lunched with two diplomatist ladies, and we had much talk about the state of German feeling. They both deny what Loftus affirms, that the feeling in the south is more hostile than a year or two years back to Prussia. But they think they are as slow and unready in the south as they well can be, and that in the event of a war with France a very marked inferiority would be shown by them in comparison with the Prussian troops.

There was a nice story of one of the South German Princes, he showing his picture gallery to a Frenchman, and saying, "C'est la gallerie du Schloss, ici sont les portraits de tous mes ânes" (*Ahnen*, German, "ancestors"). They think the pleasantest German Prince is the "poor Pretender" (to Schleswig-Holstein), the Augustenburg.

People are a little unhappy about the Artillery, as they have got to think the steel guns unsafe, the difficulty of casting them without air bubbles being so great.

The Radzivills are still in town, as are many more of my old friends, for the Reichstag sits till June, or longer, the members all at sixes and sevens as to the best way of imposing new taxes, to make up for the year's unusual deficit in the Federal Budget. Old Countess Pauline Neale I have seen, and was struck with the poetry of her expressions about her great age. "It is a great rank that I have—that God has given me, for few get to be ninety-five years of age; but I find it is a rank that weighs me down, and does not lighten life for me."

May 23.—Have seen a good deal at the club (now very nice and renewed) of a Prince Solkofski, who intends coming to England, as a diplomat, in a year or two. His mother was last year the representative of the Polish ladies who were so grateful to grandmama for the part she took in getting money for the wounded Poles.

A dinner at Lord Augustus Loftus's. There were about sixteen. Loftus goes on declaring that Germany is further off from unity than ever, and he defies anybody to bring the South Germans, "a different nation," into really close bonds with the North. He has been to Potsdam and was asked to stay to lunch, probably because they thought he must be in want of sustenance, as he took young Seckendorff for the Prince of Würtemberg, and went on "Royal Highnessing" him, to S.'s great astonishment.

May 25.—Dined with the Radziwills. Old Prince Wilhelm takes great interest in everything that goes on in England. The brother Prince Boguslave, three sons, and a daughter or two, with several nieces, represented the family, and we had besides the English military attaché, Walker, Windhorst, a former Hanoverian Minister, and Dr. Abeken, secretary to Bismarck.

Loftus against the Crown Princess going to Nordenei for bathing. He declares the feeling in Hanoverian society is still such that she will be quietly ignored, and that if she asks these people to any party they will not go. Further, that she will receive affronts that she will not be able to forget. He says at the same time, what I cannot quite understand, that it would not matter were it only the Crown Prince who was going there. "He was a Prussian, and could not help himself at the time of the war. But she is looked upon as a Hanoverian

Princess," and, if no disagreeables be created by unwise intercourse now, she may, in a few years, be of the greatest service in promoting good feeling between Prussia and Hanover. This, they say, must come soon, but it is not the time to try it yet.

The Schleinitzes, whom I saw in the evening, say that there are many people who are Prussianised in North Hanover, and they do not anticipate anything disagreeable. That "she may live in an imported Prussian society if she will." My impression is, that she will not wish to see any society except that of the bathing women. But perhaps she ought to be told what Windhorst thinks of the feeling towards her, on the part of the Hanoverians.

I dined with Bunsen and Herr von Paton the other day. The latter is a deputy who is enthusiastic about the effects of Stein and Hardenburg's Land Legislation, in creating a large class of peasant proprietors. I had been struck, while reading books on Ireland, lately, at the unanimity with which several authors who know Ireland well, wish to see a greater number of small-sized properties. On the other hand, from our own crofting experiences in the West Highlands, and from all one has heard of the misery to which one bad harvest can reduce the very small tenant class in Ireland, I was desirous of finding what there was in Germany to prevent excessive subdivision. This must, somehow or other, be guarded against in Ireland. In Germany the character and customs of the people form a sufficient guarantee against harmful subdivision. Whenever there is a Saxon population, primogeniture prevails as a rooted custom among the people. The eldest always gets the land, the younger being in some cases merely his farm labourer. In other parts of the country, where the population is not so purely Saxon, the strong Teutonic thrift and prudence again gives the land to one of the sons, not always the eldest, but sometimes to the youngest, the others being recompensed with money. I could only find one provision spoken of as a legal guard against *amoncellement*, and that amounted to nothing. It was a rule that existed in some parts against subdividing, when there was only a quarter of an acre to divide.

This would not do in Ireland. In the Provinces on the Rhine the Code Napoleon prevails and equal subdivision of land among sons is the law. But here the evil effects that would follow from such a course do not exist, for there are factories, large towns, etc., which give employment, and another string to a man's bow, so that it is not necessary for him to live by agriculture alone. Here there is the vine, which, I take it, is a more valuable crop than anything Ireland can produce. Seven or eight acres was given me as the amount of land on which a man in the Rhine Provinces could live, if subsisting only on the produce of his property. But this is the smallest minimum possible.

At the same time one can imagine a man, desirous of improving the land, laying out every penny he has on it, if it is his own freehold. Mayo, in his speech of last year, laid great stress upon the rarity of a farmer being found in the Fenian organisation. Why not, then, increase as far as possible the class whose interest in the land makes their existence a guarantee of peace? If they are inclined to be peaceful as tenants, they will be still more anxious for quiet if they are possessors of small properties. In the neighbourhood of towns, and where there are factories, properties even in Ireland might be very small. In the southern parts I think it would be necessary that they be of some size. Excessive subdivision ought there to be guarded against, if possible, by only allowing a man with some capital to profit by the advance of money by the Rent Banks, or whatever equivalent may in future be provided in Ireland, as the machinery through which (the landlord being willing) a tenant might purchase his farm. Herr von Paton and Bunsen both agreed in ascribing the content among the Prussian Poles to the Stein-Hardenberg Land Legislation. It was this too, they say, as provided in the plans of Russian statesmen for serfs, that rendered the last insurrection ineffectual. This may hardly be the case as regards Russian Poland, but I do not think it is possible to exaggerate the beneficial effects that must follow from the possibility of people possessing land of their own, where land can support them even in bad seasons.

In Ireland the extreme improvidence of the people in allowing every child a plot must be guarded against.

Educational difficulties are being discussed in Germany. Theirs do not seem as great as ours. The Roman Catholic demands are much less moderate with us than in Germany. Here they do not object to the compulsory school attendance, although it obliges children where the majority are Protestants to attend a school whose secular teaching is taught by a Protestant. They can always retire when religious teaching begins, and sometimes, when the minority is a considerable one, they have "parallel" religious classes, to which they can go to hear their own priest.

Old Prince Radziwill, when I talked to him about these schools where the population is mixed, said with reference to the minorities, "Of course, then they have to submit," as if no other thing were possible or desirable, and he is an earnest Roman Catholic.

It may be right to allow the new Central Board for Education that is to be created in Scotland to advise where Privy Council grants are still to be given to R.C. schools in the large towns, but for our landward districts I cannot see why the R.C.

Church should not be satisfied with a good Conscience Clause, and Protestant schools.

THE FATHERLAND

"Where lies the German Fatherland?"
　Asked poets in Napoleon's day:
'Tis where the Hohenzollerns stand,
　"From rock to sea"[1] they won their way!
Leaders of men who pay the price
　That Empire claims—self-sacrifice!

Imperial rule of peoples strong,
　Who strike to flank—behind—before,—
Who bore upon their limbs too long
　The armour's weight that served of yore.
But now spring forth, from lumber free,
　To fight, one host, "from rock to sea."

Bismarck and Moltke—brain, and force—
　And their old king shall aye be known,
Like those who o'er the Tiber's course
　Saved Rome, till conquest's seed was sown,
To grow to brave all tempest's shock,
　"From rock to sea," from sea to rock!

Temple of Union—Citadel
　Of Creed of German Brotherhood,—
Guarding great Fritz's lessons well,
　"From rock to sea" thy kings have stood,—
Whilst their Faith thine—what foe shall win
　Thy Brandenburger Gate, Berlin?

London, *June* 12, 1869.—From Berlin I railed to Cologne and Coblentz, and visited Gerald Talbot, a nephew of Lord Shrewsbury's, at one of the excellent Prussian War Schools (Schloss Engers),

---

[1] The Hohenzollern motto "Vom Fels zum Meer"—"From Rock to Sea," *i.e.* from Hohenzollern to the Baltic.

two miles down the river from Ehrenbreitstein. I wish we had some of their Kriegschule in England. They seem to me superior to our Training Academies for officers. Each man who joins the army has first to pass an exam., answering to our "Direct Commission" exam., but afterwards he is not allowed to join the regiment, whose uniform he at once dons, until he has also passed, after two years' instruction, the Kriegschule's exam. Talbot, a cavalry cornet, has to go through infantry, artillery, and engineer's instruction, as well as learn all the cavalry business. There is too much work exacted for the time given, and it must lead to cramming; still the result is that the officers are in the main infinitely better instructed than ours. Instead of having to learn their drill as ours do, from non-commissioned officers on joining the regiments, they join them thoroughly well up in drill.

The country was looking lovely, the vineyards beginning to get very green, and all the meadows near the Rhine full of white flowers.

London, 1868.—I have been dining out every day. Ireland is the subject of everybody's talk, and now men discuss the probability of the Lords throwing out the Irish Bill. I hope they will not for their own sakes, as well as for Ireland's. Young Trevelyan and the Radicals look pleased at the idea, as many wish for a stronger Bill, which they think they may get if the Lords raise an excitement in the country.

My father has come back from staying with the Queen in Scotland. People say that the difference between French and English Court at present is chiefly this : that one is too much Bal-masqué and the other is too Bal-moral.

CHAPTER XXII

Ireland

I HAD Irish relations in the Fitzgerald family, my mother's sister, Caroline, having married Lord Kildare, afterwards second Duke of Leinster. He and she were an excellent couple, devoted to Ireland, and living there during almost all the year. Their house was a large Georgian building near Dublin, where I was taken as a child, and much spoiled by the charming old Duke, who always wore a white double neck-tie and a broad smile. He delighted in showing off his house and park, taking people who visited him all over the estate in a couple of high jaunting-cars.

The first time I was there the Comte de Paris and his brother—both afterwards distinguished through the part they took in the American war, where they were called Captain Paris and Captain Charters—were of the house party. One of the interesting things about this place was the finding, in the lake in the park, which had been temporarily emptied of water, of a number of antlers of the extinct Irish elk, an animal whose horns were far bigger than the American and Canadian moose of to-day.

The Duke gave my father some fine specimens. The animal may, like the moose, have lived in wooded country, for all Ireland bears marks, in the peat and bogs, of having had a scrub growth of oak and hazel, but it is certainly wonderful how such an expanse of horn could have been guided through a thicket.

The Duke had another place called Kilkea, an ideal little castle with the battlements sloping back externally to their summits, in a manner only seen in Ireland. The place was very well restored, with the monkey crest of the Fitzgeralds, and their motto "Crom-a-boo" often repeated in the decoration.

The owner was benignity itself. Ireland's "Only Duke" he was, for the title of Abercorn received its dukedom later. There were many anecdotes told by the party there. For instance, there was an examining priest who said to a child, "Little girl, what is the state of matrimony?" "Please, sorr, it is just a state of torment and agony by which men are prepared for a better life." A catechist said, "Can a man have more than one wife?" The answer was, "Two only, as being necessary to salvation." He then made the children repeat the Creed, and they went on, one after the other, till they came to the confession of belief in the Church. A little girl then said, "Please, sorr, the boys who believe in a Holy Catholic Church are staying away to-day with a bad cold"

There was also a story told of my uncle, Lord

Carlisle. He had been saying, at a dinner at the Castle, that he thought the feeling of distrust towards ticket-of-leave men was much stronger than it ought to be. He added that for his part he would not mind having some ticket-of-leave men as servants. "Then," said an impudent dog on the other side of the table, "I think that in the morning your Excellency would be the only spoon left in the house."

The Bishop of Down talked of Archbishop Whately, who had the Protestant See of Dublin. The Bishop could not stand tobacco smoke. One day, when the Archbishop was his guest, he traced tobacco smell to a room, and entered grumbling, " Who's smoking ? " and found Whately doing his best to mitigate the crime he had committed of taking a cigar by sitting on a window-sill with his legs dangling over the wall outside, as he puffed into the open air.

During another visit to Ireland I was on the point of being arrested for a Fenian. Taking a tour to make up my mind on land tenure questions, I wanted to go by a Galway to Dublin express, which passed Sligo in the middle of the night. At the station there was no one but a fine and solitary specimen of the Irish policeman. I asked him the news, said I was waiting for the Dublin express, and, as he was communicative, we smoked cigars together in the waiting-room. He seemed very friendly, and hardly asked me any questions after

I told him I had come from Westport, when at last we heard the noise of the train's approach, and he suddenly said, "I must arrest ye."

"Why?" I said.

"Well, I'm told to," he replied, to my astonishment.

I said: "Oh, nonsense; you'll catch it for making mistakes. I'm going to the Viceregal Lodge, where they'll be after inquiring if there's an intelligent policeman at Sligo, and how can I say there is?"

"Well, what d'you call yourself? give me your card," he continued.

"I have no cards with me, but my name is So-and-so; I am going to the Viceregal Lodge. You can telegraph to watch me if you like," and I gave him another cigar, which he took thankfully.

"Well, I fear you're under arrest," he said, to my disappointment.

"Oh, rubbish; here's the train—I'm going to get in; I'm going to the Lord-Lieutenant."

He sighed. I took up my bag and went to the train. He followed. I took a seat. He went to the guard, and I heard a muttered conversation, and then the guard's voice raised louder, "What's he look like—does he look like a gintleman?"

I was pleased to hear the answer: "Yes, I think he does."

Then both came to the window. "Ye've got no cards?"

"No; I'm on a little trip to see the country, not to pay visits."

Then they withdrew and held a muttered conversation. "He's very like," I heard. "We'll telegraph; that's not him."

The constable came and said, "Well, I think I'll let you go as far as Dublin."

"All right—good-night," and the train left; and I hied in the morning to Lord Spencer, who told me that a "head-centre," as the Fenians called their officers, was being searched for, and later Lord Spencer said he saw the man in the street, and that he was so like me that he had nearly ridden up to him to greet him.

It is remarkable in Ireland how the descendants of the Norman settlers of the time of James VI. of Scotland, and also those of Cromwell's day, lead the way in any progress the country has shown. Dublin and Belfast are both fairly prosperous towns. Elsewhere there is practically nothing but jobbery, quarrelling, and stagnation, if not retrogression, in any urban centre. In politics the leaders were seldom "Milesians." Mayo, for instance, whose great-aunt married into the Gunning family, had more Norman than Celtic blood. It was this lady's daughter who became Duchess of Hamilton and then Duchess of Argyll. Lord Mayo served as Viceroy in India when my father was Secretary of State for that Empire. One day in London I was summoned by a message that

Lord Mayo

his private secretary wanted to see me, and I found him awaiting me in the hall, looking scared and very pale. He at once told me that there was shocking news from India, that the Viceroy had been murdered. Such a thing as assassination was so very rare in India that I could not at first believe it, but it was only too true. The Governor-General had been visiting the Andaman Islands, where there is a convict establishment, and one of the miscreants had sprung upon him and stabbed him between the shoulders, in the back. The funeral took place in Dublin, and I rode with the Lord-Lieutenant, Lord Spencer, to the vessel at the wharves in the Liffey River, when the body was brought ashore, placed on a gun-carriage, and the procession was formed, and marched along the quays and streets to the barracks, where we formed up to salute as it pursued its further progress to the country place he had owned and loved.

Lord Mayo was a great loss. He was a hardworking and able man, of clear judgment, and much valued by Disraeli, who was a very good judge of character. News from Dublin is associated to me with another terrible crime—namely, the murder of Lord Frederick Cavendish by assassins who mistook him for Mr. Burke, with whom he was walking. I was at Ottawa, and had been attending a play at the theatre, and my secretary, Col. de Winton, had gone to hear a debate in the House of Commons. Returning he said there was very bad news from Ireland, and told us what it was. We had plenty of evidence of murder conspiracies among the Fenians, but that they should have thought they could further their cause by killing one of Ireland's best friends surpassed belief. I telegraphed to ask, and the cable message came back, "Only too true."

It was a time when the madness of some people made them delight to wade in the blood of those who were willing to lift their country from the slough of wretchedness into which it had been plunged by its own headlong passions. The sympathy of the loudest among the people seemed to be ever on the side of the disturbers of their progress. When the Prince of Wales, in 1871, was at the Viceregal Lodge, and a reception to men of all shades of politics was given by Lord Spencer, the opportunity was taken to hold a meeting at the Duke of Wellington's monument, to demand the release of those who were in prison for treason felony, and who in any other country would certainly have been condemned to severer punishment than a few months in prison.

Is it ever possible to content the great majority of these people, so as to leave the discontented palpably in the wrong in the eyes of all? Their own early condition, when each race among them lost its independency in turn, because fighting constantly among themselves, was one of territorial division into five provinces. Such divisions might now again be instituted with some approach to the ancient state of "self-misgovernment" in narrow limits. The politicians who in the Colonies back up Home Rule demands for Ireland do this chiefly for the sake of the Irish vote in their own countries, whose Governments would never for an instant listen to such disintegration in their own cases. Were an Irish State to be attempted anywhere, by Irish emigrants, it would soon be made to conform to the laws governing the new Dominions.

No State in the United States would venture to defy the Federal Government, nor would that Government ever allow a State or collection of States to set up any separate authority within its jurisdiction. So with Canada : no single province or collection of provinces would be set up which would ever be able to levy duties according to a separate tariff against the rest of their fellow-citizens, or be in a position to "give the go-by" to federal law and order. The same with Australia. Such separation would involve power to make tariffs for any part of the country against the rest. None who draw part of their blood from Ireland can wish the islanders aught but prosperity. How can they ever be prosperous if they are always to be encouraged to go "agin the Government" which guides the policy of the united nations of our islands?

England found the separation from Scotland intolerably mischievous. Would any sane person in England or Scotland vote now for the repeal of the Union so violently decried in Queen Anne's time? The obligations of contract between man and man are often as derided by the Separatists as are the Union provisions in our Constitution. It is certain that if Ireland were alone to-morrow she would repudiate the rents now paid to Government for the land the Government Treasury is handing over to tenants. It is unfortunate that the landowning class do not still form the bulwark for government against the idea that the diminished rents are now paid as an extra British tax instead of their being regarded as paid to the landowners only. Having failed to support the men who had property, the Government's own property in taxes will next be assaulted.

No one who knows them can fail to like Irish people, though under the name one has to like many very distinct varieties of genus *homo*. Most of us have Gaelic blood in our veins. Perhaps the men who have least are the successful men in the north of Ireland, but they largely depend on Gaelic labour. It is humiliating to us who, in Scotland, came across the narrow seas from Ireland in the ancient days, to find the men we left behind us are in two-thirds of that country little advanced from what they were before the West Highlands became Earaghael, or the Land of the Western Gael. It is still more distressing if we see that they are led by a policy that separates them from those in England with whom the Scots have united successfully. We wish our success to be theirs; and when they turn from all counsel, and desire that which no men ever receive in any civilised state—namely, complete licence and freedom from any authority and unity—we recall the worst times in our history, and sorrowfully see that our old people, where unmixed, hark back to barbarism, and seem only as a dog, in which we have pride, returning to his vomit.

It makes plainer than ever that provincial government is the outside demand that could be yielded—that is, that the supremacy of the Central Union Government must be fully and unquestionably maintained for the good of both islands.

Most of the gentlemen whose country houses I visited in 1869 thought that they would soon have to take what capital was left to them out of the country, were England to desert justice to please her enemies. And who would bring new capital in the place of that driven away? they asked.

I really think many here would like to have Protection for manufactures against England and Scotland. If they do get this, it is difficult to see how Great Britain can help treating them as she treats Colonies—that is, give no money at all. Sentiment would not provide Ireland with money. They are always complaining that they don't get enough from England. If England did not stand at Ireland's back in finance, the smaller country would have little commercial credit. Erin would get poorer and poorer. There are manufactures that employ labour in the north. Complaint is made of low wages, yet at the same time complaint is also made of emigration. Surely if emigration were stopped there would be more people, and wages would fall; unless indeed the financial idea be that a high Chinese wall of tariff against everybody would give all residents in Ireland "more and to spare." Her whole financial idea seems so topsy-turvy, that one may call it for Ireland the "murder and turf" theory, a favourite expression among her imaginative friends, who say they hate us when we feed them, and imagine that when separated and we don't feed them, they will love us dearly. I think six months or one year's experience would change their ideas again, especially as Belfast will insist on having her own Home Rule. "Facts winna ding," as the Scots say, and Ireland must face plain facts of finance. Without England she would be poorer than she was in her worst days of ancient rapine, savagery, and starvation.

If you make joint ownerships in land, such "properties" must infallibly be battle-ground. Infinitely better have at once real ownership, the tenants to get the land either for so many years' assured occupancy according to the worth of their work, or as fully seized proprietors—the landlords to be left with what they have efficiently protected according to English systems. In a country where Rundale prevailed, the pretensions to individual ownership on the part of the occupiers, and the allegation that this is founded on historical usage, are ridiculous. An old Irish clansman never had any ground he could call his own as an individual. I am all in favour of charity legislation to guarantee the poor from cruel eviction, but beyond that, interference by courts, and the institution of joint property seems to me pure mischief, and fuel for endless legal contest between the partners in ownership.

The theory that a co-proprietorship in land was given to the tenants in James I. settlements is disproved, as far as all the original Clandeboy (Lord Dufferin) grants are concerned, by the wording of these grants, still in the possession of the descendants of the men to whom they were given. If the door be opened to the recognition of tenant right where improvements have been made by tenants, the door ought to remain open for the purchase of the "right," that it be extinguished. This has been done in cases in the North, such as the Maxwell and Dufferin lands. Sound commercial leasehold security is the only good plan. If this be kept, confidence, and capital with it, will return.

I am all in favour of the State compensating landlords in Ireland and giving the peasants land under £20 or £30 yearly rent, and then supervising them as to subdivision. Everything above £30 to be left alone to be under commercial principles.

How can anything make small properties numerous, except at the start, in a country of poor land, when good trade opportunities exist to make more money away from the land?

I am struck with the undesirability of the tenant's payment to his predecessor, and with the success with which unjust claims on the in-coming man can be "compressed." Dufferin has compressed it to very little, and on Maxwell's estate it has been almost entirely bought out. On Lord Downshire's it reaches £40 per acre, and the land is really not his own. On the Londonderry estate it is £20 or £25. I heard of a bit of land being negotiated between two neighbouring proprietors, and there it fell to very little. It might be extinguished altogether. But where it exists the custom is so strong that, unless the landlord bars it, he acquiesces in it according to English custom. Under such circumstances it ought of course to be a legal claim. The tenants agree that leases override custom. Legislation ought to give inconveniences to a landlord if he does not insist on a written bargain.

Here are some smoking-room stories:

Did you ever hear of an Irishman trying to recollect a date, and, after scratching his head for some minutes, saying at last with a grin and a passing gleam of intelligence, "Shure, yer honour, it was the year the peace broke out"?

**KILKEA CASTLE,
MAGENEY.**

"Prayers! Niniche!" This is the portrait of a black poodle which assumes this attitude when told to pray. At the word "Amen" it springs down from the chair.

A DOG'S DEVOTIONS.

"Well, we'll not get Home Rule for ould Oireland, and Ireland a nation," said an Irishman, "till France, and Russia, and Germany, and may be Austria, Italy, and the United States give them blackguards of Englishmen a good hiding." Then after a pause, he added in a proud whisper: "and the whole lot of them shoved together couldn't do it. Oh, it's the grand navy we've got."

A Roman Catholic Irishman once said to me: "Yes, if our friends who speak of a separate nation in Ireland were only a little more national in their policy in religion, and less national in separate ideas, we would be happier all round. Why should we take orders from Rome? Our national church derived through John, and not through Peter. We had a separate tonsure for our clergy. We had a separate calendar. We had a separate Easter. Why, the Japs have the Shinto religion. Bedad, sorr, with Rome we have the kiss-toe religion."

Among the many puzzles Ireland affords it is curious that many clamour for land there, and when they can't get all they want cross over to the United States, where they can have land to their hearts' content, and become independent farmers, and yet, when on American soil, they seldom seem to want any of it, and prefer to become labourers in the mining centres, or to remain in the great towns. You meet all over the United States and Canada any number of English and Scottish settlers who have taken up farms, but the Irish are rarely met with doing "that same," unless, indeed, they come from Ulster.

A man was tried for moonlighting, or trying to murder by night, and the evidence was overwhelming. It was a district where there was much intimidation. The judge charged the jury very strongly in favour of conviction. The jury immediately brought in a verdict of "Not guilty." The counsel for the prosecution started up indignantly. "Do you call this law, my lord?" The judge answered even quicker than had the jury: "No, sor, I call it jurisprudence."

A certain prominent Irishman protested against Irishmen being sent out to the Front to be killed, and then to come back to spend the remainder of their days in an Irish workhouse.

The same gentleman's knowledge of the anatomy of Scotchmen was evidenced in the statement that "as brave a heart beats beneath the tunic of an Irish Fusilier as beneath the kilt of a Gordon Highlander."

One of his colleagues announced, "I am now going to repeat what I was prevented from saying."

In eulogising the bravery of the Swiss, it was said that among those who took the field were "the beardless boy of sixteen and the grey-headed burglar of sixty."

Prisoner appears in dock.
Magistrate: "Well, what brings you here?"

Prisoner: "Two policemen, sor."
Magistrate: "Drunk, I suppose?"
Prisoner: "Yes, sor, both of *them*!"
Magistrate: "£2, or a month!"
Prisoner: "I'll take the money, rather than the month, thank yer honour."

Sergeant: "Why aren't you smarter? Look at your jacket."
Soldier: "I am as God made me."
Sergeant: "If I hever 'ears you mention that 'oly name in connection with such a thing as yourself, I'll have you before the Colonel."

Local steamer captain to naval officer, taking a trip on local vessel.
N. Officer: "This seems a nasty coast, full of rocks."
L. Captain: "Yes, sor, I know every one of they rocks. (Vessel strikes.) "Ah, bedad, that's one of them!"

1869.—Cork to Galway, where Barrett, Mr. Lambert's would-be assassin, had been tried a few days before. A mob collected and cheered the prisoner. They afterwards attacked a juryman who was supposed to have held out for a conviction against the majority who voted for an acquittal, although there was no doubt of his guilt. They would have killed him had he not taken refuge in a barrack. I found most of those I spoke to in favour of the mob. One said: "Oh, there's much to be said for him. He is a fine young man, sir, a very fine young man. He weighed thirteen or fourteen stone." This is much like what was said of some one being an awful sinner, when the first man who had mentioned the name said, "Sure, God Almighty would not damn a man six feet three inches in height." Some of our acquaintance might, on this theory, do anything. For instance, that excellent man the late Duke of Devonshire. He was a very tall man, and used to say that he felt so immense among foreigners, that when he was abroad attending parties in evening dress, wearing his decorations, he liked to see the company standing round him, reading the inscription on his Garter.

I have been imagining an Irish Government without a Lord-Lieutenant, and a Provincial Government based on limited delegated powers to Provincial Chambers, and with Dublin made like Washington, a separate "District of Columbia." Here a small Council of a few delegates from Provinces might have their habitation for transaction of some of the business affecting all four or five Provinces, now transacted at the Castle. This would be much like the ancient usage in Ireland of the "Five Kings."

My dear old German tutor writes apropos of this, that though I have a wide and high horizon, I have a strong fundament, which is most comforting when one meets with opposition !

CHAPTER XXIII

FRANCE

Emperor Louis Napoleon.—I knew his name first as a healer of my infant attack of chickenpox! His action when he changed his title from that of President to that of Emperor of the French afforded plenty of material to *The Illustrated London News* to picture the events at Paris, and these drawings cheered my convalescence at Castle Howard. The conflicts at Paris especially were most excellently portrayed by that friend of one's youth. The firing by high-shakoed infantry upon the Republican and Radical populace gave us most absorbing excitement. Many people disapproved of these proceedings, but they made me distinctly better, and gave me an interest in the movements of the world to which my illness had made me a stranger.

Long afterwards, Louis Napoleon's visit to England, and the kind reception given to him by our Queen, who admired the army which raised him to the headship of the Second Empire, and the beauty of his Spanish wife, the Empress Eugenie, made his career one that had much fascination for English boys. The great Whig ladies did not like him, but they all acknowledged his charming manners and the grace of the Empress. He seemed at all events to be firmly seated in the affections of the French people, and his name was in itself a talisman. It revived the memory of the glories of their arms under the leadership of his uncle. "When France and England are good friends," said almost every one, " there will be peace, for we two together can induce Europe to follow where we lead." And when, a few years later, the alliance was made which made us and the Sardinians fight side by side with the French against Russian aggression, and the Crimean campaign was undertaken, the last murmurs against Napoleon seemed to have died out, and every boy knew not only the names of the French leaders by heart, but even the uniform of every French regiment serving with our own. Tin soldiers made that possible, and more elaborate and expensive toys showing the Zouaves, the Tirailleurs, the Chasseurs d'Afrique; the Cuirassiers, the Guides, and the Generals St. Arnaud and Pelissier and their famous cook Soyer, who could prepare such good dinners in camp, all were household words to the militant schoolboy.

One good Whig dame held out stoutly during the time of his visit to England against showing him any attention. Her impudent boys determined to see if she would persevere in her attitude. Getting a photograph of Louis Napoleon, they sent it to her, and wrote underneath, "With the homage of Louis Napoleon," and imitated his handwriting. The lady, who was obliged as a great personage to be civil to all who were honoured by her sovereign, was "put in a state of mind" at this supposed civility on the part of her *bête noir*. "Oh, what shall I do? How can I write my name in his book? Why should he wish to be civil to me? I must ask Lord Palmerston's advice." I forget what the end of the affair was, but I think the boys confessed, and so relieved their mother's feelings, and excused her from any "reciprocity." She would certainly rather have died than send her photograph in return, although it was of course delicately suggested to her by the boys that it was the very smallest thing in the way of civility that she could possibly do to the head of the French State.

The English loved, as they always will love, to visit Paris; but "Society" did not go there to be entertained at the Tuileries. Those who frequented the French Court were few. Yet it was well worth while to see one of the great fêtes in those fine rooms which were levelled with the dust at the time of the Commune. There was one especially elaborate entertainment, when a ball was given and arrangements were made so that the guests could, from the central windows of the first floor, descend into the gardens by a temporary staircase, very handsomely designed and carried out, with a double flight of steps leading from a broad platform. Both the Emperor and the Empress were especially painstaking to be gracious in speech to all they could meet. He was naturally a silent man, and was short in figure, like his uncle, but lacked the first Napoleon's fine eyes and clear-cut features. His pointed moustache and "goatee" beard gave of course the fashion to his countrymen, and the adornment was called an "Imperial." The last time I saw him at the Tuileries, he inspected the Cavalry of the Household in the great square at the back of the palace, and went in and out along the lines on horseback. He did not ride along the last line, next the crowd which had been allowed to enter to see the sight, on the further side; and it was said that this was a precaution against assassins who were supposed to be waiting for the opportunity that might be given them if he went close to them. But it seemed more probably owing to fatigue, for the Emperor was then already feeling the malady from which he later suffered so cruelly.

When, after the final disasters to his arms and fortune, he came to England, he was very punctilious in paying visits of ceremony to those he had known. His quiet and rare, but kindly and courteous, speech was a contrast to the vivacity, unchanged as ever, of his consort. I saw him both at my father's house and at Camden Place, a house near Sevenoaks, which had been chosen for his abode by Doctor Evans and others of his old friends here. It was a pleasant residence, and is now, I think, a golf club's headquarters. The Emperor showed me the rooms ; and coming to the dining-room, which was panelled in oak in the French style of decoration, he told me, with a touch of that fatalism for which he was known, that he had bought a good deal of panelling like this on the walls at Camden House, at Paris some time ago. He had not been able to get as much of it as he wanted, for some had already been sold, the Parisian vendor could not say to whom. When the Emperor walked into the Camden House dining-room he found that the panels he wanted at Paris were in the new home chosen for him in England. He seemed to think it a sign of his curious destiny, the lot of a man to whom strange things were always happening.

CHAPTER XXIV

Letters of Congratulation on Marriage

CLANDEBOYS,
Oct. 11, 1870, 10 a.m.

Dearest Duchess,

I need not say with what delight I congratulate you. When I saw where Lorne had been, I guessed what was going to happen. The marriage has my entire approval, and I am prepared to give the young couple my blessing on the first occasion. Seriously, though, I do not think he could have picked out of all England a lovelier or more charming lady, and, in common with every one else, I have felt her attraction very forcibly. I write to catch the post, and will say no more at present.

Yours affectionately,
DUFFERIN.

Mr. Disraeli, with his humble duty, thanks Your Majesty for your gracious kindness in communicating to him, through Lady Eley, the truly happy news of the approaching marriage of the Princess Louise.

From an engraving

Louise Caroline Alberta
1874

PRINCESS LOUISE, MARCHIONESS OF LORNE.

The engaging demeanour of H.R.H., her beauty, her sensibility, and refined taste, had always interested him in her career, and made him desirous that her lot should be worthy of a nature so full of sweetness and promise.

What is about to happen seems to him as wise as it is romantic. Your Majesty has decided, with deep discrimination, to terminate an etiquette which had become sterile, and the change will be effected under every circumstance that can command the sympathy of the country.

Knowing the depth of Your Majesty's affections, which cares of State and the splendour of existence have never for a moment diminished or disturbed, Mr. D. feels that he will be pardoned if he presumes to offer to Your Majesty his sincere congratulations on an event which will consolidate the happiness of your hearth. There is no greater risk, perhaps, than matrimony, but there is nothing happier than a happy marriage. Though Your Majesty must at first inevitably feel the absence of the Princess from the accustomed scene, the pang will soften under the recollection that she is near you; and by the spell of frequent intercourse, you will miss her, Madam, only like the stars, that return in their constant season, and with all their brightness.

Lady Disraeli thanks Your Majesty for your gracious inquiry after her. She is, I am happy to say, quite well, and singularly interested in the subject of Lady Eley's communication.

Dean of Westminster to the Duchess of Argyll

DEANERY, WESTMINSTER,
Oct. 15, 1870.

MY DEAR DUCHESS OF ARGYLL,

You must let me send a few words of congratulation to you, on the wonderfully interesting event which has occupied our thoughts for the last two days. You know how very deeply we feel anything which brings new opportunities for usefulness and honour to you and yours, and you know also, perhaps, how very highly we think of the Princess Louise, and how greatly we have desired that she should find a husband worthy of her. There ought to be, and is, a splendid career open to such a marriage—full of difficulties no doubt—but as Grotius said in a sentence that I am fond of quoting, "Nothing is so worthy of princes and prince-like persons, as that which is difficult even to desperation." May all blessings rest upon them, and flow from them.

We are at home now, reserving ourselves for a start abroad, if we may have the chance of seeing Paris and Rome once more, after the astonishing events which have befallen each of them. We still remain faithful to the P. in spite of their prosperity. We earnestly hope that they will find some way out of their pandemonium, of which they have been the innocent creators. . . .

As for the Pope, I cannot look with unmixed joy

on his fall; partly because I feel that his ecclesiastical power will increase as his regal power diminishes, partly because I cannot reconcile myself to Rome becoming a commonplace city. Still I suppose it is right.

Yours sincerely,
A. P. STANLEY.

Oct. 1870. *Marriage Announcement*

Forster is enchanted; quite an ideal marriage, he says, with tears in his eyes.

Lord Derby writes very heartily, and says, " It will be undoubtedly popular."

Everybody at Balmoral is delighted, and they all speak with great affection of her.

LINES SENT BY PRINCIPAL SHAIRP OF ST. ANDREWS

While round thee many at this hour rejoice,
   And kind hopes are expressed,
One voice, I ween, you miss—one gentle voice,
   More kind than all the rest.

One heart that day by day unceasing prayer
   Had lifted for her boy,
Called to go forth, a worthy part to bear
   In his Queen's high employ.

Oft will your spirit turn to her lone rest—
   The lady most benign—
There, where blue waters of the well-loved West
   Round the dark hills entwine.

Yet doubt not thou, the prayers for thee she made,
   Long years since, are not lost,
But stored to fall with blessings on thy head
   When thou shalt need it most.

And the good spirit which made pure her heart
   Through all her earthly day,
Shall go beside thee, whereso'er thou art,
   To sanctify thy way.

Keep faith with that good past, and so unite
   With ever strengthening band
The love of a young people to the Might
   Of the old Imperial land.

Many the leal hearts that are waiting there,
   Upon that Western shore,
To hail Victoria's child, and him the heir
   Of the MacCailein Mor.

Many, but none more than the men who dwell
   By vast Ontario,
Speaking the ancient tongue, and guarding well
   The love of long ago.

Go, and all good go with you—seek to gain
   Not momentary cheers
Of shouting crowds, but that that shall remain
   To bless the future years.

Set forward truth and right in those wide lands,
   A builder unreproved
Of that still Kingdom, fashioned not with hands,
   Which cannot be removed.

Autumn, 1878.

                   KENSINGTON,
                      July 24, 1878.

My interview with Dizzy to-day was so exactly what I had expected that I begin to believe that ten days' yachting in the Hebrides entails the possession of second sight.

I had hardly been shown into the large room, with columns and the picture of Sir R. Walpole, before I was asked to go across the staircase-head to Dizzy's own room. When near the door I saw him (in a looking-glass) rise hastily to receive me, and he came towards me, and led me to a large red leather-covered armchair, he taking another. I told him I was glad to hear that all at Osborne thought him in good health, and he said he was, but had suffered from throat, which fortunately only troubled him first at Berlin when the heavy part of his task was done. I congratulated him again, and waited for him to open fire, which he did at once, saying that he wished to see me about a very important matter, namely, that one of "our great Viceroyalties" was vacant and that he wished me to take it. Then full stop, to see if I was surprised, which I was not, having seen all in a vision beforehand.

I expressed my sense of the honour done me by the confidence, but said there were other better men who had had administrative experience. Had he thought of Sir J. Fergusson? Oh yes, he had thought of all that, and was of opinion that I should be a better G.G. "than Fergusson." The Duke of Manchester I suggested. No, he was most anxious that I should take it, and believed I had abilities. A bow on my part, and another question, "Had Dufferin suggested me?" "No, it would have been impertinent to do so," was the answer; and then he continued,

"The Queen, when I first spoke of it, thought that she would not like her daughter to be so far, but on considering that Canada is now only ten days off, and that you might come home for a time every year, and after sleeping over it, she was quite in favour of the proposal." So I said that I must have time for consideration. He said I might come away in a year, two years, three years, if I liked. So I made my bow and left, he showing me the way.

SCHLOSS, COBURG,
Sept. 2, 1878.

We are lodged in the rooms the Queen occupies in the Palace, a big building not unlike a plain Burleigh House, and with a large place in front, nicely ornamented with flower-beds and cut trees. Opposite to us, a theatre and the Duke of Edinburgh's house, and on one side a handsome stone Italian terrace which fences in the public park, rising on a hillside, which is well timbered, up to the very picturesque old fortress on the crest, an English half-mile off. The houses in the town are very quaint and remind me often of bits of Nuremberg. We have been driving much about in the neighbourhood to various houses and castles belonging to the Duke, and went through the collection in the fortress this afternoon, besides visiting several old Court gentlemen and servants who were anxious to see L. She has not been here for thirteen years, but finds no changes. I never saw a town more cleanly kept. One could imagine one's self in a Dutch street if cleanliness alone were in question.

The armour, birds, old glass, cabinets, and weapons in the "Festung" are well worth seeing. One room is inlaid all round with hunting pictures of old battues, etc., of the seventeenth century, in coloured woods, and is a most curious picture gallery of the sports of that time. There is an immense collection of prints and drawings by old masters; the place is larger and handsomer and more interesting, far, than I expected.

I had a visit to-day from a Craignish Campbell, who is a lieutenant in the Prussian Army. He was the first of his regiment in a French battery, at Mars-la-Tour, the second of the awful battles round Gravelotte. He got hold of the French regiment's flag, and was cut over the head and breast, and shot through the hand and arm, while his horse was killed under him.

The views from the hills to-day have been most beautiful, and I do not wonder at the Prince Consort's homesickness for this place.

CHAPTER XXV

The Churches.—This is a formidable title for these pages, but no one will come to blows with me or their neighbours if they read it. At the last great Edinburgh Volunteer Review, I went down to Holyrood to mount a horse, and observed to the English groom who had the care of the charger that there was hardly space enough in the Holyrood stables for the demands that might be made upon them for the housing of horses. Could not a piece of land at the back of the single row of stalls be obtained, I suggested, for more animals?

"Well, I don't know," was the answer, "they do say as how the space at the back belongs to some Persuasion—Presbyterians, I think they calls them."

"Good heavens, man, don't you know that the Presbyterians are the Church of this country recognised by the State? Theirs is the Church of this land—theirs is the Established Church!"

He looked amazed and doubtful if he heard aright. He seemed to think I was joking, and that no State could possibly call the Presbyterians a "Church." Well, I have heard the same apparent belief expressed in less bald terms by others, better informed than he. " Oh, I thought you were a Churchman ! " some have said. Others take refuge from the difficulty by calling the Scottish Churches " Kirks," as if the old Saxon word relieved them of any obligation to recognise that Kirk means Church, and *vice versa.* I was brought up in the " Persuasion," and still think it the best form of ecclesiastical government, unless the German Protestantism that has " prelates " simply as inspectors and district officers be an advance in the good government of " Persuasions." I was prepared and examined before taking my first communion by Dr. Norman MacLeod, well known in England as well as in Scotland as the editor of *Good Words*, a most excellent, broad-minded Churchman—or if you like, "Kirkman"—who was an honour to his communion and an example to all Christians.

I have always liked the fancy that the faith fell to earth as a great crystal globe might fall, and that when it broke in its fall among men, each band of believers got a piece of the shining ball, and has it now. When people call themselves Catholics or Churchmen to the exclusion of all others, they don't see the piece of the crystal globe that their brethren have. Perhaps they think their neighbours have been able to swallow it, or sell it, or put it in a mud-hole. They are mistaken. They may have advantages over others in some points, but those whom they look upon as outsiders have the better of them in others. Some think themselves personally insulted if you criticise their form of Christianity.

Not at all. They are not insulted because others see that their bit of the globe has some sharp edges, and maybe some fractures. The power of thinking for themselves can never be denied to civilised mankind, and faith with charity is better than obedience with anathema, cloaking real doubt.

I have often wished that with freedom of worship were joined in some church a practice of using the most beautiful prayers and the best forms of devotion of many others. The Russian, the Roman, the Protestant Churches, all have forms worthy of adaptation. It is curious that the only common form is the practice of singing the Psalms of the Jews, and the prayer of our Lord. Jew and Gentile, when they turn to King David for expression, are often united. Would that all could go further in a common worship of the one Creator of all! Would that each " persuasion " did not insist so strenuously on having its own patent medicine only, and cease to declare that this " is necessary to salvation " ! Could it be believed that He who formed the infinite variety of man condemns to eternal torment the vast majority of His creatures? Certainly no assumed superiority tends to peace on earth and goodwill among men. Nor does it bless those who dress themselves in the robes of religious pride. On the contrary, they attract against themselves and their professions the natural dislike of those who feel themselves despised or disregarded.

One good thing this Church of Scotland has accomplished which will not be denounced by her greatest disparagers. She has been enabled to secure that her clergy shall not have stipends of less than £200 a year. In England unfortunately there are many who have to live on incomes below that sum. In 1875 I proposed that a fund be raised to secure that all parsons in England should have the same. We held a meeting at which the Archbishop of Canterbury and Lord Selborne and others spoke, and spoke most eloquently. This proposal succeeded in raising a fund, large, but not nearly large enough, and it still continues, and is still open to subscriptions, under the name conferred upon it some time after we raised it, of the Queen Victoria Fund. The first secretary was Canon Troutbeck, one of the Westminster clergy, who worked most zealously with me, and whose name should be remembered for an effort which is at the present moment doing much good, an effort which should be supported by the whole of the Anglican laity and clergy.

One finds intolerance among the hot-headed in every communion. The Papacy says all that does not follow it is "anathema." But its bad opinion of neighbours is not worse than the complacency with which Highlanders of the Protestant form of faith sometimes make up their minds that their brothers, cousins, and others not belonging to their "Persuasion" will suffer badly in the next world.

Lately an English visitor when out deer-stalking conversed with a ghillie, who belonged to the Free Church, as to the difference between his Church and the Established. The Englishman said he had attended the services of both Churches, and had heard their ministers talk in private, and could make out no difference at all between the faith and practice of worship between the two.

"Och, yes," answered Tonal, "there is a great difference!"

"What is it? I can't see it."

"Och, its just this: that we'll have grace, and the others will be gralloched [disembowelled as stags are], and burned in the everlasting fire. It's just that they'll be tamned, and we'll be singing."

This always in all communities seems to be a most comforting thought. But I don't think it has any "justification by faith"!

The Girls.—A society the Princess and I started about this time has had a very great success. This is the Girls' Public Day School Company, which now has schools all over England, giving girls a most excellent and cheap education. We had a little Educational Parliament at 1 Grosvenor Square, where we were then living, getting the leading educationists together; and, unlike the case of boys' schools in England, we have never had any strife, for the good reason that we do not depend on the rates for the maintenance of our schools!

This is the letter which started the Clergy Fund:

KENSINGTON PALACE, *July* 22, 1875.

MY LORD,

I venture to ask your Lordship if you will have the kindness to consider whether you can see your way to recommending to the support of the clergy and the laity in your diocese the Church of England Incumbents' Sustentation Fund, which was established, as you are aware, two years ago, and met with the express approval of the archbishops and bishops, and of the Upper House of Convocation of the Province of Canterbury. The exact mode in which this should be done I do not take the liberty of suggesting; but I beg to bring forward certain statements in support of this appeal, which may possibly also be of use for the basis of the recommendation which I trust you may feel yourself able to give.

It is not necessary that I should point out the evil which this Fund proposes to remedy. Your Lordship must have many more opportunities than I have of estimating its gravity. Its magnitude may be gathered from the tables of the report of which I have the honour to send you a copy. These tables show that there are nearly 4,000 benefices in England under £200 a year. Without entering into the question as to any amelioration which might be effected by a judicious union of rural benefices, I desire to bring under your notice that a careful estimate shows that a sum not far short of seven millions (£7,000,000) would be required to raise all existing benefices to £200 a year. At first this sum might appear to be so great as to be quite out of reach, but when it is remembered that from so much as is complete of the return recently ordered to be made to the House of Lords, respecting the amount spent on the restoration of churches during the last forty years, the expectation is warranted that the total sum thus expended will be found not to have fallen far short of thirty millions (£30,000,000), as was pointed out at the public meeting held in behalf of this Fund on June 30, 1875, the sum the Council proposes to raise appears insignificant in comparison. Besides, the work of restoration of the fabrics of churches having now been carried so far towards completion, the opportunity seems to present itself to the Church for taking up a task the importance of which, as regards her stability and usefulness, is certainly not second to that of the conservation of her buildings.

The promoters of this movement are not unmindful that there are similar agencies, national and local, already in existence, but they desire to supplement and accelerate—not to supersede—the work of these various bodies. It is well known that the Ecclesiastical Commissioners, whose action, it should be remembered, is not confined to benefices under £200 a year in value, are obliged from year to year to decline at least two-thirds of the benefactions offered in behalf of benefices, as being unable to meet them with grants; and the Council of this Fund hope that they may be able to secure for the Church some of the benefactions which are thus in danger of being lost altogether. I may also mention that the grants from this Fund will be invested separately, and not used as benefactions to be subsequently offered to the Ecclesiastical Commissioners or to the governors of Queen Anne's Bounty, so as to push forward as rapidly as possible the work of endowment of poor benefices, and not to make the funds at the disposal of these bodies the only measure of the rate of progress.

The governors of Queen Anne's Bounty have kindly undertaken to receive and hold in trust benefactions of money, and the grants made to meet them, and this without expense to this Fund. The cost of perpetual management will also be saved, for the interest arising from the investments will be paid from the Bounty Office as it becomes due.

These benefactions and grants may, if required, be applied through the agency of the Bounty Office in the purchase or erection of a parsonage. It is hoped that the annual cost of the machinery of the Fund will continue to be small. For the two years during which the Fund has been in existence the expenditure on machinery, deducting from it the amount received as interest on donations, etc., on deposit, has only slightly exceeded one and a half per cent. per annum on the amount secured to the Church by means of the Fund.

The Council are particularly desirous to work in harmony with diocesan societies having a kindred object, and if any scheme for organised co-operation presents itself to your Lordship, the Council have said they would be ready to consider it. There certainly seems to be room for both national and local efforts in the same direction. Some persons would prefer the one mode of working and some the other; and this fund, in combination with diocesan societies, offers a choice to all. A national scheme would naturally attract any who are not specially bound by local ties, and has the advantage of giving the abundance of one part of the country an opportunity of supplying the want of another. Any suggestion which your Lordship may see fit to make as to the working of the Fund would be most gratefully and carefully considered.

I venture to remark in conclusion, that it seems to be specially desirable that the objects of the fund should be brought before each parish in England and Wales. If annual contributions from each parish, even if of small amount, could be secured, so as to supply a steady income, a good hope could be entertained as to the completion of our undertaking within a reasonable time.

  I have the honour to be, my Lord,
    Your obedient servant,
      LORNE.

CHAPTER XXVI

1878-1883

NOVA SCOTIA

White-lipped is Fundy's racing tide,
   Swift charging fair Acadia's shore,
That glistens red, when far and wide
   The Ebb swings back to Ocean's roar.

But ever on its restless toil
   The orchards of the Province smile,—
Green woods of fruit that gem the soil
   In apple harvests, mile on mile.

Here Scotland and her old ally,
   Fair France, both gave the land a name;
And proudly she has sought to vie,
   Through Nature's bounty, with their fame.

Her orchards' fruit in maidens' cheek
   Its hues in gentler beauty leave,
While Flood and Ebb unite to speak
   The gallant deeds her sons achieve.

S.S. "Sarmatian," 14 miles off Halifax, *Nov. 23, 1878.*—We are close on our destination, but dark has come on and the captain says he must lie to, to the disgust of the ladies, who have another night of rolling in the trough of the sea before them. We cannot see the lights at the entrance of the harbour, and it is not supposed to be safe, in the dirty weather, to go any further. We have not seen the *Sirius*, one of the warships which was to have met us to-day, sixty miles from Halifax, and must have missed her, as the weather was hazy, although we passed over the spot the Admiralty indicated as the place where she would be.

6 *a.m.*—We have made the lights, and are going in. The rain is making the deck wretched, but the captain's anxieties seem to be over. Yesterday I caught one of the gulls which have followed us right across the Atlantic, and made a drawing of him. I think it is a kittiwake, but am not sure. He was caught by a simple long piece of twine left to fly in the wind from one of the ship's ropes, and, coming against it, entangled his wings, without being hurt. It is the old English schoolboy way of catching swallows by strings attached to church steeples.

Dr. A. Clark has made himself very useful, although he himself was not always comfortable. He says he believes sea-sickness is caused by the variation of atmospheric pressure on the fluids in the brain, just as one sees the mercury in a barometer rise and fall, owing to the difference of atmospheric pressure, when the vessel rises and falls, or her side is lifted or depressed in rolling. The mercury rises or falls three-tenths of an inch sometimes with a bad roll, which shows what a sudden change of atmospheric pressure is brought about.[1]

---

[1] The change of *height* of mercury *in barometer* is due to the ship rolling and so inclining the tube—and not due to change of atmospheric pressure. There is no change of *level*. An aneroid does *not* show a change.

Halifax Harbour, *Monday,* 25.—Steamed in late on Saturday night, after in vain trying to get a pilot, the sea being rough, and the people apparently thinking that the *Sarmatian* needed no guidance. A Yankee steamer passing under our stern outward bound for Portland, Maine, shouts, "The fleet have been looking for you all the afternoon."

After many blue lights have been let off, and cannon fired from our decks for the pilot who won't come, the captain pities the ladies and runs in and anchors. Soon afterwards we are boarded by the mail tender, and then up comes a steam launch from the *Black Prince*, which had arrived safely three days ago, with the Duke of Edinburgh. Then there was much conversation in my cabin, where I had turned in, till past midnight, to the wrath of Dr. Clark, who wanted L. to go to bed. The *Black Prince* had come by a southerly course and had escaped bad weather, but ninety of her men were on the "light duty" or sick list, with Cyprus fever and hard work.

Sunday was bright, with a cold wind. There is no snow on the ground as yet. Sir Patrick McDougall, the Commander-in-Chief, a pleasant, tall, long-nosed Scotsman, came on board with the Lieutenant-Governor of Nova Scotia, Mr. Archibald, a good-natured, clever-looking lawyer and politician. Sir Hugh Allan, the head of the house owning these fine steamships, appeared, having come up from Montreal, very anxious as to whether a great St.

Andrews Society Ball was to be attended by us. The whole afternoon was spent by me in writing answers to thirteen addresses. Colonel Littleton came from Ottawa, also Moreton, having arranged things up-country. The people on shore are reported as being "drunk with joy." The Prime Minister sent to say that he could not pay his respects until Monday, as he had got lumbago. We are now under weigh again to steam to our moorings, and the fleet are to salute, so I stop this till this evening.

Admiralty House, Halifax.—The landing was the prettiest sight imaginable—the town looking its best in bright sunshine, with its many steeples, and houses covered with flags. All ships in the harbour, which is a very fine one, dressed, and six men-of-war, two of them almost the largest in the service, manning yards and firing salutes, while the citadel's guns answered from above the closely packed buildings. At the landings, evergreen arches, volunteers, regulars, and Ministers. Sir J. MacDonald and his Minister of Public Works, Mr. Tupper.

Sir John in full uniform. We got into the carriage, after all the rest of the party had gone on ahead in theirs, being the seventh in a string, a very large staff riding behind. The streets were a mass of bunting, and the people had put up over twenty great arches. "Ne obliviscaris" everywhere. The regulars, the 101st, fresh,

Halifax

or rather jaded, from Cyprus, some artillery batteries, and much militia, lined the whole route.

At the Legislative Council building we found the staircases lined with troops, and finally went into a large hall, with daïs, throne, and Council-table, at which were all the Cabinet. My swearing-in followed, and after the ceremonial and a reply to an address from the town we were allowed two hours' quiet here, only varied by the excitement of one of the maids having lost the keys of the jewel-case, which had to be broken open by Admiral Sir E. Inglefield, who is a mechanical genius, and who hammered away at the locks until they broke, getting himself very hot in his full uniform during the operation which proceeded, with the maids in tears, and A. and I both "in full fig," holding the beautiful but unfortunate case.

The dinner at the Lieutenant-Governor's was given to about forty, many of the Ministers being there and the Roman Catholic Archbishop. A drawing-room defile, of the whole adult population who could appear in evening clothes in Halifax, followed, and we did not get home till past twelve o'clock. The Admiral has made us very comfortable. He is a good artist, and a great lover of china.

Nothing could have been more pleasant than the welcome given by Halifax, the capital of the first Canadian Province we have visited.

1878.—It is curious how old monarchical ways, no longer known in Great Britain, still survive in some forms in the free and self-governing Colonies. For instance, now that I have taken up my work, and attend at the Government Buildings to all the papers that are brought before me, I am sometimes told that my predecessors used to attend also the meetings of the Cabinet quite as we may suppose the Stuart monarchs may have presided at their Council of State when their Ministers deliberated. Now you know well, or ought to know, that the Queen and the sovereigns before her since the Revolution have done this but seldom. When the Queen nominally presides at a Council, it is only a form, for all decisions have been previously taken. She has seen the papers that led to the decision, and she may herself, or through her secretary, have taken part in written or oral discussion, but with each Minister or the Prime Minister singly, and not in Cabinet conclave. But the Governor-General in Canada has often himself sat and spoken in the Cabinet conclave. To prove this to me I was shown the Council Room, in which a high-backed, decorated chair was placed at the head of the long table, and ranged along the table at each side were the chairs for the Ministers. I said as soon as I saw this Cabinet throne that I would not be representing the Queen in occupying it when Ministers were engaged in consulting each other about any Bill they proposed to bring forward in the House, and that I would never use it. Nor did I do so even for the formality of assenting to Bills passed, which was done by signing " Privy Council Orders."

On the other hand, I took great pains to show that all papers regarding executive action were studied before being signed, and if there was anything that seemed wrong either in the preparation of a measure, or in the measure itself, when approved by the Privy Council or Cabinet, Ministers were asked to come to me and talk the matter over. One of the first things that happened to me after my arrival at Ottawa was the presentation to me for signature of a whole bevy of Privy Council Orders dismissing many officials in the civil, and some in the militia service. I sent them all back unsigned, asking that a reason should in the case of every dismissal be given, and so placed on record. The Government of Sir John MacDonald had just come in, and the "spoils of office" system, so harmful in the United States, seemed through these dismissals to be repeated on a small scale in Canada.

This was pointed out to the Government, and they, averring that each dismissal was fully justified on account of the officials having taken part against them in the late political contest, yet diminished greatly the number of dismissals, which they returned to me with the repeated request to sign them. I acknowledged that for a permanent official to take part in political contest was wrong, and conceded signatures to all dismissals where this was proved to have taken place. In many cases, however, the threatened man continued in office, because nothing could be alleged against him save that the new Minister at the head of his Department wanted him removed to provide for some political friend of his own.

It would amuse you to see me making the acquaintance of the Canadian M.P.'s. The Parliamentary Buildings are very picturesque. High towers and steep mansard roofs rise over three blocks or ranges of stonework. These are placed on a beautiful cliff, "cedar"-covered, and look down on the wide Ottawa River, here expanding into a great basin, but still foam-flecked with the excitement of its struggle and escape after falling in a roaring cascade over the Chaudière Rocks. Endless stacks of timber encumber the banks near the Falls, for there whole forests are brought to be cut in immense sawmills. The city stretches around the Parliament blocks, paying due respect to them by keeping wide grass-plots clear within their enclosing space. Wide streets, rarely bounded by stone houses, but always nicely planted and fringed with substantial brick residences, open out in every direction, often overlooking the river, giving a view of the broad water expanse and the low shore opposite. This eastern shore is fringed with the wooden houses of Hull, a French quarter, in the

THE ST. LAWRENCE AND BATTLE-FIELD OF QUEBEC, FROM THE RAMPARTS.

The point of land on the right is Wolfe's Creek, where he landed.

From drawings by Lord A. Campbell, 1880.

WOLFE'S CREEK, QUEBEC, OLD RAMPARTS, AND A PART OF THE BATTLE-FIELD.

Province of Quebec, whose low hills rise covered with forests, but all the nearer land is cleared for farms.

From hundreds of miles of such partially cleared country come the French Canadian Members of Parliament. From districts nearly as well wooded come most of the English-speaking members. But there are others who represent the prosperous cities of Montreal and Toronto, and the good and comparatively old cleared lands of Ontario and the Eastern Atlantic Provinces. The prairie country is yet in its infancy, and the Pacific " slope " is only represented by a few who come from Vancouver Island.

Ottawa, 1878.—I never saw anything like the heartiness of the people. Leaders of deputations conclude reading their addresses with swimming eyes; the members nearly shake one's hand off. An enthusiastic working-man M.P., an Irishman named O'Donoghue, said he represented the tagrag and bobtail, and that there was not a workman or newsboy in the street who did not feel as joyous at our coming as Sir H. Allan, "the richest man in the country." It is a very remarkable display of sentiment.

We gave our first big dinner yesterday, in the handsome Ballroom here, and had all the Cabinet, many of their wives, and three judges of the Supreme Court of Ottawa, making a party of nearly forty. To-morrow we have a large military dinner— all the superior officers of corps in town, the general commanding the Dominion Militia, and the officers of the Bodyguard (which is a very well got up battalion), making in all forty-six.

All snow has left the ground. There was only a little of it before, and a thaw last night has made it disappear.

I suppose we must get regular winter weather soon, but as yet, with the exception of some sharp nips of frost, it has not been so cold as in England. People declare that the climate is changing.

ONTARIO

> Lands yet more happy than Europe's, for here
> We mould the young nation for Freedom to rear;
> Full strongly we build, and have nought to pull down,
> For true to ourselves, we are true to the Crown;
> The Will of the People, its honour shows forth
> As pole star whose radiance points steadfastly north.

Ottawa, *Jan.* 2, 1879.—We have spent a very quiet Christmas and New Year time, and are only now beginning to see a few people at private dinner-parties. I send you a Memorandum which I have given to Sir J. MacDonald as showing what I think of the Constitutional aspect of the Quebec business (the dismissal of Lieutenant-Governor Letellier). I was delighted to find after it had been written and sent that Dufferin in 1876, when he had a hot discussion with some of his Ministers, wrote most strongly on his absolute right, within the walls of the Privy Council, to express his opinion or feeling as freely as any of his Ministers. Mr. Blake had told him that Canada was not a Crown Colony, and that he had no right to press his views, and he replies that "it is true Canada is not a Crown Colony, but neither is it a Republic, and if it became one Mr. Blake would find a President imposed on him who would be found a much severer master than a Governor-General." Dufferin had expressly left a copy of the paper in which he had said this, in 1876, in the office, sealed, and to be opened by his successor.

The cold is perceptible just now. When we walk or drive, the hair about the mouth becomes as stiff as an icicle with the breath. Gas lighting by the finger touch is most successfully carried on. On Christmas Day the feat was performed, and it is useful, for one can do without matches in a dark room, provided it is warm enough to make the air quite dry. All that is necessary is to rub the feet on the carpet a good deal, and then if the gas is turned on a touch of the finger on the gas-burner will be quite enough to send the flame rushing up.

G.-G.'s Office at the Houses of Parliament, *Jan.*, 1879.—Mr. Sydney Hall came back two days ago from a place one hundred and fifty miles up the Ottawa River, where he went with Harbord to see moose-hunting. They had rail for one hundred miles, then twelve hours' sleighing, and then a day's march to a shanty, where they got a certain amount of night shelter. Harbord is still there, wishing to have another week of it. The snow was very heavy, and they only got one "cow," whose upper lip and huge hoof were brought back in triumph. Harbord's gun had got snow in it, and he could not fire, and the Canadian hunter with the party, a man six feet five inches in height, found his rifle of no use, for it snapped, and the beast fell to the rifle of an Indian. They all seem to have enjoyed their time very much, although Hall's nose was once completely frost-bitten, and he had to go back at once to the shanty, on the discovery that he might lose it altogether. He was luckily close to home, and was directed to hold his nose in cold water for a quarter of an hour, and to rub it gently, when animation, flexibility, lightness in weight, and colour gradually returned, to his great relief, and he has been caressing his proboscis ever since, to make sure it has not disappeared. That same day he had seen the half of an Indian boy's face black and covered with a blue mould in consequence of a frost-bite, so his feelings may be imagined. They saw few birds, but found many traces of the "partridge," the wood-grouse which burrows in the snow. The hunter said he had seen them take headers into the snow, straight down, like a gannet, from a tree, and there in the snow they remain often for a long time. No traces of bear were seen, only a "deadfall" trap in a hollow tree, which had killed two bears, and then, accidentally, a favourite cow. Places where moose had lain were frequently seen, and there was good hope that Harbord would get a good one.

The snow was not yet deep enough for the beasts to "yard" or herd together in a trampled place, and the hunting was all "still" hunting—creeping through the woods and looking out. The moose is said, when started, to have a curious habit, when he has distanced his pursuer, of turning round so that his track forms a loop, and of coming back to near the path he took some time before, in order that he may wait and see his pursuer pass, calculate the amount of time it will take the hunters to get round the bend, and so have a comfortable time to rest before again starting.

We go on having constant dinners, and have made the acquaintance of a great many people, many of whom are very agreeable. There is always plenty of exercise to be got, the tobogganing being great fun. On a fine frosty day the thing goes down at a tremendous speed, the snow rising in dust clouds behind it; and when at the end of the course there is an upset, the cedar thickets ring with laughter. Sir Edward and Lady Thornton both went down in the most plucky manner, but both looking as if they did not expect to survive. They nearly came to a sad end near Niagara when they left. I gave them a special train from beyond Toronto to Niagara; and owing, I suppose, to the great cold, a piston-rod gave way while a high bridge was being crossed. The engine left the track, and it seems almost miraculous that the train did not go over and make the forty-foot drop into the river below.

Parliament opens on February 13. On the whole affairs do not look bad, as British Columbia is likely to be satisfied about the railway. There may be a row about the slight raising of the tariff after the Government friends have been taught to expect a much lighter protection, and the Letellier business is a shell that must explode soon. But as Dizzy says, "Difficulties vanish when encountered," and there is no reason for looking for evil. Distress is not so great here as in England, and the Government are determined to practise the most scraping economy. I cannot get them up to the mark this year about embodying any regiments, although I believe Sir John was really anxious it should be done. We are to have another curling match. Here men play with iron stones, and put their foot into a hole cut in the ice to keep steady in delivering a stone. Everybody wears goloshes, called "gums," and they say: "Mary is coming in directly, but she is wiping her gums on the mat." There is another charming expression: if a man is a donkey, he is called "quite an outside fool."

The Colorado beetle makes good potatoes scarce. I am told that millions of these insects were washed over by winds across the great lakes, and lay in lines along the shores, unfortunately still alive, and have devastated Canadian potato-fields ever since. The only hope is that a small red parasite upon them may multiply, for it kills them.

Feb. 24, 1879.—I am very busy seeing all the senators and M.P.s, beginning at 8 o'clock with them, and going on till 1.30. I am struck with the very American look of the New Brunswick people. The senators from that Province have much of the Boston cut, which is not wonderful, as they live so near and are the same people. The men from Ontario are the most British in appearance. The French from Quebec show a great liking to be addressed in their own language. Sir John has nominated a French Canadian as Speaker, and he at once asserted the privilege of his people by reading the usual Commons' demand for free access, etc., to the Governor-General in French before he read it in English. Some of the representatives of the old French families are very pleasant people; for instance, both the present Prime Minister in Quebec, Mr. Joly, and the head of the Provincial Opposition, M. de Boucherville, are most agreeable. De Boucherville's ancestor was governor of the "Three Rivers," an old French colony in the St. Lawrence, in 1650.

M. Masson, the Minister for Defence and Militia, fell down in a fainting-fit two days ago, while seconding a vote of condolence to the Queen, on Princess Alice's death, and I hear that his heart is so much affected that he will be obliged to leave public life, for which I shall be very sorry.

We have a good physician, Dr. Grant, who has treated diphtheria with the greatest success lately, by placing patients in mustard baths and inducing a violent skin action. He feeds up with beef tea, etc., only, no alcohol, and paints the throat inside and out. This winter he has recovered some desperate cases. Formerly, with old prescribed treatment, he confesses he lost numbers, but now he is pretty confident of saving any case, if called in in time.

There are many applications for rewards for saving life here, and I think the Humane Society in England, whose recognition is much valued, should undertake to recognise these acts, when duly authenticated. I am sending home one proof of gallantry now, and am making the request that the society should reward Canadian " braves."

We have three rinks of curlers, all playing at the same time on the skating-pond here. The Scotsmen think more of one's attending curling matches than of any amount of business capacity!

Ottawa, *March* 13, 1879.—I find my acquaintance-making with the M.P.s exceedingly interesting. Yesterday I saw a Mr. Skinner from Sutherland, who remembers dearest Mama teaching the school at Golspie. He is now a Colonel of a Highland regiment at Hamilton in Ontario.

We are trying to dine and entertain all the M.P.s, and give three dinners of fifty-four each a week, besides two theatrical parties of three hundred and fifty each next week and the week after. There are about eighty senators, and 205 M.P.s. Soon there must be more, as Manitoba is settling up so fast. There are the most extraordinary franchises here. P. Edward's Island has Manhood Suffrage, so has British Columbia, but the other provinces have plans to keep out the "residuum" and insist on a man having one hundred dollars real property or some amount of income, and it answers well.

This part of the country is rich in the most heavy hematite, and other iron ore, and it is the dream of the people all over the provinces that they can work their native mines remuneratively. There is plenty of coal, on both great oceans, to work the iron.

There is a wonderful white marble hill in Nova Scotia, and they want to try to work that with a little protection. And so it goes on, but there is a great desire to discriminate in favour of England, and the tariff does go against the Americans more than any other country. I have sent the complaining answer from England in my cypher telegram to the Government; but they were elected to try protection, and do not give the country half as much as it asked.

March, 1879.—They have found lately, about seventy miles up the river from here, in a place near the bank, an old astrolabe, an instrument for taking observations, which seems to have been lost by the great French discoverer Champlain in 1613. He mentions in his diary that he had a difficult journey on that day, having to carry boats, etc., to avoid a rapid, and in the following days and during the rest of the journey he does not mention that he took any observations, although he mentions them regularly up to that day, so there is pretty strong presumptive evidence in favour of the old instrument having been lost by him.

The tariff which is making England so angry is well received here, and the United States seem to wonder that it has not been tried long ago. I have sent a long despatch home, giving a Government view as to the extent to which they favour England. They are certainly desirous to do so, but they think they can't raise revenue by any direct taxation, and must raise some of it by English goods. Several companies are of course springing up to forward manufactories in different parts of the country. Without protection it is difficult to see how they can have manufactures, and our neighbours " cut rates " and " dump " at low prices to prevent manufactories arising. Bastiat and Cobden are being " made to take a back seat."

Sir Edward Thornton took my message regarding Sitting Bull to Evarts and read it to him. He was pleased, but takes a most unsatisfactory view of the Indian question, holding us responsible, when it is only the American bad conduct towards the tribes that has driven them over ; and knowing that we have no force on the western plains strong enough at present to menace the Indians, who amount to several thousand excellently armed and well mounted men, Evarts insists on calling Sitting Bull our Indian, when he is theirs, and we must not have this affiliation order acquiesced in. The Americans refuse the Indians any decently good terms, and, as the people can't starve, it is difficult to see how they can avoid crossing the line to get food, when fighting must begin.

We are strengthening our excellent mounted police to five hundred men, but they have to keep a frontier of about one thousand miles. I am now seeing what can be done to quietly arrest Sitting Bull and get him from his people, and in custody, supposing such a strong step to become necessary, but I believe it would be a most dangerous proceeding. To send our militia out there to keep order would, I think, be a bad thing, and it would be best to let the Americans come over and avenge any attack on them than to embroil the Indians with our red coats. The Cabinet never thought of doing anything but remonstrating with the Americans as to the expense we are put to in helping the Indians to live. This is all very well, but would not be thought to have satisfied international fairness, if the tribes attack the troops, and no warning to the savages had been given that if they behave badly their blood must be on their heads.

About the "use of Colonies," surely it is better to

have 20 per cent. only levied against English goods than an American 50 per cent. Besides, per head the Colonies do buy immensely more from us than any foreigners, and their ports are open and their men are always ready to bear their burden in fighting.

If we had had a Russian war, we should have had a first levy of ten thousand men at once, and now no end of the militia officers here are volunteering for the Cape. Besides, one Colony provides a berth for your son, which, to say the least, should make you a confirmed "Imperialist" in spite of your having the misfortune of having Mr. Lowe and Mr. Gladstone as friends!

We had a very successful private theatrical party last night—four hundred and fifty people.

The Opposition are trying to make out that I am "embroiled" with my Ministry, and each handshake is watched by the bloodshot eyes of angry politicos.

I send a card showing an invention of a gate which is exhibited. The bar from which the suspended rope or hanging handle is swung is so long that before coming up to the gate one can easily pull the rope, when the gate at once rises and goes sideways, and when you have driven through the posts you pull the corresponding hanger on the other bar, and the gate rises and replaces itself. It is ingenious and very easily made.

Colonel Gzowski, who has spent a day or two here, has given me the following hints, which are worth knowing.

1. Grapes, if one wishes them to last during the winter, are not to be cut off from the vine, but the vine to be left with the bunches on it. When the last bunch has been cut for the table, the vine to be taken down, the waste wood cut off, and the stock laid along the ground covered with some sheltering brush. He says he always pursued that plan.

2. He declares that it is a great mistake to have apples ranged singly on horizontal frames, as done in England, in the apple store-houses. This treatment is quite right for pears, but not for apples. Apples should be put in barrels, and left in them, and they will keep much longer, and preserve their flavour better, and no fruit merchant here ever dreams of unpacking their fruit barrels. Every one takes apples from the barrel as they are wanted for the table.

3. That by far the best way of sending game, poultry, etc., long distances is to do as follows: Take a large barrel, and through the centre put a stovepipe. Insert in this stovepipe, which should be round, a square-cut column of ice, and fill in the space between the square surfaces of the ice column and the round of the iron pipe with sawdust. Jam into the barrel round the pipe all the game you want sent, and shut up as usual each end of the barrel. The Colonel declares that birds thus packed will keep for a long time.

Here is a prologue I wrote for recitation at

our first dramatic performance at Government House, Ottawa, in honour of my predecessor, Lord Dufferin :

> A moment's pause before we play our parts,
> To speak the thought that reigns within our hearts.—
> Now, from this Future's hours, and unknown days,
> Affection turns, and with the Past delays ;
> For countless voices in our mighty land
> Speak the fond praises of a vanished hand ;
> And shall to mightier ages yet proclaim
> The happy memories linked with Dufferin's name !
>
> Missed here is he, to whom each class and creed
> Among our people lately bade " God-speed " ;
> Missed when each winter sees the skater wheel
> In ringing circle on the flashing steel ;
> Missed in the spring, in summer and in fall,
> In many a hut, as in the Council Hall ;
> Wherein his wanderings on Duty's hest
> Evoked his glowing speech, his genial jest ;
> We mourn his absence, though we joy that now
> Old England's honours cluster round his brow,
> And that he left us, but to serve again
> Our Queen and Empire on the Neva's plain !
>
> Amidst the honoured roll of those whose fate
> It was to crown our fair Canadian State,
> And bind in one bright diadem alone
> Each glorious province, each resplendent stone,
> His name shall last, and his example give
> To all her sons a lesson how to live,—
> How every task, if met with heart as bold,
> Proved the hard rock is seamed with precious gold ;
> And labour, when with Love and Mirth allied
> Finds friends far stronger than in Force and Pride ;
> And sympathy and kindness can be made
> The potent weapons by which men are swayed.—
> He proved a nation's trust can well be won
> By loyal work, and constant duty done ;
> The wit that winged the wisdom of his word
> Set forth our glories till all Europe heard

How wide the room our Western World can spare
For all who'll nobly toil and bravely dare,—
And while the Statesman we revere, we know
In him the Friend is gone to whom we owe
So much of gaiety, so much that made
Life's duller days to seem with joy repaid.
These little festivals by him made bright
With grateful thoughts of him renewed to-night,
Remind us less of her who deigned to grace
This mimic world, and fill therein her place
With the sweet dignity and gracious mien
The race of Hamilton has often seen,
But never shown upon the wider stage
Where the great "cast" is writ on History's page,
More purely, nobly, than by her, whose voice
Here moved to tears or made the heart rejoice;
And who in act and word, at home, or far
Shone with calm beauty like the Northern Star!

Green as the shamrock of their native isle
Their memory lives, and babes unborn shall smile
And share in happiness the pride that blends
Our country's name with her belovéd friends!

NEW BRUNSWICK

Oh, the lovely river there
Made all Nature yet more fair!
Wooded hills and azure air
Kissed, quivering in the stream they share.
Plunged the salmon, waging feud
'Gainst the jewelled insect brood;
From aërial solitude
An eagle's shadow crossed the wood;
Flapped the heron, and the gray
Halcyon talked from cedar's spray;
Drummed the partridge far away;—
Ah, could we choose to live as they!

Government House, New Brunswick, *August* 1, 1879.—Here we have been shown some "Albertite." It is like Cannel coal to look at—very black and polished, and like compressed and polished bitumen. They say that it is being worked out in Albert County, in this Province, the only place where it has as yet been found.

A tremendous storm burst while we were at Moncton the other day, and we have since heard that the poor French Acadians who came there to greet us found on their return to their homes that many of their houses had been spirited away by a whirlwind. Three people were killed, and many odd things happened. A horse tethered to a building was found all right fifty yards away, although nothing but the débris of the building could be found. A man was sitting in his room when the roof was blown off, and he himself was summarily ejected through the window, which with the walls remained standing. Some furniture followed its owner through the window, and was, with the owner, much bruised. A church remained as it stood, but minus the spire, and one set of pews only, in the body of the church, was thrown against the side wall, while their neighbour pews remained piously quiet.

The river, about half a mile wide, flows close past the front windows of this house—a very comfortable, solidly built, " family mansion " sort of place. The stream is here slow, and all the river we have seen above St. John itself is a series of placid reaches, bordered by a great deal of pretty, rich meadow country, flat but nicely wooded. It is like some Dutch stream scenery. Extraordinary-looking steamers, with the wheel placed at the stern, fly up and down at a great pace.

St. John, New Brunswick, *August* 7, 1879.—We have been most kindly received here. Arches everywhere, my birthday remembered on them. An immense crowd, many Americans, and illuminations as if the town had never known poverty, although it is only eighteen months since the great fire which levelled nearly all the town, and from which many of the people are still suffering so much. The Mayor speaks a great deal of your visit, and Major Domville avoided this time all possibility of a train running past him and his cavalry, by coming to the terminus and awaiting us in the city.

I have been going about the harbour in a thick fog, looking at old forts on the island in the bay, and a fort which is named after Dufferin and which is all slipping into the sea, and at the fishermen off the breakwater, who have long nets stretching driftnet-wise from boat to boat, and catching many fine salmon within ten minutes' steaming of the wharves. A fine seal was disporting himself inside the breakwater, and wonderfully tame, considering that the steamer I was on was about the ugliest and most repulsive thing of its kind ever built. To-day there is hot sun and much dust. We have been visiting institutions, and have been again cheered by all the population of the place—and many more.

To-night there is a Drawing-room and Levee. I

spoke out a little in my replies to addresses against any looking towards the States in time of depression, and held the flag high, and made " Imperial perorations."

Why is Dizzy speaking at the Mansion House in August instead of in November, or besides doing it in November? It looks like a projected early dissolution.

We could not see much of the country you admired between Moncton and St. John's, as the rain and fog were heavy. At Moncton all the local government met us, with the Lieutenant-Governor, a wonderful old man of eighty, and not looking fifty, and they were all drenched at a function there by the most severe rain I have seen since Jamaica days.

Prince Edward Island, *Aug.* 14, 1879.—We had a long day after leaving Fredericktown. First five hours of the river, then a duty drive through St. John, then three and a half hours' sail, and a final departure from Shadiac in the yacht, and arrival next morning at Pictou, in Nova Scotia. Then, after a stay of a day there, we started for this place last night, arriving in the harbour this morning, escorted by the Admiral in his gigantic ironclad the *Bellerophon*, and two other fine vessels.

Everywhere in New Brunswick, in Nova Scotia, and here we have been received by enormous crowds, and have had to reply to many addresses, all of which have been most kindly expressed. The Pictou visit interested me, for I visited there the finest coal-mine I have ever seen. There is enough coal to supply the world. The galleries are gigantic, and the seams of coal are by no means exhausted by the galleries, for there is usually twenty or thirty feet of coal under them. The workmen can always work perfectly upright in them and have more than room to swing their picks. The ventilation is so good that they can almost always use powder to help themselves along, and during all the time the mine has been worked—fourteen years—they have only once had a partial accident. The depth is great, for one goes down 960 feet by the shaft, and the sloping galleries carried us down fully 1,100 feet in all. Our fleet is supplied at Halifax by coal from another mine not far off from that we visited. There is very little sulphur in the coal, which makes it good for machine-making work and forges of all sizes and kinds.

Very many of the people in the neighbourhood are Highlanders. There are over 30,000 of them, and there is often more Gaelic heard than English. One regiment of whom I saw something were all Gaelic men, and were much pleased with a Bienachlave, or "Good-bye" (I can't spell it), with which I concluded my thanks to them for turning out in the middle of their hay-making time. The men came twenty-five and thirty miles at half a day's notice to attend.

The Admiral, both at Pictou and here, has been manning yards and firing salutes, and I have got him to promise to come up to Quebec with us, and repeat the same performance there, so that the two French war vessels there will have good company.

Sir Edward Inglefield was employed on three Arctic expeditions, and he tells me what I had never heard before, and what is known only to a few, I think—that Captain Hall, the American Arctic explorer who died a year or two ago, obtained good evidence that Franklin's party were murdered by the Esquimaux. This evidence has not been published, because Hall did not wish that it should be so; but the Admiral has read three volumes of Hall's journals, in which all the story is told. The Esquimaux said that they were obliged to kill the Europeans because there was not food enough for so many. The English got all the seals, bears, etc., there were to be got with their guns; and although there were not many new mouths after Franklin's death and the thinning of the original number, yet there were too many, and the Esquimaux killed them, only one big man— an officer—escaping, getting away eight miles, and then perishing. The Esquimaux showed the place, and on the snow being searched the remains of a body were found and collected. There was gold in the teeth, showing that it was an officer, and a peculiarity in the jaw, for the eye-teeth were missing, and Huxley, to whom the skull was shown, said they had been pulled out when the man was young. This identified the skull as that of one of the officers, who was known to have had these teeth taken out.

This island is all red sandstone. The streets of the town are deserts of dust in this hot weather.

We are to entertain the people by having a review of the Naval Brigade, and of course there is the usual " Drawing-room " to be held.

At Shadiac, where a number of people had got up a very pretty reception, I met several of the French Acadian priests interested in the people who suffered in the recent tornado. They say that the damage was very serious, very many houses having been blown down or pitched away into fields and woods, and five people killed outright, while many have been wounded. We have sent a large subscription for them, and the Province of New Brunswick is doing a great deal.

The *Kearsarge*, the American vessel which sank the *Alabama* during the great war, was at Pictou, having come back from a cruise on the Canadian fishery coasts, where she has been to convey a commission appointed by Evarts, to take evidence about the alleged grievances of the American fishermen. Mr. Babson, the Commissioner, is getting up a case against us for subsequent use. The Americans contend that the Treaty of Washington gives their fishermen unlimited rights. We contend that it only gives the rights given to our own fishermen, and that we never intended to give to foreigners rights which we deny to our people.

October, 1879.—The Americans are coming into Manitoba, after all, so Dizzy turns out to be a prophet. They say that over two thousand have come in during the last month from the States.

I have had very interesting talks with Sir Leonard Tilley, who has just returned from Washington, whither he had gone to study the American banking system. Of all things, finance is to me the most puzzling. Here we have an odious system of supporting all sorts of banks by giving them Government deposits. This lays the ministry of the day open to all phases of political pressure for the support and patronage of bad banks, and we are going to change the system; and the question is, how to do it. We shall probably have some Act passed next Session, as the Bank Charters expire now, amending the present practice, and they will probably not have any Government deposits placed in any banks which do not hold a corresponding amount of Government securities. The Admiralty have consented to send the North American Squadron every summer to the waters of the St. Lawrence.

We have made several pleasant acquaintances at Toronto, besides Professor Wilson, there being a large and very literary society there. The Chancellor of the University, Mr. Blake, who was also Minister of Justice in the last Government, is a very able man, and, even when one does not agree with him, is most agreeable. He made a capital speech in a little ceremony we got up for the benefit of Mr. Evarts, the U.S.A. Secretary of State. I was to receive an address from the Bar of Ontario in their very fine building, Osgoode Hall, and I asked Mr. Blake to arrange that after the address he should stand up and welcome Mr. Evarts on the part of the Ontario Bar, as the most distinguished member of the United States Bar. Mr. E. was much pleased, and made a very good speech in reply. It was almost the only public reception that could fitly have been given him without making the demonstration look like a political performance, and so I thought it very fortunate that opportunity presented itself, and that I was able to make the most of it. We took Mr. E. to the University Reception, and to the Exhibition. He was pleasant and reasonable in conversation.

Toronto really looks most flourishing, and everybody says that a revival of trade is at hand. At Ottawa the lumber people are all busy, and large quantities of deals were being shipped off. Squared timber was still on hand and unsaleable, so I suppose you may expect your Rosneath bays to be choked up for some time to come, which you will not be sorry for. The export of cattle and sheep from this country is going to be quite enormous. One vessel lately took three thousand sheep and six hundred head of cattle; I think the only chance a

British farmer will soon have will be to buy over here, or in South America, and fatten and sell at home. Freight only gives about fifteen per cent. protection to the Britishers. In the matter of furniture-making there is so much now done here, and the furniture is so well packed in pieces, that five per cent. is all that freight will cost ; and in cases where furniture must be packed whole, the freight costs thirty per cent. There will always be something to pay for freight in the case of packed meat, but very little, and the freight of live animals will also become very cheap.

At a "Boys' Home" Institution this morning, I found the chief lady of the Managing Board was a Dunlop, from Campbelltown, who remembers you as a boy there, and Aunt Emma accompanied by the sergeant in red who used to walk round the harbour with her. A grandson of Grant, the Balmoral gamekeeper, is here, and then we hear of a Mrs. Bailie who wants to see me because she nursed Colin and Evey. At every turn one meets people from the old country who knew members of the families, and your arms are emblazoned in every street. The schools, colleges, etc., here are excellent. Now there are Highland games to be attended to. On Wednesday there is another public dinner. To-morrow a public ball.

Nov. 11, 1879.—Nothing makes one see the value of the independent territorial politicians of England more than residence in America, where as a rule the rich get rich too late for public life, or if they give their sons a fortune, and they are rich men, they do not inherit anything beyond the taste for enjoying the late-earned luxury of their father in spending the fortune left them. The father did not, in all probability, care for politics except in so far as to express the opinion that most public men are blackguards, and the sons don't see why they should bother themselves so long as politics will leave them alone.

Then the people who do go into politics are not sufficiently well off to ward off the suspicion that they go in for politics to make money by the choice of profession—by contract getting, and by various jobs. Where in England it would be monstrous, useless, and absurd to charge men with dishonesty in politics, such charges are on this continent too often the commonplaces of political life. There is hardly a man in public life against whom such accusations are not made; and they are made because in a country where there are few men of independent fortune, men who must live somehow live by taking toll of their fellows. The accusations are made because the temptation to profit by political life is so great that it is not uncommon to do so. I do not think it is possible to value too highly the class we have of professional independent politicians. This class is mainly derived from possessors of entailed estates, and their value is greater than that of some undrained land. I do not, however, see why the draining should not go on, and why the estates which are hopelessly in debt should not, in spite of entails, be sold in an encumbered Estate Court. But a chance should be given to the family and estate, that it should not succumb and be destroyed by the wickedness of one man. Where property means employment of labour one should not frighten capitalists from enjoying it at home. Taxes and burdens should be placed on men who employ foreign labour.

November 29, 1879.—What a terrible exertion you have gone through, in that tremendous meeting at Leeds! If assemblages of that size are to be the rule in future, we shall have to get men stationed like telegraph-poles down the room, to repeat the orator's sentences to the masses who cannot be near the platform. You seem to have managed to get them pretty well in hand and quiet during the last part of the speech, which was very eloquent, especially about the Moors in Spain, and the farewell shot on the famous ramparts of Corunna. How well I remember you repeating those lines to us chicks in the old dressing-room at Rosneath! but, by the bye, it was the "foe" who fired the random and distant shot, and the burial was done quietly to prevent the enemy knowing of the British whereabouts. "What inaccuracy!" we shall hear Lord Salisbury say.

I send an extract about an old man reported to have died lately at the age of one hundred and seven, and a native of Inveraray. It would be interesting to find out from the Parish Registry if McNair's age was as great as stated.

I have been corresponding directly with Lord Salisbury—not through *The Times*—about the position to be given in England to Canadian Representatives. English Ministers do not seem to understand what is wanted, but they offer the title of " Commissioner"; and if they will really give the Canadian equal chances with their diplomats of knowing what is going on, and will enforce and urge his demands on foreign powers with the same zeal they employ in furthering the interests of the British Isles, essentials will have been conceded.

Sir John and Lady Glover, who have been staying here, gave what is to me a new account of the use of dogs for catching fish. They say that the dogs employed by the Labrador factories as sledge dogs in winter are not fed at all by their masters in the summer. The packs go out by themselves, fishing morning and evening, and provide their own fish for breakfast and supper. They catch capelin and trout, and they do it by putting the ends of their paws, or, if a dog has a particularly pretty paw, the whole paw, in the water! The fish are attracted by this curious object, and perhaps by its smell, and come to the surface to see what it is, when the dog snaps and catches and eats them! Lady Glover, whom I believe, although she may have an Irish imagination, says that she has seen dogs in Newfoundland going out to fish in the same way, only along the shore. Nice beasts! A dog with a white spot on the paw is always the most successful fisherdog.

Sir John's account of his Ashantee and Lagos experiences is very interesting and should be put into a popular book. His plan, before Wolseley was sent out, was to raise the interior tribes against the Ashantees and to come down upon them from the interior. He says he does not believe in the interior country being much more healthy for Europeans than the sea-coast. The amount of gold, oil, and ivory to be got is, he thinks, still immense. There were great gold treasures at Coomassie in the tombs of the kings which we never reached. Much severe fighting took place between his column and the Ashantees, who " ought to have eaten him up." He is a thickset, dark man, with close-cropped grey hair, and French-cut moustache and beard. He was severely wounded while fighting against the Burmese, a bullet having entered near an eye, where there is still a great hole, and came out near the ear. On recovering consciousness, he had to walk ten miles before he got into safety.

The Press takes up the Canadian Academy project well, and there are favourable leading articles in several of the papers about it.

I have sent three fine owl-skins to you. We had a great flock of the pine-grosbeak about the house, evidently a flock passing from the north to some other feeding-place—where I do not know, as these birds do not, I think, go beyond the winter snow zone. They were almost all young birds or females.

A corroboration of the snake's love of milk comes from Kingston, Ontario. A cow kept in a large byre with a lot of others was seen to be uneasy and terrified. A snake four feet long was found near her, and when killed was full of milk.

Mr. Drummond, of the British Legation at Washington, tells me that when he was at Buenos Ayres he heard of many cases where not only cows but women asleep had been sucked by snakes. The husband of one woman told him he found a snake sucking his wife's breast, and the baby had hold of the snake's tail and was sucking that!

The great Railway Debate goes on, speeches of six, five, and three hours long being not uncommon. I do not think the Opposition is making any headway against the proposal, although they have done their best to excite the country.

Jan. 13, 1880.—A January thaw, which is a regular phenomenon here, has prevailed for the last few days, and has been succeeded by heavy frost, so that the whole of the snow has been covered by a coating of ice, so thick that a man can stand on it without breaking through. The moose cannot do this, being too heavy, and their feet go through the crust, and I expect to hear of Bagot and Harbord having good sport up the river, if they fall in with beasts at all.

The statue designed for a sundial, which I am making with Van Luppen, approaches completion, and I must say I think it is not at all a bad figure. I shall have it photographed and send the photos to you that you may judge. The Academy Exhibition will not be open till February 20. I think myself lucky to have been able to get it on foot, "off my own bat," the first year, as it will be a lasting thing, and grow with the nation's development.

Feb. 16, 1880.—We have had a narrow escape here, having been run away with and upset, and then dragged for four hundred yards the other night, when on our way into town for the drawing-room. L. has been much hurt, and it is a wonder that her skull was not fractured. The muscles of the neck, shoulder, and back are much strained, and the lobe of one ear was cut in two. As we pounded along, I expected the sides of the carriage to give way every moment, when we should probably have been all killed. As it was, L. was the only one much hurt, although Mrs. Langham was a great deal bruised. McNeill and I escaped almost untouched. Willy Bagot behaved very well, jumping with a groom from his sleigh, and sticking to the hold he got at the horses' heads till they stopped, although he was bruised about the knees by the beasts.

May 10, 1880.—Mr. Bierstadt, who is now here, is going to send me from New York photographs of some very curious cliff dwellings in Northern Mexico and Central America. He has had these done for the purpose of drawing up a report on the remains of ancient people, and photographs are to be taken of everything of interest. They show an absence of anything approaching to good art that is remarkable; for the masonry in the south is excellent, and the population seems to have been very dense along the great rivers.

Report speaks just now of a little difficulty with Indians at one of the posts on account of squaws. At one place there are Crees, and it is urged that we should send women for wives to the N.W., otherwise we shall "*Cree-mate*" the whole of the police. Lately there was a question as to the paternity of a baby on one of the Railway Sections, and the evidence reported was: "Well, it's half Injun and half engineer."

I hear of a negro who was canvassed for his vote, but declined to give it, on the ground that "there are so many humours (rumours) flying, that one must remain mutual (neutral)."

Young McNeill, Sir John's nephew, came up to Ottawa the other day, and dined with me. He seems to be getting on very well in his farm in Western Ontario, and likes the country. He is four miles from a railroad station, speaks highly of the crops he raises, of the hard work, and the prospect of getting on in cattle breeding. This he has not yet begun, but it is going to be one of Canada's greatest industries, and the London (England) market will take all that he can send.

Lowe and Bright have both given utterance to expressions which show them to be lukewarm about anything Colonial; although Bright is ready to lick the dust off the foreigners' shoes, and Gladstone, probably unwarrantably, is also supposed not to care twopence if the connection is severed. Hartington's language was very good on the subject, and is being quoted here.

L. is going about again. We visited a nunnery which has charge of a school and hospital, and she has attended a judgment-giving in a constitutional case, and one or two debates in the Commons, going again to-day for a grand set-to between Government and Opposition about the Pacific Railway, which the Liberals—as is usual at home, when anything national and necessary costs money— think too expensive a scheme.

Canadian goldfinches have been added to the aviary. They merit the name far more than do their English cousins, being of the brightest yellow with black crest and wings and tail. Then a green and rather ugly crossbill has been captured, and looks very solemn and cross among the other birds. The plumage of the snow-bunting is far more handsome in summer than in winter, being well marked in cream, white, and black,

I am glad that Sir Alexander Galt is in England to "post" people on the Canadian questions. Too often when Canadian interests have been fought (as in the Ashburton Treaty, and the San Juan business) the result has been a series of scandalous concessions by England. Too often in treaty-making Canada has been simply ignored. Even with high tariff, she takes far more English goods than do foreigners. Her goodwill is worth keeping, and if her representative is allowed scope to work for her in treaty-making, that goodwill cannot be lost. Other Colonies when confederated are sure to follow Canada's example, and when we make treaties we can do so by machinery that will represent a greater industrial population than that of any other national combination in the world.

Yesterday the Academy opening took place, and was a great ceremony. The Exhibition is really very good, quantities of pictures having been rejected, and many good ones being exhibited on loan. The Queen gave a commission to the President, Mr. O'Brien, to paint something of Quebec. The tapestries, the old Rosneath one, and a large Gobelin we had at Dornden, looked very well. I shall send you a photo of a statue designed for a sundial, which was supposed also to be good. The Press is very enthusiastic on the subject of this push given to art.

I got Sir John MacDonald to send a telegram

direct to the great Indian Sioux chief, Sitting Bull, who is, they say, preparing to make a raid from our side on the Yankee posts, warning him solemnly that the "Great Mother" would not stand attacks being made on her allies from our frontier. I wrote the message, which was approved of by Sir John, and should have reached our officer commanding the North-west Police two days ago. Yesterday I saw in the paper that the Washington Cabinet had resolved to represent to us the case, and we shall now be able to say that we lost not a moment in sending a peremptory message to the creatures to behave themselves. The question is becoming a difficult one in the north-west, for our neighbours' treatment of the Indians has been so bad that the redskins have come over to our side in great numbers, but are dependent for their food on the buffalo, and the beasts won't stay up in the north to be killed, and the Indians must follow to live, and then they came in contact with the Americans who abuse us. They say that we have between thirty and forty thousand of our own wild Indians between Red River and the Rockies, and there are large forces of the Sioux over with us. Our men manage them capitally, and we have not had a single row. We have sent a remonstrance to Washington against the policy which keeps the additional horde over with us, as we have been to great expense to keep them quiet and look after them.

QUEBEC.
From New Liverpool, July 15, 1881.

From sketches by the Duke of Argyll.

QUEBEC, JULY 15, 1881.

QUEBEC

Who hath not known delight whose feet
   Have paced thy streets or terrace way;
   From rampart sod, or bastion grey,
Hath marked thy sea-like river greet
The bright and peopled banks that shine
In front of the far mountain's line;
   Thy glittering roofs below, the play
Of currents where the ships entwine
   Their spars, or laden pass away?

QUEBEC TO QUEEN VICTORIA

(From a poem in French by Mr. Louis Frechetti, the French Canadian Author.)

Before thy golden sceptre Despots, cowed,
Resigned their ancient might of fire and cloud,
   And held afar a darksome way;
And men shall hail this time Republican,—
These sixty years of glory that began,
   Victoria, in thy maiden day.

Light lies on us thy sceptre, gracious Queen!
War against tyrants oft has glorious been,
   For Freedom lives through Battle's stress;
But who strikes down his brave defender's arm?
What child, with base ingratitude, would harm
   The mother hand, stretched forth to bless?

So I, no courtier, who by creed and race
Cherish French memories, that thou canst not grace,
   Yet to thy flag bear homage true;
Thy race's flag! Thereafter mine! Proud symbol, known
Where'er the sun has shone; can it for me atone
   That victor once o'er France it flew?

Yes! Without yielding faith or pride in aught
When of thy great example I have thought,
   And of thine era, free, serene,
I, subject-citizen, Republican and free,
Feel I can wholly render loyalty to thee,
   And, Frenchman, bless thy flag, my Queen!

Montreal, *May* 29, 1880.—The place is in great beauty, the avenues of trees in the streets in full foliage, half hiding the well-built villas of limestone, of which all the upper part of the town is constructed, and giving very pleasant shade in the hot weather. Yesterday we had 86° in the shade, and I hear from New York that they are enjoying 111° in the shade there! Quebec was glorious in its spring dress. About a hundred ships lay beneath the citadel or at the wharfs, many of them showing some marks about their bows of the ice they had met with in the Gulf. No heavier ice has come from the north or from the rivers for years, and several ships were caught in the field floes and detained for a week or ten days and in some danger of being battered by the lift and swing of the pack.

The *Sardinian*, which brought Prince Leopold's party, saw several icebergs and was herself in the floe for some hours. The experience was a rare and fortunate one for the travellers, and the contrast between the cold weather in the neighbourhood of Newfoundland and the most tropical sun met with at Quebec must have given a curious impression of the climate. The review went off very well, and was a beautiful sight. French- and English-speaking regiments fought over the old battleground ; and as there was nothing in the programme at all like the events of 1759, all were pleased.

River Cascapedia, Province of Quebec, *June,*

MIDDLE CAMP, CASCAPEDIA, 1880.
The Governor-General's Camp. Tents on the left. Tiko Hill in distance.

From drawings by Lord A. Campbel.
LUNCH HOUR ON THE CASCAPEDIA, ABOVE TRACKETY.
Louis Jerome and M., 1880

1880.—We have a house, with capacious loft for servants, a good-sized sitting-room, kitchen, large verandah, and four bedrooms, each large enough for two. I bought it at Quebec, and the workmen are not yet out of it, as there was a little delay in choosing the site. At first we thought of putting it up on the opposite side and at the bend of the river below. Then it was found that the place might be damp, and the spring for the house supply a little far, so now we have placed it on the lower end of the spur that comes down, opposite.

Camp, *July* 2, 1880.—Archie and I have ascended in canoes ten miles above this, and have to-day returned to our tents, having put up in a "shelter"—that is, a cloth put gipsy fashion over boughs—when sleeping out last night. The salmon are as yet scarce in the upper reaches, and the flies are everywhere very numerous. Yesterday we slept on a piece of shore, fondly imagining that it would be wind swept. It turned out to be a lovely inferno, the sandflies swarming on it to such an extent that the flyproof lumbermen and Indians with us could not sleep, although they kept up a big fire. Close to us we found the dung of a bear; and Archie, who had borne up pretty well, at last broke out into disjointed plaints: "Oh dear—lovely—most lovely—but, dear me—quelle profonde misère! Delicious wilderness, but quite savage—bears making dung almost over one's breakfast-cloth, and ants as big as the knife handles walking over it!" He is in a constant alternation of rapture and despair, and had unalloyed satisfaction in seeing a beaver-retreat among the logs of a small "jam" or mass of logs on a bar. Many of the sticks bore marks of the beast's teeth, and his entrances to his den could be seen. A nest of a sandpiper was found with four eggs. Ground-colour, clay with brown blotches, some towards the larger end big. Also a red merganser like those you saw, and a young one, killed (as they destroy fish, a justifiable murder). We saw two squirrels swimming rapids in the river, and when I was fishing one suddenly appeared in the water, ran up the pole of the man who was holding the canoe in position, and disported itself by running fore and aft along the gunwales, until we tried to catch it, when it leaped off and continued its swim across the river, going at a great pace down and aslant very rough water.

There are many fine pieces of jasper on the gravel beaches, and I got a good piece of white agate, and some amethystine quartz. Archie caught two 23 lb. salmon on our way back this evening, and lost another which the men vow was a forty-pounder. The trout are magnificent in this river, and average 2 lb. and are very often $2\frac{1}{2}$ and 3 lb. They are fresh from the sea, and when large have some red in the centre of many of the pale spots with which you remember they are all covered here. The red spots in the pale dottings are not

From sketches by the Duke of Argyll.

THE CASCAPEDIA.
From my tent, 1880.

QUEBEC.
July 21, 1882.

seen at all in the smaller ones. One grilse of 11 lb. has been caught, but it is very rare to get them, and it is a mystery why all the fish should always be above 20 lb.

There are plenty of night herons—some owls and small hawks; no eagles have as yet been seen, nor have I shot any small birds, the redstart you shot last year being the only small bird I have seen. The birch partridge is a grey grouse, something like a grey hen, and different from a spruce partridge, which is a smaller bird. The birch partridge drums with its wings during the hatching of its young, and pleases itself so much with the noise that people can get near enough for a shot. The sound is like a heavy waggon when it passes under an archway over rough pavement. A muffled thumping, that comes from them, we have often heard during the last few days.

Near the camp is an old bear-trap—a "deadfall," the construction of which is curious. A palisade ensures that the bear shall not approach except from one side. The bait is put on a withy, which is twisted round a down-pointing hook, and when dragged off this the "deadfall," a heavy log weighted with other logs, comes down on the bear's back, and either breaks it or keeps him "in the stocks" till the hunter comes and kills him. They have for beavers and otters "deadfalls" of the same sort, but the animal is also made to bring the weight on himself by pushing a stick with his breast.

I am much pleased at getting two Canadian

porcupines, from a lighthouse keeper, who, being an educated man, but ruined, is very sorry for himself in his lonely position, and spends all his spare time in sport. The porcupines do not of course pay him, but each seal is worth a pound sterling, and he and his son sometimes get a hundred in the winter. He chases the porcupine with dogs and gets many of them. The two we have taken off as prisoners feed greedily off potato or any vegetable given them, and may breed in confinement.

The whole north shore is covered with immense boulders, but apparently only near the shore, forming a boulder-strewn river terrace. We stationed ourselves each on a boulder, and cast into the sea-water flowing up into the stream, and found that the fish rose freely, for we got twenty or thirty in a short time. The water is so clear that you can see twenty feet deep easily, and the view of the boulder-strewn floors is most beautiful, for the great rounded masses shine green-white with barnacles, and you see the fish moving over them.

August 22, 1880.—Our cruise has been of late a good deal on wheels, as I have been visiting all the Nova Scotia towns on the Bay of Fundy, and then Cape Breton again by boat. At all the places we stopped at, about a dozen, there has been an address presentation, and the consequent speechifying, and I am glad that after Sunday, when we visit Mirimichi, in New Brunswick, it will be over for a short time at least.

"TRAKADY" ON THE CASCAPEDIA.

River Bonaventure, county Canada, fifteen miles beyond middle Camp, where we had No 2 Camp

From drawings by Lord A. Campbell.

CHELSEA, OTTAWA RIVER.

Lumber men drawing logs floated down into the river with long poles. The initials of the owners are cut on the top of the logs, or other marks known to these men at a glance.

We expect a heavy mail at Chatham on the Mirimichi, and after digesting it shall go by rail back to Quebec, having been away since the beginning of the month.

They say that the vast flocks of Brent geese that visit this part of the country invariably leave exactly on the 9th and 10th of June. They are never a day earlier or later. This makes the movements of that portion of the bird army, which you write so interestingly about in the *Contemporary*, more regular than I had ever imagined them to be.

Of the things which we have seen lately, three have chiefly interested me. First the Grand Pré country of *Evangeline*; secondly, the old French forts, or rather their remains at Louisburg, in Cape Breton; and thirdly, the number of Highlanders settled at several of the places we have visited.

The Grand Pré country is perfectly lovely—such rich lands on new red sandstone soil, such width of great sea-meadow covered with the richest grass, such hundreds of happy, prosperous-looking homesteads, surrounded by their orchards and cornfields. One never sees a poor-looking person, and the land is as garden-like as any part of England. No rugged pine-forest outline meets the eye, but great willows, elms and oaks, and birch clumps have been left here and there. From the top of a steep hill which we climbed in search of agates, the view was like that over the weald of Kent.

At Louisburg, the plan of the old French citadel and great fortress besieged and taken by Wolfe is clearly to be seen. The rampart lines remain, and several of the bomb-proof casements, although our troops did their best to blow up the whole place. A little digging brought to light a quantity of relics of the fights—old gun-barrels, buttons, bits of bridles, broken hand-grenades, tomahawk and brown-billheads, axes, and several swords—all rusted and decayed, except where the metal was brass, when it remains almost as good as ever. It is strange that so much is still left in the ground when one hears that shiploads of things have been taken away.

The Highlanders at Antigonish, Pictou, and Sydney in Cape Breton are chiefly from the Hebrides and west coast, and are most enthusiastic. They kissed my hand and behaved like their ancestors, who were proud to follow to death. All speak Gaelic and English equally well, and grin with delight if one says a word to them in the ancient tongue. You never saw such happy, prosperous-looking people. They have farms of two, three, and four hundred acres apiece, and are steadily turning all the country around them into a well-settled, happy district.

At Antigonish they are all Roman Catholics, and have built a great stone church which overlooks the neatest-looking town imaginable hidden away among well-cultivated hills.

THE CASCAPEDIA.

Cottage, July, 1882.

From sketches by the Duke of Argyll.

THE CASCAPEDIA.

Middle Camp Pool.

Here at Charlottetown I have been shown by an old gentleman, the father of one of my Ministers, named Pope, a letter from you dated Inverarary, 1848, when you had made inquiries of him as to the capabilities of this island for the sake of the Tyree and Ross of Mull men.

My Esquimaux dog steals all the newspapers, and after reading them tears them to pieces. She is also very fond of taking the stockings and boots of one of the party by night, and putting them into another man's cabin. Sometimes slippers disappear until they are searched for on deck, where they are found half full of rain-water. No curious fish have been caught, except a hideous red thing. Many most delicate mackerel and cod, and a skate or two. Sharks have been very common about New York, and have attacked boats passing through their schools, but we have seen none.

The amethysts of Cape Blomidon (a Cape mentioned in *Evangeline*) are most lovely, and I have ordered some to be sent to me at Ottawa. There had been too many boys and servants picking up specimens for us to find good ones during our short scramble among the rocks. The Bay of Fundy tide we also did not see to much advantage, as it is only during spring tides that it raises a "bore" in the rivers. The great red flats left at ordinary low water are, however, sufficiently striking. A large iron-mine was interesting at a place called Londonderry. I have been preaching the commencement of iron ship building, for we have the coal and iron to any extent together at the water's edge.

Sept. 18, 1880.—The great railway scheme seems to have been arranged. If it has been well done, it will be a great triumph for Sir John MacDonald. Parliament will probably have to meet a little earlier to discuss the whole thing.

Ottawa, *Nov.* 18, 1880.—Colonel Gzowski of Toronto, aide-de-camp to the Queen, goes home this week, and wishes to be introduced to you. His wife also goes home for the winter, wishing to be with her daughter, who is the widow of Colonel Northey, of the 60th, killed at Ulundi. He has done a great deal to encourage the militia in Canada, taking a team almost every year to Wimbledon.

His history is remarkable. A son of a Russian Governor, he joined in the revolt of the Poles, when a military cadet. He fought the Russians for a whole year, and retreated with the Polish army, 17,000 strong, across the Galician frontier, retiring before 70,000 Russian troops. He came to America with nothing in his pocket, and unable to speak a word of English.

He made the acquaintance of Sir William Bagot, who helped him. He became one of the first Civil Engineers in Canada, built the great International bridge above Niagara, and is well off and deservedly influential. . . .

December, 1880.—A dear old Irish senator, Mr. Ryan, his wife and daughters, and Col. Dyde are with me, besides Mrs. Stephenson. Col. Dyde is eighty-six, and younger than most men of forty, six feet three inches high, very good-looking, and remembers Napoleon "looking like one of our Indians" in 1802!

Parliament opens to-morrow. Sir John MacDonald is by no means well, and I am afraid will not last long—but he has great recovering power.

Dizzy writes me a mournful letter apropos of Ireland and Bright's utterance about the Lords.

My exercise consists of golf and tennis. I am endeavouring to get Mr. Blaine, the new American Secretary of State, to pay me a visit during the first week of July, and then Westward Ho! for the great plains and rivers, and the wild Indians. We shall hold great councils of these, and hope to have some effect in satisfying them, and getting them to take to the agricultural life which can now alone save them.

I am a great admirer of our Ontario Self-government, and think that it would form a good foundation for home legislation in the same line. Freeholders can vote for the County Council (answering to Grand Jury, or Commissioners of Supply) if possessed as a freeholder of two hundred dollars, and as a tenant of four hundred. These men have therefore the franchise only, and they in each township elect a "reeve" and "deputy reeve"—

these reeves must be men having eight hundred dollars. They come together once or twice a year, form the County Council, and assess rates for the county under the presidency of a Warden, whom they elect to hold office for one year. The only objection to the plan is that some counties have too large a council—one, for instance, has fifty-three. This could be obviated by one reeve instead of two being chosen for each township.

I have a lady staying in the house, who says she has made the voyage through the Hudson Straits three times and found it very pleasant, with such bright and smooth seas, although she was only in an old-fashioned sailing vessel.

Judge Johnson, who has been staying with us, gave me two fine walrus tusks the other day, which he found on the shore of Magdalen Island. It seems that a lot of this ivory can be got from the clay there.

We had a most successful opening of the third annual exhibition of the Canadian Academy of Arts last night. Some very good paintings were shown. My other Canadian child, the Royal Society for Literature and Science, promises very well. This morning Principal Dawson came to have a long consultation thereanent. All the men invited have most thankfully accepted the honour of nomination.

Your Mull leaf-beds seem threatened with an Eocene origin. A great dispute is raging about the age of Bovey Tracey; and although the animal life on this continent shows much difference between the Upper Cretaceous and the Eocene, the plant life in America and Canada seems almost the same from the Cretaceous right up into the Miocene.

The ghastly Irish mess becomes more terrible every hour. I am not at all sure that local Provincial Government would be a bad thing. It would give each Province Denominational Education, which the priests want and which the British Parliament will never give. The powers given to Provincial Assemblies might be jealously enough curtailed, and I should not be at all sorry to see education handled for Scotland by a Scots Provincial Assembly. Civil rights would be too large a concession to give any such bodies now, although it answers to give it them here.

May, 1881.—Dizzy's claims to national gratitude, quite independently of personal feelings towards him, seem to me to be his latterly constant care not to embarass a Government, however hostile he may have been to it, during any international negotiations; his firm determination to put aside the spreading parochialism and narrowness in national policy, and the warm encouragement he gave to arts.

I have persuaded Sir John McDonald to go to England, and have got the Cabinet to give him an Emigration Mission to make it possible, as, to his great honour be it said, he is poorer than any church mouse.

June 27, 1881.—Dr. Macgregor arrived this morning brimming over with enthusiasm. I wish you could have seen him at the Hotel Dieu, a great establishment of nuns living in a building which has belonged to the order since the first stone was laid in 1639, under the auspices of the Duchess d'Aiguillon. We had visited the hospital where the sick are tended by the nuns, and, after rambling over endless old corridors, were shown into a hall where the novices and postulants for admission to the order were drawn up in a row.

The Rev. Dr. Macgregor had been making copious notes of everything, and was not to be stopped or daunted by an array of lovely novices. So out came the notebook again, and the great little man took up his position like an inspecting officer calling a roll-call in front of troops, and many questions came pouring from his lips, accompanied by groans of approbation, curiosity, and admiration of the saintly womanhood before him. These questions were at first quite harmless, and related only to the names of the different articles of their attire, and the nuns didn't mind, although skirts were particularly inquired after for their ecclesiastical title. But the demureness and quiet meekness of the women's faces quite altered when the great little man in his enthusiasm went on to ask about their underclothing, and what they wore below that, wishing apparently to get at a hair shirt, but getting only a general giggle from the whole line. After that he was hurried away.

We leave to-morrow for Halifax. One German and two French corvettes are to be there besides our squadron. We shall have between three and four thousand militia in a New Brunswick valley, and after the dissipations on the Atlantic seaboard we begin our great western journey.

Out of sight of shore, Lake Superior, *July,* 1881.—We have been steaming steadily for three days and nights, and yet we cannot reach Thunder Bay at the north-west corner of the lake till to-morrow at one o'clock. This morning we could just see the high hills on the north shore in the distance, but we shall come in sight of the high basaltic cliffs of Thunder Island to-morrow. Absolute calm has been our fortunate lot. The party consists of Dr. "Hamish" McGregor, of St. Cuthbert's, Edinburgh; Austin, who writes for *The Times*; a Canadian correspondent; Sydney Hall, for *The Graphic*; Roche, for *The Telegraph*; Dr. Colin Sewell; my cousin Bagot; Captain Chater, of the 91st Regiment; Major de Winton; little Campbell, the shorthand writer; and Captain C. Percival, formerly 2nd Life Guards. The coolness of these waters, making all the air pleasant, is delightful after the heat we had passing through western Canada, where dust, sun, and speechifying took much out of one.

The people at Collingwood were mostly Highlanders, very many hailing from Tyree and Islay. They were most affectionate, crowding round to get a shake of the hand—old men and women hobbling out to have a word, and blessing one in Gaelic. The Rev. Doctor Hamish was deeply touched and interested. One good-looking old lady we saw sitting at the verandah door of a charming house. There were three generations at least around her, and some of them very pretty young women. We asked who she was. " Oh, she came from Islay." So the doctor and I got out of the carriage, stopping the long caravan of gigs which accompanied us, and went to speak to her. She had not a word of English, although all her descendants spoke nothing else.

Another very old man had been there sixty years and came from Bowmore, and there is a Bowmore near Collingwood, and it is a more thriving place than the original by far. He remembered your grandfather. All the people say that they are as prosperous as possible, and that is saying much. We visited some interesting copper-mines on a big island in Lake Superior. The ore is beautiful, pure mosslike branches of copper showing in the conglomerate of amygdaloid trap, of which all the island contains bands. Agates are very common, but as a rule small.

We have met at several places Indians, but mostly much mixed in blood. At one meeting, however, some pure bloods sent a deputation about grievances, and a grand old man perpetually in his speech addressed me, who might have been his grandson, as "father." It is astonishing to see along the north side of the lake how the settlements are increasing in number, mostly with people from Ontario, but many English and Scots also.

Georgian Bay—a misnomer, for it is a part of Lake Huron—possesses a lovely archipelago, and the islands are literally countless and of all sizes, and even the most minute bears a tree or two.

Qu'appelle River, ninety miles west of Fort Ellen, *Aug.* 16, 1881.—We have got beyond the limits, even as enlarged recently, of Manitoba. You would never complain of the want of bird life in this part of the Dominion. Every one of the 100,000 ponds and lakes we passed on the prairies swarms with wild fowl. Small birds are very numerous, and so are hawks. The ducks hitherto shot are a small kind of merganser, blue and green teal, American widgeon, the "stalk" duck, a small black-headed duck, the shoveller, with long enlarged bill and white wing coverts. Hawks, buzzards, a lovely white-rumped, ringed red hawk, fine cranes, standing about four feet high, and many sharp-tailed grouse. To-day, for instance, there were fifteen of these grouse and twenty duck of various kinds killed merely by the "trail" side as we made two halts to rest the horses. It is amusing to see the ducks taking possession of the tops of the muskrat's houses, as affording a good point of observation of their pond domain. The rats' abodes are conical heaps of decayed reed or sedge, and stick out of the water in many of these dark pools. Much of the muskrat fur is sold in London as sealskin, and the profit on the transaction must be great, for 70,000 ratskins were brought in last year to one Hudson Bay trading-port alone.

The whole land is a grass meadow, very green, sometimes undulating, sometimes spread in great level plains, usually bordered by ridges more gravelly in character, and full of clumps of poplar copse. The river valleys look like broad bands of plain somehow suddenly let down bodily two hundred feet or so. The bottom of the valleys, down which the rivers twist in the most violent loops, is as flat as the plains. The poplar wood is stronger about the river banks, and is mixed with small trees of hardwood. No pines or firs since leaving Winnipeg, three hundred and fifty miles away.

I have a great Indian Council to-morrow. The wretches have been having a sun-dance, *i.e.* torturing themselves after the customs described by Catlin. All seem very friendly, but all ask for impossible things. A squaw we saw the other day had killed nine American babies; fortunately she did not demand more! Many of the Indians have very striking heads. One old strong-featured man at Ellice had a profile the very image of Mr. Gladstone's. If Mr. Gladstone had long black hair parted in the middle and smoothed back, and were a little bedaubed with brick-dust, there would be no

From a drawing by Sydney Hall, Esq.

RED INDIANS.

difference in the likeness. On inquiring we found that the name of this chief was Way-wa-sa-ka-po, or " the man who is always right ! "

We have had no post since leaving Winnipeg, since August 7. I do not expect to get any till we reach the Rockies, another twenty days.

There are great numbers of the small ground-squirrel they call the gophir all over the plains. Some are a yellow ochre colour, some are striped with brown and yellow-white, and have spots to vary the lines. Their tails are short, but with long hairs growing like the squirrel's, only not so long.

It is astonishing to hear the good opinion of the land even from men who have just had the trouble of the first rough life on arrival in the country. Directly a man gets in his first crop and has spent a winter here, there are no terms of praise that he will not use for the land. Old men come from comfortable farms in Ontario are as loud and emphatic in their praise as are the young. Some say they like the Ontario winters better, but they are in a hopeless minority.

Fort Qu'appelle, *Aug.* 16.—We have a large number of Indians. Considering the starving state of many of them in the winter, it is amazing how well we get on with them. The great object with them now is to persuade them to begin agricultural work in their reserves, and naturally it is difficult to change suddenly a people's whole habit and manner of living. Still, many of them are making most laudable efforts, although they work by fits and starts. Agricultural instructors are appointed to the reserves, and some way is being made. To-day there were two addresses presented by Indians —one in French from half-breeds, and one in English from the settlers. Land claims are being taken up very fast. The Hudson Bay Company are busily engaged in the same work of sale, and they have much to dispose of, one-twentieth being theirs.

We have two lakes, each about two miles long, occupying the valley near this place, and they are full of very fine white fish, like those found in Superior, Huron, etc.

We dismiss part of our escort after this, and travel northward to Battleford in light marching order. Hitherto we have had ninety-six horse, seventy-seven men, and twenty-one tents. It has been very pretty to see the train winding in single file over the plains.

Dr. Mcgregor has quite got over his indisposition, and is by far the most active and intelligent of the party; but he preached (unconsciously) for an hour and a half at Ellice, after promising, on account of other arrangements, to be very short!

On the Saskatchewan, *Aug.* 28.—The long jolt, jolt of the waggons is interrupted for three days, and we have the benefit of a steamer to get to Battleford up this most noble river. We are on the North Branch, and crossed the South Branch in order to arrive at these banks. Both branches are about equal in length, one being 1,050 miles, the other 1,090. This one is about 350 yards wide, flowing along through a valley that slopes down gradually to it, the banks often covered with balsam and white poplar. The sunniness and greenness of the whole is wonderful, and not half enough described in the accounts I have seen. The dews prevent it from drying too much, as the American prairie does. The woods would be much heavier, were it not for the fires carelessly originated, usually in September. The Indian never sets the plain on fire. Whites and half-breeds often do so by not putting out camp-fires on leaving them. You should have seen Dr. Hamish the other day, putting out a prairie fire with his coat, looking like a benevolent demon.

The variety of sand-piper plovers has been endless. Since I last wrote I have seen a prairie owl, but not one of the burrowing kind. They live with rattlesnakes further south. We have seen considerable flocks of pelican, white with black wing feathers, Canada geese, and two wild swans. The ducks are endless.

All the settlements near Prince Albert are full of Scots. We have not yet met a man sorry to have come, and all say they like the climate, as well as the soil, better than that of Ontario. Our steamer has a paddle like a wheelbarrow placed astern, and the motion makes much shaking. Next year a new company is going to put several steamers on the river, and there is much need of them, for enough freight for six is now left at the mouth of Lake Winnipeg, and cannot be got to the people till next spring. The river seems to open and close with ice at just the same time as the Ottawa—that is, it opens on April 20, and closes with ice November 15.

Most of the men we have met hereabouts came here with from two to three hundred dollars. But I should advise a start from Great Britain with eight hundred or one thousand—that is, £200 or, say, £180.

The Indian women are very ugly, but *faute de mieux* the Hudson Bay people have taken them often, and half their officers are married to half-breeds, very nice ladylike people often, and usually talking " very Highland," their fathers being Scots.

Fort McLeod, N.W. Territories, *Sept.* 17, 1881.—We have had no means of receiving letters between Winnipeg and Calgary—a place called after the one of that name in Mull, but there are no people at the Canadian Calgary as yet. It may become more than a name [1]—that is, for eight hundred miles as the crow flies, and for a very much longer distance by the route we took. At Calgary we got a mail, which was taken from McLeod to that place, 104 miles, by two of

[1] 1907. Calgary has now about 18,000 inhabitants.

FROM OUR CAMP ON ELBOW RIVER, NEAR CALGARY,
SEPTEMBER, 1881.

From sketches by the Duke of Argyll.

RIVER SASKATCHEWAN, TOUCHWOOD HILLS.

our mounted police troopers, in 12½ hours—a good ride, which did the boys credit. One of them came from Ottawa. The force of police is an excellent one, chiefly recruited in Ontario, and consisting of a lot of very strong handy young fellows, who have occasion often to act with much tact and pluck in dealing with the Indians. One of their number, a Corporal Graburne, was shot by a young Indian near this place last year, and the presumed murderer is now awaiting his trial, which is to take place next week. The case illustrates our difficulties here, for the boy shot the policeman under the impression that it was a duty he owed to his father. The old man in dying declared that want, owing to the absence of the buffalo, had killed him. The want of the buffalo was owing to the white men, and his children should revenge him. "Starlight," one of his sons, took his opportunity, caught Graburne alone, and shot him.

Instead of the myriad herds of buffalo, which used regularly to come to feed on our green northern prairies when the southern grasses got burnt up, there are now only small herds, and the tribes are often in great want, and must be fed and clothed—all this involving tremendous outlay. The buffalo was everything to them. His skin gave them clothing and tent cover; his meat food for all the year, for it was dried and made into pemmican, which will keep for ever. His sinews gave them thread, his dung gave them fuel. Now that they can no longer find any, they wear wretched blankets and live in cold cotton tents, and many cough their lives away. At all the meetings I have held with them we have strongly counselled work on the reserves of land, to which instructors are now appointed, and some have made good progress.

I am sorry to turn from the world of mountains, and to see yet more of the world of sward, instead of piercing those beautiful gorges before us and getting down to the Pacific. We shall just touch the hills, for we visit a Government farm thirty miles off, at their base, and then our march south will allow us to see a mountain lake, which is still on our territory. After camping there we shall cross to American ground, and visit Fort Shaw, where General Ruger, in command of the U.S.A. frontier forces, is stationed. He will probably help us in getting food transport, and I want to talk to him about frontier Indian troubles. From near Helena we should get the railway to Winnipeg (four days), where I have to speak—and then I shall go on (four more days) by rail, *viâ* Chicago to Ottawa. There I hope to give Dr. Macgregor three or four days before he sails by the boat, leaving Quebec on the 15th of October.

We have been lucky hitherto in our weather, and escaped a terrible hailstorm which beat an unfortunate surveying party black and blue. They said if it had lasted ten minutes more it must have killed them all. With us the last week has been like a time in an English June.

I have procured one carved stone. Nothing is more curious in this country than the entire absence of all tradition among the savages as to their own origin, or as to any former people living there. One entrenchment we have examined, and this carved stone shows that other people were there in old days. They say that the same carving was produced by the Pacific Coast Indians. The Assiniboins, cousins of the Sioux, have a tradition that they came from the sea, but that is all. The languages of the Sioux, the Blackfeet, the Crees, and others are perfectly distinct and utterly unlike each other.

As soon as I get back to Ottawa, I am going to set about the founding of a Canadian Scientific and Literary Institute, an interesting undertaking which will require a good deal of trouble and correspondence to bring about. I was provoked the other day to find that one carved stone had been carried off by Americans to the Smithsonian Institute at Washington, and these things are sure to happen until we have some such Association of our own.

We have seen plenty of natural curiosities—wild swan, "wavy" geese (so called because of their wavy line of flight), many brown cranes, badgers, porcupines, antelopes (*Anticapra furcifer*), buffaloes (we killed three), black bears, Canadian geese, avocets. There is a small red duck that is new to me, and we have caught two kinds of trout (red belly with many black spots on back, and white belly with red spots on side), and a fish like a bream with great golden eyes.

I have great hope that this journey may be of some use to the country in making the Indians take to quiet settlement, and in *advertising the new territories*. We have not wasted a day, and tomorrow there is again a gathering of over two thousand Blackfeet, and the Council will last all day.

Cascapedia River, *July* 12, 1882.—I have just come back from a stay of three days up the river, and killed eight salmon, of an average weight of 31 lb. The biggest was $42\frac{1}{2}$ lb. They are all in perfect condition. About 150 lb. of trout were also caught. This morning I killed two splendid fish, of 5 lb. each.

People are clearing out here, for the north-west. That is, the English people—the French Canadians remain and multiply faster than ever. The story goes that as it is the custom to give the twenty-sixth part of everything to the priest of the parish, a man who was horrified at being presented by his wife with a twenty-sixth child, gave it to the priest.

CALIFORNIA

The dirty and horrible fellows!
  Why tolerate any Chinese?
Mr. West Slope abusively bellows
  To win a political breeze.
Yet when to perdition he's sunk 'em,
  What sight at his hearthstone one sees!
Lo! all that he hath, save his buncombe,
  Is run by the Heathen Chinese.
His bakehouse, his laundry, his kitchen,
  His table, his garden, his trees,
His wife from the East, so bewitchin'—
  Are tended by "filthy Chinese."
How touching are then all his speeches
  And promise to send over seas
The men his experience teaches
  Are the cheap, if the nasty, Chinese!
How nasty! for what with their deepness
  Some gold out of nothing they squeeze,
And, bad as their work is, its cheapness
  "Takes the starch out of white labour's knees."
White voters, then, vote for your living,
  And swear that their moral disease
Must keep a good Christian from giving
  Employment to Pagan Chinese.
Sweet Hoodlum of Rum and of virtue
  If your delegate talks as you please,
Do leave him one vice that can't hurt you,
  One noxious, but little, Chinese.

San Francisco, *September,* 1882.—At Omaha we saw a good deal of General Howard. He commands a military district now, having been shifted from the West Point Military School, where he has for some years acted as Commandant. He is a kindly, excellent man.

The wheat crops on the prairie had all been cut when we passed. The corn still stood. I never saw such a horrid desert as that formed by the alkali plains of Nevada. White glare of powdery salt clay, partially covered with sage-brush, where a gigantic grouse is at home. After reaching the western slopes of the Sierra Nevada, there is a sudden change, tall pines appearing everywhere, and the mountain views being often very fine. Unluckily we had to make most of the journey from the mountain-tops to the sea by night.

The country about 'Frisco is very dry-looking, but there are fine crops on all the levels. The city is placed on an enormous harbour, with a narrow hillocked entrance, and sandy hills back all the town. The principal streets have enormous stone and brick buildings with fine shops, and the side streets and environs are full of wooden houses, built of a red pine which smoulders but does not easily burn, and are considered as safe from fire as are the stone buildings. A very crowded ferry steamer took us across the bay after we had been received at the station by all the notables, the chief of these being General McDowell, who commanded the first Federal armies during the war. A southern pink haze veils generally the dry, bare hills, the islands, and wide sweep of the bay. Many ships, chiefly English, are at anchor—among them the white-painted corvette, the *Comus*, which is to take us north.

I have been writing to tell Mr. Gladstone what Irish priests say about Irish Local Government in Canada. I hope to see certain things given over to Irish Provincial Assemblies—education, local administration, etc.

BRITISH COLUMBIA

Coal beneath her giant firs,
Gold in river, mount, and glen,
Peaks and fairy isles are hers!
Peace of God, goodwill to men!
Quiet havens, teaming floods—
Fringed with green Madrona leaves,
Forest aisles, and ocean caves;
Fields of fruit, and harvest sheaves.
She haunts at will her snowy range
Or shores of green that never change.

British Columbia, *Oct.* 6, 1882.—We are in the midst of our Canadian Switzerland. The archipelago of wood-covered islands in the straits between the main and Vancouver Island makes the sea a very sheltered one, and we were not at all unhappy when the steamer touched on a sand-bar at the mouth of the river, which has several mouths and a large delta flat. We were off again very soon, and, anchoring for the night, waited the arrival of a flat-bottomed vessel to take us the following morning upstream. Salmon were seen leaping out of the brackish water as we approached land, and here I may at once tell you all we have heard about these fish. We know they never take the fly, though they can be caught with bait and trolling or spinning tackle. I can't help thinking that their habits have not been sufficiently studied, for it is declared that they have never been seen descending the water. This can be easily understood in the case of the Fraser, for the water is muddy, and they can't be seen ; but in the rivers that flow into the Fraser (the two Thompsons, for instance) the water is clear, and observations could be made.

The number of salmon that enter at different times of year, and the number of apparent species, is very curious. The Indians say that there are seven different kinds, probably including two kinds of sea-trout, but the whites say that there are certainly five kinds. One of these is hump-backed and tasteless and poor-coloured in flesh—not so red as the others—and has a great hooked bill, and many think that this is a spent fish ; but he too, like the rest, comes straight from the sea, so that, combined with the fact that he is apparently not spent, but goes up the river to spawn (he comes only every second year), the puzzle is great. All kinds thrust themselves up the rivers for a thousand miles or more, and are found dying, often in myriads, from exhaustion. The Indians spear them and scoop them up in hand nets, and dry them in thousands. Where we now are, up one of the Thompsons, we see their camps at every mile, and at each camp horizontal poles stretched on the banks under the woods have strings of split salmon hanging from them.

The Indians on the Lower Fraser are almost entirely fish-feeding. Here they have farms as well as fisheries, and ride horses, and are finer men than those below, who from always sitting in canoes are bred

From sketches by the Duke of Argyll.

INDIAN TORCHLIGHT PROCESSION AT NEW WESTMINSTER, 1882.

FRASER RIVER, AT ENTRANCE.

with big upper bodies and big arms, and short and not very straight legs. They are all " good Indians," and have none of the dislike or contempt of work shown by the Blackfeet and others of the plains. The steamer we have now is worked by them, and they demand vehemently to have better schools.

Before leaving for the up-country I went to a fir-covered inlet to which the Canadian Pacific Railway is to be brought, and where there are many magnificent Douglas firs, as well as gigantic yellow cedars and red firs. These woods certainly put one quite out of conceit with those at Inveraray. The height of the trees is marvellous. The lumberers have an ugly way of cutting them down about ten feet from the ground. Spring boards are driven into the trunk for the men to stand on, and perched on these they deliver their axe blows with great effect, and after about three hours' chopping the giants fall crashing in whatever direction may be wished.

The road along the Fraser Gorge is frightful. Parapet or protection of any kind at the side of the road there is none, and for sixty miles the heavy lumbering coach with its four horses is constantly swinging along ledges within six inches of destruction. Of course nothing could save one at these places, for the precipice is often absolutely sheer for hundreds of feet, with the torrent, probably another hundred feet in depth, just below. The scenery is magnificent, for the rock walls rise two or three thousand feet high, and then come slopes on the mountain sides with rich green firs and varied with yellow and red autumntinted maples, and then two thousand feet higher yet more rocks, and often bits of snow-field. Big glaciers there are none, except on the Skeena River further north, where a glacier seven miles long and four hundred feet in ice-height overhangs the river.

As one gets further up the Fraser, there is the occasional relief of seeing a little foreground between one's self and profundity. Where the Thompson joins there are most curious elevated benches or great terraces. At whatever height the road reaches, the cuttings all show rounded gravel deposits. Sometimes great portions of these "benches" slide down, trees and all, and dam the river back for a short while, but very soon the obstruction is cut through by the waters.

After about eighty miles of our travels had been passed, the country opened out considerably, and gave evidence of much greater dryness. Sagebush and cactus appeared. The pines were fonder of the mountain tops than of the rolling hills in the straths below. The water in the streams was of a clear blue-green. There were cattle, and considerable tracts of enclosed land; and some houses, which were often better than log cabins, put up by Government for railway engineers, offered us hospitality. The road had still some *mauvais quart-d'heures* to give us, but we found ourselves luckily yesterday not far from an hostelry by a lakeside, when one of our axles broke. So a three-mile walk brought us to a steamer, which

GOVERNMENT HOUSE, BRITISH COLUMBIA, SEPTEMBER, 1882.

From sketches by the Duke of Argyll.
THE CASCAPEDIA, JULY 6, 1879.

we have since employed and which is now in the centre of a most lovely lake, helpless, for a snag has broken our wheel (an only one at the stern) and it will take some hours to repair it. Luckily the weather is fine, for, with the usual recklessness of this country, we have no small boat attached to us for emergencies.

Kamloops was the first lake we saw, and, ascending the Thompson, we have reached the Shuswap Lakes, which a map will show you. We are only one hundred and ninety miles from a point we reached on the other side of the Rockies last year. All round us are hills and mountains covered with Douglas firs, for the rainfall in the belt is again greater, and the pines are consequently less frequent. The Thompson, where we tracked it to-day, was a beautifully clear-flowing shallow stream, full of salmon, that had evidently long used the gravel-beds as their spawning-ground, for the bottom was all in furrows, ridged by their noses. The trout seem also very fine and very numerous, and they will take the fly. What a pleasure-ground this country will be for the future tourist, and how delightful a good hotel and plenty of row-boats and trolling tackle would be on this long lake! The railroad will skirt it, so it will be easily reached, and mosquitoes will form the only drawback, but this only during the heat of summer. Our engineer who is now labouring at the broken wheel is a Scots piper, with piping prizes.

We are going another hundred miles to get some prairie chicken and grouse shooting.

Victoria, British Columbia, *October* 23, 1882.—Returned yesterday after three weeks' travelling, having passed over a thousand miles of ground. The puzzle about the salmon never descending was partly solved to me by the fact that we found one, on lifting a net near the mouth of the Fraser River, which was evidently trying to descend, a most hideous brute, and belonging to one of the previous "runs." He had immense jagged teeth as well as hooks on the end of his jaws, and was green and ghastly. Next to him, entangled in the meshes, was a fresh good fish of the run now coming in, called the Cohoes. He was a full squab-shaped salmon of good silvery colour, but unlike ours he had the back of the head, body, fins, and tail all covered with dark spots.

We much admired Lake Shuswap, which consists of four great fresh-water lochs joined together at a place where the land leaves only a narrow strip of water. Everywhere the hills rise abruptly, breaking away only in one or two places so as to give a view of higher summits beyond. Where we entered a shallow river which was to take us onward for another thirty miles, there were some wild swans, many duck and teal, and some geese. In the river-woods we found several white-headed eagles, who watched our ascent from the withered tree-tops, as we stuck for some time on a sand-bar, but we had time to

THE FOUR SISTERS.
Fraser River, British Columbia, October, 1882.

From sketches by the Duke of Argyll.

THE FOUR SISTERS.
Fraser River, British Columbia, October, 1882.

catch some trout with brick-coloured backs, and another fish which was more pretty than edible, herring-like, with a quantity of small bones. Twenty more miles through a beautiful valley brought us to our shooting-ground, an open country near another beautiful lake. Sage and bunch-grass covered the curious terraces, which are universal in this country near river and lake. Near it was a poplar-bordered creek and open prairie. On this we found numbers of the sharp-tailed grouse, and killed eighteen and a half brace in about four hours. There is a lovely yellow-chested lark which sings well, and does not belong to any family represented in England. It has a long bill, and a devious flight. We saw some snipe. The woodcock is said not to exist east of the mountains, although one man tells me he could have sworn to having seen it in Oregon. It might certainly be introduced.

A small lake, two and a half miles long by three quarters of a mile broad, had around it an extraordinary beaver-dyke of earth. The water lay in a glen which had a level bottom, so the lake is shallow. The beavers seem afraid that when the water is high the shallow at this end would prove dangerous to their young. Around the whole circumference of the lake, which is fringed only occasionally with poplar, they have built a " fail dyke " about three feet high, so that if there is any overflow the water at the sides remains pretty deep, and the young may kick their heels and flap their broad tails in security. There are very many bears about this country; and at Okanagan, where we now are, the nasty cinnamon bear, which is so savage that it attacks man without provocation and by preference, is frequently found. Their skins only fetch seven dollars—less than the small black bear, whom the cattlemen sometimes lasso, and have great sport. The grizzly is not uncommon. Panthers exist only near the sea apparently, but where they appear the wolves disappear. One coyote wolf only came to look at our proceedings. He is more like a grey fox than a wolf, but is very impudent, and carries off chickens from the settlers' houses.

Returning to steamboat travel, we made a roundabout and passed some lovely scenery. The Ponderosa and Douglas forests were all varied by the gold of the poplar, and it looked sometimes as if a garden had been arranged to please, where the old lava torrents had flamed. The maples further down looked as if they would themselves light the road in a dark night, so intense was the yellow. One lake was said to be composed entirely of soda-water, but I am afraid that taste did not, and analysis will not, bear out the assertion.

I preferred riding to driving through the canyons, and got a horse, and rode in three days ninety miles. We saw Douglas logs being cut up at a saw-mill. A forty-inch stick square of ninety feet in length

SHUSWAP LAKE, BRITISH COLUMBIA.
October, 1882.

From sketches by the Duke of Argyll.

THE FOUR SISTERS, AND MOUNT HOPE.
Fraser River, 1882.

was being operated upon. A tree still standing was about three hundred feet high and over ten in diameter.

On Vancouver Island the coal-mines which are in the middle of the forest were found by an old Scotsman, Mr. Dunsmuir. He had tried a bad small vein in a rock twenty years ago. While powder was being put in, he walked away, and fell in the dense brush near a root of a fallen tree. Grasping at this to help himself, he found on rising that his hand was full of coal. He acquired a title to the land, and bored, and now receives £60,000 a year from this mine, so accidentally acquired. It is cretacious coal, but of excellent quality, and fetches the highest price in the San Francisco market.

Government House, British Columbia, *Nov.* 3, 1882.—We are established in a sort of rival of your Cannes villa Poralto, with a far grander range than that of the Esterelles opposite us, on the other side of the straits of San Juan. An old volcano, now prosaically called Mount Baker, is the finest hill visible. It is 11,000 feet in height, and is isolated from the rest, dwarfing them all. The air is quite mild at this season, much like that of the Isle of Wight, and snow never remains long on the ground at any time in the winter. This is owing to the Japan current, a Pacific Gulf Stream, which makes the whole seaboard warm. We delight in the place so much that instead of only staying three weeks, as intended, we shall stay till the end of the month.

You never saw such marvellous kelp tangle as there is fringing all this coast. The weed is over ten fathoms in length in many parts. The smaller kinds near the shore have an odd bulbous root growing, not in, but above the ground, and attached by threads to the rock. The Indians use the finer portions of this extraordinary weed for ropes, and the hollow bulb and root portion for bottles, and keep their oil, got from fish, in them.

Indians are very expert in using many of the natural products. Excellent nets are made by them from nettles, and the spruce root is much used for smaller ropes, and for their fishing sea-tackle or traps.

I had a pleasant journey into the interior of the island. There are very fair roads, chiefly made at the time of the great gold excitement here in 1860. Gold seems to be everywhere, but not in paying quantities. When that railway is made they will be able to get quartz-crushing works, and then make it pay. At present any one can get a dollar or two every day, if he chooses to wash for it, on the sand-bars of the Fraser, but at other work they can get far more in wages.

There are almost as many "celestials" in the province as there are whites. The Indians number 30,000, and the whites and Chinese each about 12,000. Emigration does not come because there

MOUNT BAKER, BRITISH COLUMBIA,

From Vancouver Island. Dutch Shooting Lagoon, Victoria. The Capital lies in the Bay in the direction of the Mountains.

From sketches by the Duke of Argyll.

MOUNT BAKER, BRITISH COLUMBIA,

Seen through a field-glass, 1882.

are no railways as yet, but the whites put the blame on the "pig-tails," and wish that they were all banished. Any eloquence would be vain in telling them that Chinese labour would help. They say, "We will go it blind," and would rather not have the railway than have it built by the "heathen Chinee." The Scots are chiefly in the coal-mines seventy miles from this, and do not seem to make so much fuss about the invaders as the English, who are used in the galleries to shunt and push the coal trucks. It is an odd thing to see a mine worked, as those near Nanaimo are, in the middle of a dense forest.

We had an affectionate send-off from British Columbia. Their community is still much more like the Crown Colony than any of our other provinces. There is an upper stratum of intensely British Englishmen, and then comes an extraordinarily mixed lot of Chinese, Indians, foreigners, and half-breeds. There is a want of the "I'll stand on my own feet" feeling, which is strong in Canada. They won't get better or richer (they are very comfortable now) until the railway, and with it fresh blood, reaches them.

We have been making many duck-shooting excursions—often into the woods to lakes and marshes. Except for the presence of the large red-stemmed arbutus and bigger trees, one can sometimes hardly believe that one is not in some part of the Inveraray woods; but the sal-lal gives an undergrowth we have not, and it is a charming plant, never higher than five or six feet and always green. It makes a capital cover for woodcock or pheasant. The bracken was all turned to its glorious russet of death, and none of the ferns were whitened as with us. Some large varieties growing on rocks seemed evergreen. The trees, young and old, are much covered with long, grey, hanging moss. It is a great change to come as we have done, in sixty-two hours, from all this moisture and firwood vegetation to the South-of-Spain-like atmosphere and dryness of San Francisco. The sandy yellow-grey hills have tried to put on a little green, but are always very arid-looking.

General Scholfield is in command of the whole of the western slope of the United States. He is very civil in offering an escort of troops to us while we pass over the "cowboy" haunted plains near Mexico. Some trains have recently been robbed by desperadoes on that line. We shall stay for a while at Los Angeles, and shall meet our British warship from Washington or Charlestown about January 26, and hope to see the President.

Santa Barbara, *Christmas Day,* 1882.—We took a charming drive the last day we were at Monterey. Leaving our pine-grove and the hotel, we drove past the town, a little place full of sun-baked clay walls and heavy Spanish tile roofs, and went on past the promontory that forms the horns of the wide sandy bay.

Here a forest of the pine which looks half like

the Scots fir, half like the "Maritima," began, and we left its shelter only when, after three miles, we came out on a sand-blown place of level ground. Here there was a great noise and a horrible smell. These came from a very heavy surf and the guano left on jagged sandstone rocks by myriads of birds—cormorants, gulls, small dusky albatross, and dark pelicans. The stink was so great that we were obliged to go, and found a space of beautiful shore further on, free not only from all objection, but most delightful. Here we saw two flocks of Californian quail, which had apparently been enjoying a bask in the sand above high-water mark.

A terrace of green turf lay between a magnificent grove of Monterey cedar and the surf-lashed beach of rock and sand. The cedars were worthy of their cousins at Chiswick and Whitton, but the trunks of this species are whiter and more gnarled. They looked very grand, their dark, horizontally spreading, massive foliage shown against the wild spray mists of the heavy breakers, which dashed so violently against the rocks that columns of spume were rising constantly into the air.

Then the details in the life of this scene were enchanting. In the coves were many shells that I had only known from collectors' cabinets. The "Venus' ear" were common as oysters near Colchester in England. In whole shells or in broken bits, their wonderful colours of prismatic mother-of-pearl shone at every yard. Pieces of red coarse coral, many forms of zoophyte, and long strips of a graceful laminaria lay in every rocky pool, whole surfaces of rock being one mass of sea-anemone. As at home, soldier crabs had appropriated every spiral shell they could find, and were happily quarrelling. Immense barnacles were common; but what was most curious was to find the barnacle animal without the shell, but occupying little rock rifts, and living in single blessedness with odd limpets and quaint periwinkles for company.

We found that this point was the first place where the cedars came close to the water. For three miles this tree took the place of the pine, and clothed finely formed hills looking mysterious in the mist raised by the surf. Where some cutting had been done for the levelling of the road, great quantities of the "Venus' ear" were observable under the sod, and it was evident that they formed the "kitchen heap" of some old Indian encampment. The Chinese had two villages, or pescaderos, and at each of these they were eating the animal. We took one home and tried it for dinner. Most of us rather liked the dish, and no one was ill afterwards. The shell is so large that one shell-fish gives a good supper.

From Monterey we went to San Francisco, and then due south on a dry, flat plain, with distant mountains in sight. From Los Angeles, a great place for orange culture, we came here by steamer in eight hours, and shall stay till January 5. This is a scattered town with the usual rectangular streets. Shanties and brick walls are spread over a plain near the sea, and the dusty roads are bordered with pepper-trees and eucalyptus.

Some Mexicans gave an exhibition of horse-riding skill in front of the hotel this morning. At full gallop they try to pick up a dollar from the ground. Only one man, after half an hour, succeeded, but the others often raised the sand in their hand. There is a ridge four thousand feet high behind us, and the people grow wheat and grapes and honey for the 'Frisco market. Spanish seems to be as much spoken as English, but the blood is chiefly Indian, and English is taught and spoken only in the schools.

February 3, 1883.—I had an interesting three days at Washington, where all were most courteous, Canada being honoured as a big fact by the President's returning a G.G.'s call—this is the first time it has ever been done.

The dinner given at the White House was a most handsome affair, and very well done. Canoe and snowshoe devices on the table in white and red carnations were very pretty, and there were some beautiful ladies present, notably, as Mr. Gladstone would say, a niece of General Sherman.

General Sherman looked older, but very well, and bright in conversation. He also gave a dinner. The chief people at the receptions were: Story, the sculptor; Senator Sherman; Bancroft, the historian, a wonderful man, now eighty-five and as lively as a kitten; Secretary Lincoln, War Minister, a son of old Abe's, but not the least like him, young for his post and resembling a good-natured German; the Chief Justice, a man with force and character; Pierpont, former Minister to England; Admiral Porter, carrying his years marvellously, and always imagining that torpedoes of his own invention will whip floating creation—a nice old sailor, lean and dark, with a sharp eye; General McClellan, most agreeable and like the Duc d'Aumale, now Minister, a great friend of poor Gambetta's; then some pleasant Supreme Court Judges; also Blaine, kindly and agreeable. Washington was wet and slushy. The streets are now beautifully asphalted.

The new Government buildings are fine, but rather too much divided up in decoration. The Capitol seemed to me more imposing than ever. I had to hold quite a "levee" of members, and of senators in the Senate, and do about five hours' talking at the receptions each evening. At New York I saw General Grant, who is in great good health, and surrounded by pretty things collected in a comfortable house looking on to Central Park.

Cascapedia Cottage, *June* 23, 1883.—We have had so much rain that the river is still very high. I only tried one pool to-day, and caught a salmon of thirty pounds. He was very sulky, took the fly under water and remained there, firm

SEAL SHOOTING, EGG ISLAND.
Among the Boulders, August 5, 1880.

From sketches by the Duke of Argyll.

FROM OUR SCOW, UPPER DECK, JULY 20, 1879.
Luggage Scow crossing the river.

as a rock, except for two minutes when he made a rush. I was half an hour getting him, and the single gut casting-line parted, just as he was gaffed. The other pools were left for the other rods to try this evening.

At the same place, as we were poling up, my "ghillie" Barter, who was in the bow, heard a scratching noise, and could not make out what it was. Soon his eye caught a little black mass up a tree. There was another black mass below. He called to me, but the cedars were thick, close over my head, and I did not at once see the little bears—for such they were. When I had got my gun, the only weapon I had ready, the little brutes were scampering up a steep bank. It was useless to fire at them there, with Number 5 shot. I think they must have been eating the sweet young shoots of the spruce. There were the size of medium Newfoundland dogs.

Middle Camp, Cascapedia River, *July*, 1883.— This morning gave good sport. I was up at 3 a.m. as there is no use fishing with the sun on the pools, and poled up-stream. Two pools only were fished. The first yielded the biggest trout I have seen on this stream, a seven-pounder. Then came a salmon of twenty-one pounds. Then another of eighteen and a half, then a big fellow of twenty-nine, and a fourth of twenty-one and a half. The sun by this time began to illuminate all the wood slopes, so I floated down to the next pool, where I got a twenty-three-pound fish, making five salmon, one big and four smaller trout, between the hours of 4 and 6 a.m. Not a fin would stir when the sun struck the water.

Sunday afternoon was spent in investigating freshly made beaver dams near this, in a "bogan," or backwater. I send a plan of their works.

There was a difference of level of from one foot to three feet between the water surfaces on different sides of each dam. An old beaver-house and a new one were found at the places marked. The new mansion had apparently all "modern improvements," being raised six feet out of the water, whereas the old tenement was not above three feet in height. We could not see the beasts, the wood being thick and the water deep in mud, so that wading would have been unpleasant, and besides, the swarms of sandflies were merciless. The most curious part of the beaver's work was, I thought, a canal dug to the depth of three feet across a little island, about fifteen feet wide at the part intersected by the water, so that there was swimming access from one artificial pool to the other. The dams were made of brush, few big sticks having been used. The brush is fortified, as in the case also of the house, by banked-up mud. The roof of the house is covered with this, but the brush projects out of the water, like a *chevaux de frise*, all the sticks being cleanly cut and arranged up and down stream. Footmarks showed the animals had been working just before we came.

The trappers used steel traps, which they place in an opening they make in the dam. The beaver goes to repair damage, and is caught. The men declare that a lazy beaver who won't work is driven away by the rest of the family, and that he wanders by himself along the river shores, and is known as a "bank beaver."

You will see that the Canadian Government thanked me for the line I took, through Sir Alexander Campbell, who in Sir J. MacDonald's absence was senior member of the Privy Council at Ottawa. I only made one long speech, at a dinner given by the Toronto Club, and this was well received by the newspapers. At Hamilton I met McKellar, our head fisherman's cousin, a very stately and clever-looking sheriff. This was at a reception at the Court House, and directly afterwards I met old Isaac Buchanan, whose people came from Rosneath and who has been a prominent politician in Ontario. At Hamilton we were put up at Dundurn, the place which belonged to Sir A. MacNab, and where he is buried. There is a pretty view over the lake, and an old-fashioned kitchen garden. I never saw a more Scotch crowd than at Guelph; but Hamilton, London, and Toronto were all full of Scotsmen, and the St. Andrews Society's games were the best-attended meetings we saw. This place seems the most blessed peace and rest after the constant crowds and noise, but to-morrow we have the prize-giving of the Rifle Association, and a big agricultural "Fair" to attend, and to reply to addresses on the 24th, and several Lieutenant-Governors and other magnates have come from the remotest regions to attend it. I shall soon only be fit for the uses to which our phosphates are put! We have great exhibits from Manitoba, and eight riflemen have come from there, all of them about six feet four inches high, and covered as to their tops with immense black hats.

What a wonderful speech Dizzy seems to have made about Canada! Nobody is a friend like Dizzy, but the Vale of Aylesbury is famous for its ducks, which are, however, usually white; and so are Dizzy's fibs—beautiful white oriental fibs, which contradict Tennyson's assertion that a fib which is a half-truth is a black fib. The Americans *are* fond of coming here, and Mr. Evarts was immensely surprised the other day in Toronto to find himself the object of an ovation, by some hundreds of his misguided countrymen, whom he imagined were all staying at home.

Citadel, Quebec, *Sept.* 1883.—The two moose have grown immensely, and are dear beasts, coming up to be fed as tamely as ever, although we have been rather long away from them. Jack's horns are now two feet long; and with his long legs, and long ears, and long nose, he looks like some gigantic insect with antennæ coming towards one.

Nothing could have possibly gone off better than the farewell visit to Toronto. On the first day when the Exhibition was opened we had fine weather. On the second, at a presentation of an address in the park, we had deluges of rain. But on both occasions there were thousands present, and the best feeling shown. Lord and Lady Carnarvon were much pleased with all they saw, and I am glad that his lordship will have an opportunity of making a speech at a public dinner they are going to give him at Montreal.

We came down from Kingston by steamer and had a perfect day for the Rapids. The captain of the boat, named Sinclair, told me he came out from Islay in 1883, and that he and three hundred more came away entirely of their own accord, having heard good accounts of Ontario; that although they were sorry to go, yet that they were cheerful enough on the voyage, and had nine pipers on board and went straight to their destination, and none had ever regretted the move.

Long Point, Lake Erie, *Oct.* 3, 1883.—I have been enjoying two very pleasant days duck-shooting, and am off again to-night to Ottawa, where we shall have Pacific Railway upon the brain for the next few months, Ministers having returned, and all the business having to be talked over, and the time arranged for the meeting of Parliament to ratify the bargain finally made. Before getting to this shooting-ground, we had a reception from Highlanders at St. Thomas's which was in its way most touching.

There never was such a Paradise for ducks and all water-fowl as Long Point, twenty miles long, and only just above the water, jutting out into the sea-like lake. Where there is soil on this bar, heavy timber grows, and on approaching the place by steamer the trees look as if they were standing in water. On one side the lake is pretty deep, and the west winds bring up thundering waves. On the east side the water is very shallow, and for miles along the highest part of the spit there is a plateau of mud and peat covered only with from six inches to three feet of water. All over this wide tract the water finds its way through islands of reeds, sedge, and rice-beds, which are alive with birds. The rice looks like fine straw, but without gloss, more slender, and with grass-like heads containing the rice-seed. There are also vast beds of wild celery; but this grows under water, its seed vessel, like a thin peacod, floating near the surface at the end of a long spiral stalk. I am sending a lot of this to the head gardener, in hopes that you may acclimatise it with you. It should not be put out at first in any place where it can be got at by wildfowl, but should be carefully allowed to spread itself in some nook of a pond, or prepared place, where it may have two or three feet of water and soft bottom.

The whole of Long Point is the property of a club, or company. Each man pays about four thousand dollars for his share of sport, the season lasting all October, during which time the shooting is uniformly abundant, the opening day being no better than any other. The club has a charter from the Provincial Government, which has passed very strict game laws. No night shooting is allowed. Trespassers in pursuit of game are severely punished by fine and imprisonment. Keepers are engaged and paid by the club, and live on the island, for such it has now become, the lake having for the last forty years separated it from the mainland. The head quarters form a village of neat huts built on platforms resting on piles in the marsh and reeds at the edge of the lake, and at the opening of one of the sedge-flanked natural canals that lead into the interior of the duck wilderness.

Here, at Duckopolis, each man lives like an old lake-dweller, and has his hut, which is usually arranged to give him a sleeping-room, a little parlour, and a place to hang up his ducks and store away his boats and decoys, while an inclined plane fitted with rollers allows him in his boat to sally out on the creek at any moment; for unless he take exercise on the island where the firm land and the woods are, he is as dependent on his canoe-punt as is a Venetian on his gondola. The canoes are made so as to hold the shooter and the punter only, space sufficient remaining for the storage of the dead game and for the decoys. These are made of wood, and painted to look like different kinds of ducks, with lead at the bottom to keep them upright, and a piece of twine about four feet long attached to them with another weight at the end of the string, to anchor them.

As soon as the place chosen by lot for each shooter is reached, the decoys are put out immediately round a "hide," made simply by two rows of reed bunches stuck down into the mud. Sometimes where there is more water than usual stakes are driven in on each side of the little punt, connected with each other by a double cord, and between these cords are fastened the sedges; but the boat, by having a board fastened along inside of the ribs, can always be fitted with more bunches, so as to hide it from all sides, although the ducks flying directly overhead can usually see it.

Many more birds arrive a fortnight hence, and we are a little too early. There are no canvas-back, and only a few redhead. I shot four of these last. They feed as a rule with the canvas-back, who, being a stronger bird, allows the redhead to pull up the weeds, and then drives him off and devours the products of the dive. Although some of the best ducks have not yet arrived, there are many different sorts here—the two teal, the green- and the blue-winged; the "blue-bill," a "squabby" little dark duck with a slate-coloured rather turned up nose; the "spoonbill," or shoveller; pintails; the American widgeon; the black duck, a large thing like a dark female common wild duck, or mallard; the mallard himself, and his wife; the lovely wood-duck, who does not quack, but makes a plaintive squeaky wailing noise, and coot in any number, are all here.

I send you the score of the two days. As a rule, the decoys did not do much in the way of attraction, except with the teal. But they made the birds fly down lower than they would otherwise have done, and are well worth trying at Inveraray. I shall send skins of most of these kinds to you. The sport is the best of its kind in the world.

Besides ducks, I have shot a kind of dotterel, or "grey plover" as it is called, which is excellent to eat, some snipe, and a hawk like a sparrow-hawk, and have seen bitterns, March harriers, water-snakes swimming, and, among other curious things, a big newt, twelve inches long, with a red frill round his neck. The island is full of snakes, which climb trees and fascinate the birds. You see a bird fluttering about in apparent agony, unable to fly away from a given place, and this turns out to be "electro-biology," or magnetism of a snake's stare. If the snake is shot, the bird flies off all right, but a little more staring makes it come near enough for the reptile to strike it.

Great numbers of migratory birds are killed in the night against the lighthouse at the point. They say all migrations take place at night, and ducks and geese and small birds fly up rivers and strike against and are drowned in waterfalls. At Niagara it is the regular practice of men and boys to go down during the time of migration with lanterns at night to watch the eddies near the Falls for dead ducks and geese, and other birds, and numbers of them are got.

We are going to begin negotiations with Spain, carried on with the approval of the Foreign Office, and through them. This is a great step, and at last an acknowledgment from England that portions of the Empire having different tariffs cannot have identical arrangements with foreign countries.

. . . The night parties now being given here are the most beautiful things you can imagine—twelve to fifteen hundred people. The great snow-slides, the two skating lakes, one in the pine wood close at hand, and the other in the open, near the curling gallery, all glow with lighted cressets and fires. The snow is all around, on the cedar thickets where the boughs are piled with it, or the woods.

. . . Perhaps you may be able to help me about a Canadian contingent for the Imperial Army and Navy Reserve. Sir Patrick MacDougal says that the members of the Defence Commission have all been keenly in favour of the plan. It would show the world that for Defence the Empire swings together, and it would take from the armoury of the "Disintegrationists" the cry that the Colonies will not contribute to the general Defence. The "Disintegrationists" have already had to give up the cry that the Colonies (at least as far as Canada is concerned) won't defend themselves. It is curious how much one hears in Canada that a Liberal Government means indifference to the connection between Colonies and Mother Country, and it is of great importance that this feeling should not be allowed to have holding ground.

... I think that we in Great Britain might "take a leaf" with great advantage from the Municipal County representation in Canada. The parishes might elect a delegate each. These should vote for a representative for the County Council by numbers—say one for every 2,000 people. These representatives of 2,000 could form the County assessing board. In Education the Irish and French Roman Catholics in Ontario are perfectly content with the Law. There is no compulsory attendance. There is a compulsory education tax levied on all ratepayers. This acts in the same way, or near it, as would compulsion. The children are sent because the people want to have the value of their money. All money levies from Roman Catholics goes to Roman Catholic schools only. In Quebec Province other denominations may also have their tax money devoted to their own schools only.

Ottawa, 1883.—Here, of course, all is snow and ice, and I have one hundred and fifty people to skate and slide this afternoon. All my staff, except the Duc de Blacas, have come.

The newspapers of some of the regions through which we travelled in the west read like an uninterrupted Newgate Calendar. They do not seem to care for any news except for "Billy shot Jack in such-and-such a saloon on such-and-such a day."

There is a depression in the land at the head of the Gulf of California, which is a great many feet below the level of the sea, and is exactly in appearance like a piece of Egypt—hot yellow sand, with every now and then a ridge of limestone much worn away on the surface by the friction of wind-driven sand. Then appear the clumps of green bayonets, which you may see in English subtropical gardens, and prickly pear and other cacti are very common as soon as one passes the pure desert. In rocky passes on the American frontier there is a cactus that is like a green-fluted thorn-covered column, twenty feet high. These stand in such quantities that when I first saw them in the dusk of morning I thought they were tall tree-trunks left standing for some reason. The only birds I saw in California were a white and grey crane, and a curious thing looking like a thin grouse with a long tail on pretty tall legs and with a crest. It is called a "road runner." A red-headed woodpecker pockmarks the plane-trees with acorns laid up in the bark for food, always on the sheltered side of the tree. Various ground squirrels are common, and many hawks. In Arizona they sold bird skins at one place, and I got a fine specimen of cinnamon teal.

What interested me most was some of the Indians.

Side by side with savages like the Apaches, who only three weeks ago murdered two Englishmen and about thirty other white settlers, is an old village-building race of totally different features and habits. They are mild and unwarlike, and have excellent faces, with features like those that are seen in the south of Italy. Their houses are now built as they were when the Spaniards first found their country—in terraces, access to each floor being gained by outside ladders or, in some buildings, by trapdoors in the roof. They are the people from whom Montezuma came, and this Indian Emperor lived at or near Santa Fé. They make queer Egyptian-like pottery, and keep up a sacred eternal fire, in the flame of which they believe that Montezuma will again come to them. A most interesting people. Near Santa Fé are also the ruins of the Cliff Dwellers' habitations—again very like what are seen in parts of the East. The cliff dwellings are now deserted, but whole tribes lived in the faces of the hills, where they dotted the precipice face with the doors and windows. The pueblo, or village of the plains, is always built of "adobe," or clay sunburnt brick.

We found snow lying lightly in the north of New Mexico, although even in that region in summer one can find the enormous centipede whose bite is so poisonous that men die from it. The Kansas prairies seem excellent. How often we used to hear in days before the Civil War of the

"State of Affairs in Kansas"! We found a pleasant Governor of Missouri at Jefferson City. Dear old Virginia we found looking very white, and the Alleghanies had the streams side-bound with ice.

My Ministry have agreed to begin three infantry training schools for the militia, and have arranged the division of the territories, one of which, Alberta, is called after L.

Scots in Canada

Scene.—*Curling Rink. All playing with ear-flaps let down from their caps, on account of cold.*

John: "Why are your ears not covered? Not afraid of frost-bites, Sandy?"

Sandy: "Oh aye—but I prefer to keep my ears open."

John: "Why, in this cold! Cover them up, man."

Sandy: "No; last time I had the lug-flaps down I had a sad accident."

John: "What was that?"

Sandy: "Oh, Duncan asked me if I would have a dram, and I never heard him!"

CHAPTER XXVII

The Prairie.—Prairie—" praedia," as the Latins called the wide plains. But isn't it rather a relief to get away altogether from the ancient Roman Empire? Of this new world the Romans knew nothing. It was beyond "the utmost ocean's rim." Yet now a Latin people, the French, have bound us all down to use an old Roman word for the soil of the plains, virgin as it is of any Roman domination. Ah! the old imperial people are still able to cast the chains of their thought, expressions, and language over "regions Cæsar never knew." "Pré" for meadow, "prairie" for plain—are these not the old praedia, the corrupted "brera" of Lombardy, the Gauls' rendering of this same word?

> In measureless meadows there, gaily, all day
> The sun and the breeze with the grass are at play,
> In billows that never can break as they pass,
> But toss the gold foam of the flower-laden grass,
> The bright yellow discs of the asters upcast,
> On waves that in blossom flow silently past.

In winter, the white sea they resemble is somewhat monotonous, but in spring, summer, and autumn how beautiful! If people can rave of the yellow sands of the deserts of Egypt—horrible, sallow death-plains to my mind—how much more ought they to become delirious over the green glory of the prairie! If deserts charm in Egypt the same charm can be easily experienced in the United States, where the "American desert" stretches with alkali lakes and dreary sand wastes beyond the Salt Lake City far to the westward. There too you may have the same satisfaction, if such it be, of seeing sand-storms, and of becoming half-choked with the whirling particles which penetrate everywhere, and all you can do is to put a cloak or something over your mouth, and lie down and gasp for air. The winds, in calmer moments, have strength enough to blow the light sand over the surface, so that by the friction the wooden poles for telegraphs are slowly eaten into and cut down by the drifting and the rubbing of sand particles against them. It is only when you have hills that you can have any irrigation so as to turn desert into corn-bearing land.

The Mormons have been wonderfully successful in irrigation work. They have now ceased to have "plural marriage" and have divorced their too numerous spouses, whom they now call "deceased wives," though they be "alive and kicking," and each contents himself with one. They are a people whose Church compels them to mutual help and high taxation of a graduated kind, which ought to please modern English Socialists. A ten-per-cent. tax levied on a moderate property soon becomes a fifty-per-cent. tax on wealth exceeding a modest amount. So much so that men who become very wealthy leave the Church, unable to endure its exactions. But Mormons, if they had their drawbacks, which their friends declare no longer exist, are splendid irrigators. They know so well how to husband many waters that they no longer need to husband many wives. Many have gone to colonise Alberta, and very many Scandinavians going there become members of the Church for the aid given them as such by the older settlers. They are met at the landing on the eastern coast, they are directed to what colony to go, they are kindly received there and aid given them to build their first house, and until it is ready the hospitality of their neighbours is given them.

So have the descendants of the followers of Brigham Young improved on his example, and are now very welcome in the new lands, where they make much better citizens than do many English coming out because they are " at a loose end " at home. But it is often wonderful how English and Scotsmen contrive to find a good "location" at once. The other day I was visiting a place of mine on the Island of Lismore near Oban, in the Firth of Lorne. There was a fisherman living on the shore in a cottage, and when he kindly brought me some crabs of his catching I told him that I thought he had a brother living with him. Yes, he had, "but he's gone now,"

"Where to?"

"Oh, he's gone to Canada."

"Indeed, and to what place?"

"To a place they call Calgary, like the place in Mull."

I told him that I had camped there, and that when I was there not a soul was to be found anywhere near, and that we had spent three days fishing trout there.

"Indeed, there's 16,000 there now."

"Is it possible? And what's your brother doing?"

"Oh, he's just ranching."

"Ranching? He's a cowboy, then? How does he like that?"

"He is not a cowboy. He has cowboys under him. He has a ranch of his own. Last time he wrote he had about a hundred head of cattle."

Is it not wonderful that a poor fisherman should acquire more than a competence so soon? It was the same with a poor pier-master at a place where there were very few steamers calling and little to do. He took his family out lately, and he passed through old Canada and the flat prairie country, until he came to the rolling lands of Alberta, and there in sight of the mountains he felt more at home, and bought a section of land which he found to be good, and so cleared by nature that he could put his plough into the land and begin work at once. And more: just as though they had been the best of Mormons instead of sturdy Presbyterians and Anglicans, his neighbours turned out to raise at once the first log-house above him and his family. There were a couple of Nova Scotians, he said, and two Americans, and an Englishman, and two Canadians, who proved all most helpful neighbours, and I have no doubt that during the last year he had an excellent crop.

All that is now wanted is more railways, light or heavy. Twelve miles is about the furthest that a man can do when dragging products to the line, and dragging coal back again on his bobsleigh. But many manage to thrive far beyond such limits, ever hoping that a line will some day be made to within an easier distance for them. There are soft coal and hard coal and great irrigation works in Southern Alberta. Cement of greater strength than that of Portland is being made. Where during my visit there were on the plains perhaps 10,000 people, there are now about 900,000. One thing we hardly realised when our "trek" took us along the waters that supply the Mackenzie River flowing to the Arctic—the Saskatchewan flowing to Winnipeg and to the James Bay of the Atlantic, and the Missouri towards the Gulf of Mexico, and this one thing was the reason why cultivation made the early frosts of less severity. Early frost is the bane of the agriculturist. But these came mostly where the turf had been unbroken. When the sod had been pierced everywhere by the plough the early frosts were no longer such a terror. The reason became apparent. The matted sod held the water from sinking, and kept it, as though the grass were a waterproof garment, on the surface. As the frosts always are severest where there is some moisture, it was natural that as the plough pierced the waterproof covering, and let down the moisture into the soil below, the frost was not so much tempted to settle on the land, its moisture being lessened. Such " frigid philosophy," as Dr. Johnson would have said, comes only from experience.

The new Province of Alberta received its name when I was Governor-General and was called after the Princess, one of whose Christian names is Alberta.

ON THE NEW PROVINCE OF ALBERTA

In token of the love which thou hast shown
  For this wide land of freedom, I have named
  A province vast, and for its beauty famed,
By thy dear name to be hereafter known.
Alberta shall it be ! Her fountains thrown
  From alps unto three oceans, to all men
  Shall vaunt her loveliness e'en now ; and when,
Each little hamlet to a city grown,
And numberless as blades of prairie grass
  Or the thick leaves in distant forest bower,
Great peoples hear the giant currents pass,
  Still shall the waters, bringing wealth and power,
Speak the loved name—the land of silver springs—
Worthy the daughter of our English kings.

Canadian Prairies.—The details of the trek from east to west are interesting now that the country is filling up so fast.

Our mounted police force wore helmets and red jackets and high boots in summer. In winter they were clothed in heavy furs. They took over the whole of the duties of transport during our long prairie journey. Captain Herchmer was the Commanding Officer, and carried out his instructions most ably. He met us at what was the Railhead, near Portage la Prairie, and we arranged to go by water to Port Ella, where there was a Hudson Bay port. We were proud of the excellent appearance of our little force. No cavalry in an imperial regiment could have selected a finer body of men. We got to Qu'appelle on August 17, and there found Colonel Steele in command, an officer who, years afterwards, distinguished himself greatly with the Canadian forces in South Africa. On the 19th we started for Fort Carlton, with forty-six men and eighty-four horses. The way led us *via* Humboldt, Gabriel Dumont's Crossing, Fort Carlton, Battleford, Blackfoot Crossing, Calgary, Macleod, to Fort Shaw in Montana, United States of America. The distances marched were, in miles : First day, 5 miles ; August 9 to Big Mud Creek, 32 ; 10th to Rapids City, where no city was ; 11th, to Shoal Lake, 38 ; 12th, to Birtle, 35 ; 13th, to Ellice, 4 ; 14th, camp, 6 ; 15th, camp, 35 ; 16th, to Qu'appelle, 40 ; 17th, 34 miles ; 18th, halt ; 19th, to camp, 38 ; 20th, Edge of Salt Plain, 23 ; 21st, halt ; 22nd, to camp, 38 ; 23rd, to camp, 34 ; 24th, to Gabriel's crossing of the Saskatchewan, 36 ; 25th, to Fort

Carlton, half a day, 20; 26th to 29th, Battleford, 92; September 1, to camp, 33; 2nd, to camp, 36; 3rd, to Sounding Lake, 37; 4th, to camp, 23; 5th, to camp, 35; 6th, to camp, 30; 7th, to camp, 23; 8th, to camp, 80; 9th, Blackfoot Crossing, 34; 10th, to camp 14; 11th, to camp, 18; 14th, Calgary, 28; 15th, to High River, 27; 16th, to Willow Creek, 40; 17th, to McLeod, 25; 20th, Col. McLeid's, 40; 22nd, to camp, 28; 24th, to Cutface Bank, 38; 25th, to Birch Creek, 31; 26th, to Peton River, 68; 27th, to Fort Shaw, 28; total miles, 1,229.

You will see that "to camp" means that the place was nameless, as no one had been there to christen it. You must also remember that during the whole time we were on the prairies with no roads, and that sometimes soft places and rivers had to be crossed.

We had big gatherings of Red Indians at Fort Ellice, Fort Qu'appelle, Fort Carlton, Battleford, Blackfoot Crossing, and Fort McLeod, besides the meeting held to confer with the French half-breeds under Gabriel Dumont (who some years later led an insurrection) at Gabriel's Crossing.

We lost twenty-three horses, two dropping dead. There were no sore backs or shoulders among the horses. It was simply the strain that made us leave them behind. The care taken by the troopers of their horses was all that could be desired. At the crossing of the Saskatchewan—a difficult job—

eighty horses and nineteen waggons crossed, assisted by one scow, or boat, in five hours. The official report mentions that at Red Deer River, the guide, John Longmore, said he could go no further as the country was wholly unknown to him, and an Indian named "Poundmaker," a Cree chief who afterwards fought at Batoche against the Government forces, was our guide. We thought we had completely satisfied him and his friends, the half-breeds, but after events made them again discontented, and they broke out in the rebellion that was subdued by General Middleton.

We found plenty of water between Battleford and Red Deer River, but could find no wood except at Sounding Lake, so wood for cooking had to be carried, but we managed to get dry buffalo dung during some of the marches, which made indifferent fuel.

At Blackfoot Crossing, the officer commanding wrote very justly, "In spite of the very short notice received, that a Guard of Honour was required for the Indian Meeting, the men turned out in a manner to do credit to any troops. The Governor and party were loud in their praise of the men's appearance. Notwithstanding that the men had travelled over 850 miles of prairie, the force supplied at a moment's notice a guard of honour fit to appear at a general inspection."

On the 11th, some twenty-five miles from Calgary (then a place where no settlement existed), Lieut.-

Colonel Irvine, the Commissioner of the Forces, with Superintendent Cotton, the Adjutant, arrived in the camp, bringing a relay of horses and a supply of oats. Next day we forded the Bow river at a point Colonel Irvine had previously marked out. With ninety-nine horses we entered Fort McLeod, an old-fashioned palisaded square, with wood-built towers at the corners. When we at last arrived at the frontier of Montana, in United States Territory, we were met by an officer with a request that our little force should resume its arms, which we had, of course, carefully packed away in waggons. So we marched in to Fort Shaw, where a gallant American regiment under the command of Colonel Kent had their quarters, with all "the honours of war," and all spent a delightful time with our American friends, the men greeting our fellows as though they were old comrades. When we had to continue our journey and our men had to return to their duties in the north, Colonel Kent made his men take line with ours on parade, the red and the blue coats together, and I had the pleasure of addressing both, expressing our gratitude for the reception accorded to us.

At our own parade, which took place earlier, I told the mounted police, "You have been subjected to the most severe criticism during the long march on which you have accompanied me, for I have on my staff experienced officers of the three branches of the Service, Cavalry, Artillery, Infantry, and they one and all have expressed themselves astonished and delighted at the manner in which you have performed your arduous duties, and at your great efficiency. Your work is not only that of military men, but you are called upon to perform the important and responsible duties which devolve upon you in your civil capacities. Your officers in their capacity of magistrates, and in other lines of duty, are called upon to perform even the work of diplomacy."

CHAPTER XXVIII

I VENTURED to write after leaving Canada some notes upon Imperial Federation, and said that " for any common good we must make common sacrifices. Britain and her Colonies must hear each other's views, and have a thorough mutual comprehension of the necessarily differing wishes of the different parts of the Empire. An Imperial Union affording the largest market and the cheapest system of effectual defence for trade and homes is an alliance which would be wholly beneficial. Who shall be able to withstand the will of the many millions of English-speaking people, when they co-operate for peace and commerce? The work of Imperial federation should not be so much to make changes as to confirm the position of our Colonies where they are satisfied; to push their commercial policy wherever they think their position may be improved; to realise thoroughly ourselves the difference involved in the fiscal policy to be pursued in their behalf, as compared with what we deem best for ourselves. Each idea may find its exponent under the same flag, and prosper with different systems under an alliance giving scope to both. There is no reason why one commercial treaty with the foreigner should not embrace with its provisions different arrangements for different parts of the Empire.

"A great step would be taken towards union were a Council, with the High Commissioners for the Colonies as members, to be formed with the British Ministers for Foreign Affairs, the Secretary of State for the Colonies, the Prime Minister, and perhaps the Minister for the Board of Trade. We should derive a more intimate knowledge of the desires of each Colonial Government. There would be more opportunity than at present for Colonial envoys to bring their desires to the notice of the British Government, and of their brother colonists. They would have the opportunity to combine to further the views of one of their number, or to declare against any impracticable object. It may also be assumed that there would be less danger of any independent course being embarked upon by any independent Colony."

Since this was said the envoys of the great Colonies have been more consulted than of old. In the case of the Canadian Dominion, Sir A. Galt, Sir C. Tupper, and Lord Strathcona have been its representatives. The last has, of course, as a peer, a seat in the Upper House. The Australian Federation, still young, has not yet sent a gentleman to London with similar authority to represent all the States; but conferences have been held, and such conferences are favoured by the Imperial Government, and meet at intervals of a few years, to discuss any question which may arise. These conferences are attended by the British Secretary for the Colonies and by others of his colleagues whose Departments may be affected by the discussions. Thus consultation face to face has been brought about, and the Prime Ministers of the Colonies sit at these conferences. The Press in Great Britain has also given more opportunity for the questions regarding each Colony to become known.

The difficulty of any public discussion lies in the fact that the British Government must be responsible for imperial action, and that this cannot be undertaken except by British Ministers responsible to the British electorate alone. Where British Ministers discuss affairs among themselves, the discussion is not public. Nor are debates in Colonial Cabinets made public. The proceedings of all the Parliaments are. Are popular assemblies the best place to discuss delicate negotiations? It has been universally found that the dominant party in the Parliament thinks not. The Government formed from the majority in the popular House is entrusted in all negotiations to speak for the Parliament and nation. If their utterances are disapproved of, each nation has its remedy—the Ministers, who may be questioned in Parliament. Their answers may displace the Government, but usually only after a general election. This, however, takes time, and time for full consideration may be good. In tariff matters each people represented at the conference is independent.

As yet the Colonies have not leagued with foreign powers to the disadvantage of Great Britain in fiscal matters. It is, however, obvious that it may become the interest of the great Colonies to weigh the value of different fiscal alliances. The only commercial deterrent against fiscal arrangements which do not favour Great Britain is the protection afforded by the forces of Great Britain at sea and on land to the Colonies. A party may arise in the Colonies for the protection of their commercial interests, by leaguing themselves with foreigners who may offer fiscal advantages if the Colonies discriminate against Great Britain, but in their favour. The foreigner may say, "Deal with us, and our fleet and army practically become yours." In weighing this matter, sentiment will always have something to say.

It may be doubted if sentiment would not have been strong enough to keep the Americans one with the old country, had not the parent State unduly strained fiscal relations. It is a question of degree whether men turn from old associations to new bonds of alliance. Within certain limits "the old still holds." Exceed these limits and the enchantment of the old feelings vanishes. If the Colonies did all that their ultra-protectionists want, their tariffs would be too high for the British to keep in good temper with them. But they do not, in practice, rise higher than the limit.

The colonial citizens deem it to be necessary to encourage factories arising among them. Their policy in this respect increases rather than diminishes the strength of their Imperial Union. For if any parts of the union be weak, through want of commercial progress, the whole suffers. It is to British advantage that the Colonies should rise in commercial strength, while they form part of the British body politic. Since manufactures have been created among Colonies, as was the case in Great Britain, through tariffs, the Colonies have become much stronger. They can supply more and more each year the needs of their enormously increasing population. They can manufacture their own powder, cannon, rifles, and they can develop their country's public works, get more from their lands, and attract population. This is to our good as well as theirs. The necessity in case of trouble of being obliged to undertake single-handed their defence—a liability that existed of old—is daily being alleviated by their own efforts.

Canada's numbers are increasing so fast that in another hundred years she will probably have a larger population than England will ever be able to support. People must be fed to live. The area of England cannot feed the English. We live largely on food from over-sea. If we have strong friends over-sea calling themselves our fellow-citizens, we may be sure that in war we shall have, as years pass, less difficulty in helping them. Already "the boot has been on the other leg," and the children have come to the mother's assistance in one great imperial war. It is well worth our while, therefore, on selfish grounds alone, and without reckoning on the advantages of fostering sentiments of friendship, to see that we are not too stiff in refusing to listen to what we may think heresy in fiscal matters.

The Colonies have not found that some protection for their manufactures involves their going further and faster than they think good, along the road of protection. One interest with them, as with us, equalises another, and there will always in every country be a party against going too far in fiscal as in other matters. We have no greater tendency, but, on the contrary, less tendency to "slide" into difficulties than have our children by taking up ultra views. The language used, that it would be a crime to set our feet upon the slippery paths of protection, shows a want of confidence in the good sense of the British electorate. The Dutch, for instance, heavy as their personal build is supposed to be, have not found their three-per-cent. tariff protection a sort of fatal toboggan slide, where they must land on dangerous rocks. On the contrary, their good sense has kept them in the track they have chosen. So with us: we need not make any experiments in protection which cannot be taken back if at any time we find that they do not suit us. But there is "no harm in trying." Conservative as we are, and slow to take up any new idea, there is no fear of our being carried too far. Should we find that the nightmare of dear food be more than a nightmare, we need not fear that we may not be able to take off the tax on foreign food or manufactures that may be proved to have produced the change. We could take back anything we found to be hurtful, and the Colonies would be the last people to object were we to find that our people were less well fed than before. But with the vast food areas always open to our commerce, it is difficult to believe that the policy of saying "it pleases you and can't hurt us" to the Colonies can possibly be a disastrous one, if we impose as slight a tax as do the Dutch on foreign produce. The idea of steady, sturdy, slow John Bull becoming a flighty political acrobat, wafted about by every political breeze, and swayed violently by any of his citizens, is one of the most comical of the unfounded and imaginative hallucinations ever entertained.

From a drawing.

DUNROBIN CASTLE, 1860.

CHAPTER XXIX

Dunrobin.—Dunrobin is remarkable for two things, namely, its castle and the sea-serpent! To take the last mentioned first, as the greatest wonder. It is only here that a man known as an accurate observer and distinguished naturalist, namely, Mr. Joass, has actually noted and described what he saw one fine morning when walking on the sands not far from the castle. He had not been thinking of Norse tales of sea-dragons, of "Krakens," or anything else but his work of teaching, and of the beauty of sea and shore, when suddenly out of the same lovely water rolling so peacefully in long gentle lines of waves to his feet he saw, not far from the margin of the shore, a long head and a sinuous body, in apparent vertical undulations, swimming along. He could not, he declared, have been mistaken. There was the break in the surface and the great head, and the evidence of a long serpent's body making a great trail and disappearing. Of course no one but his friends believed him, although there was a lady with him to bear witness to the accuracy of his description. But one word from Mr. Joass on such a subject is worth many words from many ordinary mortals, and so we may confidently place his experience on a level with that of the captain of the *Dædalus*, who saw, with his whole crew, a monster very much like that described at Dunrobin, but further south in warmer seas. But the sea is warm enough around the coasts of Sutherland and Norway to bring a sea-snake to the north.

The Gulf Stream is so strong that it takes drift-timber all the way to Iceland, and it keeps open fiords and lochs in Norway during the winter, and even as far north as the neighbourhood of the Russian frontier; in one fiord, only thirty miles from the Norwegian open ocean shore, the ice never forms to any thickness. Nor does the temperature of the sea vary more than on the Irish Channel, where indeed it can be cold enough. Once, when travelling *via* Stranraer to Ireland with a friend, I found all the Scots coast so deep under snow and ice that I said to the conductor in the early morning as we looked out of the carriage, "Dear me, what can have become of the Gulf Stream?" He did not seem to understand the connection between ocean currents and temperature, and said, as if struck by an inspiration, "Oh, he'll be here presently; he's only washing his hands. I'll take out his luggage." My friend was much flattered at being mistaken for such a powerful and warm natural phenomenon!

But if the Gulf Stream brings nuts and drift-wood and sharks and fish like the opahs to our shores, why should not the Norwegians have been correct when they declared of old that the Kraken, the great sea-serpent, comes sometimes to pay them a visit? The old tales are full of them; and if the serpents exist, as the captain and crew of the *Dædalus* swore they do in the south, and as Mr. Joass says they do off Dunrobin, why not give some credence to the allegation, and why try to do the difficult operation called " proving a negative " ? Some people will of course never believe in them till they swim up the Thames and look in through the windows at a sitting of the House of Commons. The surviving followers of Mr. Gladstone will then probably very hastily move for " a committee of examination and inquiry," if any M.P.'s remain in their seats to go through any of the familiar forms in presence of anything so unfamiliar.

The sea is indeed teeming off the Sutherland shore. I have seen young herring thrown up in such millions that the coast was all silvered by them, and we took the fish up from the shore in pails. They were of the size of large sardines, and must have jumped ashore and committed suicide to save themselves from the jaws of Kraken or some other marine horror equally terrible.

Above a wide bay, upon which, clad in heather, rocks, and pine woods, the height of Ben Verâgy looks down, stands, on what the geologists call " the old sea-margin," a very handsome pile of buildings. With many turrets, whose high " extinguisher "- pointed tops break the outline of the French roofs beyond them, and with a great central tower similarly adorned, the walls of the castle rise in imposing array above a high-walled terrace. Flights of steps lead down to a lovely garden, rich in colour and in fountains, and round it and the white castle are good woods of sycamore, beech, and ash. This singularly beautiful building encloses within its walls, like a kernel in fruit, the castle of old days, a much more modest fortalice, and of very ancient date.

For many years after the Countess of Sutherland, the owner in her own right of great domains in this part of the country, married my great-grandfather, the first Duke of his name, she was content to spend money only among the people, and in entertaining the comparatively few visitors who came so far north. But Harriet, Duchess of Sutherland, employed the people also in building the French-like chateau now existing, and the work of improvement went on for many years, until at last a palace stood there worthy of the great estate its owners possessed. The west coast of Sutherland also became theirs when the Mackay family were obliged to sell it to refill their empty purses, the usual heritage of Scottish chiefs, whose families, generation after generation, had no profession but that of arms, and became gradually poorer and poorer as the claims on them from their clansmen remained the same, and the means of meeting them diminished through the generosity habitually exercised. When the potato famine came and the people seemed likely to starve, for no prudence had withheld them from multiplying on a wretched soil, the wealth derived from the south was poured out most lavishly to help them.

Had the people been dependent on Scottish sources alone, it is probable that disappearance by starvation and fever would have killed them off. But the Sutherland people had now the resources of Staffordshire and Shropshire at their backs, through the benevolence and good government of their landowners, and thousands were helped, and hundreds more sent to the happier shores of Canada. Of course the usual misrepresentations followed, and the "Sutherland clearances" were abused as cruelties—when the victims of the "cruelties" were saved from death, and in comfort heard of their hardships from the newspapers which followed them to the new homes they had been helped to build upon Canadian soil.

Readers who care for facts should read the reports of Lord Loch's grandfather on the subject. He was the manager of the estates. The people had, throughout all known history, had occasion, as they had during the famine, to love the family dwelling at Dunrobin. They had been led by them for centuries to take the side of order and good government, through the long period of the contests of the Clans. They had through them been able to withstand Danish and North Sea rovers' incursions, and had in the eighteenth century been able to keep the north for the enlightened rule which was represented by the Guelph Dynasty. Peace reigned after the insurrections of 1715–1745, which the Sutherland men helped to subdue. It is almost without parallel that whole districts in the Highlands should for so many centuries have been so wisely led. The heiress who brought all this country to the House of Gower represented the oldest earldom in Scotland, and was herself a charming and clever woman, a good artist, a good wife and mother, whose portrait by Romney makes one understand the influence she possessed and used so well.

Wherever you find the word "Dun" you may be sure that a place of strength stood there in olden times. From London to Dunrobin, and further north, you find the name. It is the old British name for a fort. From the most distant times the Robert's Fort, or Dunrobin, has stood a centre of strength and civilisation in the east angle of Sutherland—the "land of the south," as the Caithness, Shetland, and Orkney northerners called it. It saw Scandinavian pirates often at its gates, and from its shelter the swordsmen came forth who kept the wilder tribes to the east in order; and, ever fighting on the side of the descendants of the Bruce, of whose family they themselves came, the old knights and earls made their fastness a citadel for all that was progressive and successful in the policy of the realm.

The only warfare any one living can remember

at this ancient " Dun " was a lovely mimic battle waged with cardboard lances and staves with bladders, in mimic lists, a "tournament" held by children on the landward front, when all the windows and all the grassy slopes on which they looked were filled with spectators, and the organiser of the "jousting" was Lord Dufferin, afterwards Viceroy in Canada and India, and Ambassador at Paris, Rome, and St. Petersburg.

There was a stand erected in which sat a fairy-like queen of beauty, whose court was composed only of pretty little maidens. The boys were on somewhat obstinate highland ponies, so bedecked with gorgeous caparison that but very little was visible of them or their steeds. Full-grown heralds and pursuivants, with trumpets and tabards (all of real size), made the chargers look even smaller than was respectful to their real powers. Very light armour was sufficient to withstand the thrust of the lances when boys and ponies met in full career; and alas! some of the lances would bend double instead of splintering as they should have done on the ferocious impact! Some even broke of their own weight, or with the wind. But the sight of the gay crowd of combatants was beautiful; and when the knights advanced one by one to the Queen of Beauty, and recited verses Lord Dufferin had composed, the acclamations of the crowd could be heard on the top of Ben Verâg.

We used to be very fond of riding out to that

hill to investigate the remains of yet older "doons" or forts than that of Earl Robert. For there, on the steep slopes of granite and heather, were two splendid specimens of the "bourgs" or stone circular keeps that the ancient people who lived here before the Normans came to England erected as fastnesses against the Danish invaders. They are mysterious abodes with massive stone walls, built without mortar, and having staircases in the thickness of the great round walls for their inhabitants to ascend to a second stone gallery, which ran round the tower and gave access to tiny sleeping-places. These forts are very often placed in pairs, almost within bowshot the one of the other. They have often suffered even from the depredations of the descendants of their masters, who have used their stones for dykes or field divisions, or for houses; but in the case of those at Dunrobin, the stones are so large and heavy that they have been allowed in great part to remain "time defying, centuries old."

CHAPTER XXX

Iona

The quiet clouds within the west
  Have built white domes above the Isles,
And o'er the leagues of sea at rest
  The azure calm of summer smiles.

The sheldrake and the eider float
  In peace along each sandy bay;
And softly with the rock-dove's nest
  The caverns greet the warmth of day.

The purple beds of deep sea-weed
  Scarce wave their fronds around the Ross;
And silence blesses croft and mead,
  Each sculptured and knitted cross.

The lark may sing in sunlit air
  And through the clover hum the bees;
They yield the only sounds of care
  Where warred and toiled the pure Culdees.

And yonder grey square minster tower
  For orisons in silence calls
To where, enshrined in turf and flower
  Kings guard the ruined chapel walls.

Iona, "island of the wave,"
  Faith's ancient fort and armoury,
Tomb of the holy and the brave,
  Our sires' first pledge of Calvary;

Christ's mission soil, O sacred sand
  That knew His first apostle's tread!
O rocks of refuge, whence our land
  Was first with living waters fed!

Mysteriously Columba's time
    Foretold a second deluge dark
When they who on thy hill may climb
    Shall find in thee their safety's ark.

Though hushed awhile, the hymns of praise
    Again shall rise where feed the kine,—
Once more along thy grassy ways
    Religion's long processions shine.

Shall then each morn and evening late
    Unfolded see the illumined scroll,
While, echoed over shore and strait,
    The sea-like organ-surges roll?

O Saint and Prophet, doth thy word
    Foretell an earthly Church's reign,
Firm as thine island rocks, unstirred
    By tempests of the northern main?

Perchance! Thy wasted walls have seen
    The incense round the altars rise,
When cloister, tower, and cell have been
    To Pagan rage a sacrifice.

But if the old Cathedral ne'er
    Again shall send such children forth
Like those who with the arms of prayer
    Were conquerors of the Pictish north,

Yet hath that vanguard set and cast
    Such light upon our age's tide
That o'er life's trackless ocean vast
    Secure we sail or, anchored, ride.

And pilgrims to his grave shall tell
    The prophet's meaning, where he trod,
And in Columba's spirit dwell,
    Safe-isled, within the fear of God.

It was only in 1906 that a crofter, when digging in his garden, near a spot said by tradition to have been the place where Columba was buried, came on some large flat stones. Lifting these, he

IONA.

From an engraving

found that underneath was a cavity too large for the grave of a man. But there were bones lying on the sand within it—what were they? They crumbled at the touch, but some big teeth proved that a horse had been buried there with extraordinary care. The teeth were those of an old pony. Now, in Adamnan's life of the saint there is a pathetic story of the saint's fondness for his old white pony. His favourite companion was brought to the dying saint to receive his blessing. It is extremely improbable that so much care would have been taken in the burial of any horse's carcase, unless it were the body of a warrior's charger, or some specially beloved animal belonging to Columba. A warrior's horse would not be old and small. We are therefore probably right in thinking that this grave is the sepulchre of this very pony, the aged white beast described in the fifth century as the favourite of the founder. Horse trappings are usually found on a Viking's horse's tomb. In this there were none, and a rope bridle probably contented the monk. When he left Ireland and his rank as a king's son there, and turned his back, "Cull-ri-Erinn," on the vanities of Celtic rank and station, he would have no panoply or costly bridle-bit for his pony, whose bones, crumbling in the hands of its finder, after the lapse of fourteen centuries, is a curious testimony to the accuracy of the history of Adamnan.

One of the strange fulfilments of the sayings of

the holy man is often talked of in the island. Among the evils which which Iona was never to be afflicted was the hated presence of snakes, common on the near shore of the larger island of Mull. There adders are often met with; in Iona never. A few years ago a child saw what it thought was an eel in the froth of the tide on the sands in a bay of Iona. He got the dying thing, which proved to be an adder, and took it home, but it was dead by the time the house was reached. It had swum from Mull across the Sound, but had died in the attempt to violate the sanctity of the isle!

From the place where this enterprising snake attempted to land the view of the opposite coast is remarkable for its vivid colouring. The great sharp outlines of the Benmore range, the more distant mainland mountains showing beneath clouds in purple and indigo, the light red granites of the Ross, the deep blue of the sea changing to green over the pure white sands of the bays, the greys and light greens and yellows and browns of the rocks and marbles, the bright umber of the tangles—all make one think that it is a pity that the stones that seem so bright on a summer's day are not more used in decoration. But the granites and marbles are being shipped and used for London adornment, and Gorringe's great house near Buckingham Palace is lined with the rock from that opposite shore.

A fine vein of light green marble with light splashes of colour on a white ground is also worked.

From a photograph.

FROM THE CATHEDRAL, IONA.
Showing St. Martin's Cross.

It is part of a lime deposit that appears with a fuller tint in Ireland, in Ulster, on Iona, and in Glen Tilt, and then once more in Sweden, and certainly has a great delicacy in its beauty.

I have been fortunate in the innkeeper, Mr. Ritchie, who has great taste, and has encouraged the reproduction of all the best of the old patterns on the sepulchral slabs, both in wood and in metal.

Iona is one of those spots where one feels it to be a desecration to pass without spending two or three days, that mind and body may be refreshed by the bathing from its snowlike sands, the boating along its many-coloured rocks, the peace of its old ruined churches, and the walks on its delightful, natural close-turfed lawns. "Ces pelouses naturelles," as a friend of mine enthusiastically called its verdant little plains and terraces.

In the library of St. Ambrogio at Milan are preserved some MSS. written on vellum in Latin from the monastery of Alessandria, near Turin. On the wide margins of these volumes are notes in ink, which is now of a deep brown colour, but very distinct, and written in the Irish, or Erse, or Gaelic tongue. The author was Columbanus, a missionary monk from Iona, called after Columba, the founder of the church at Iona. The books are of the eighth or ninth century. Columba's settlement was centuries earlier, but the Columban church was ever able, from the time of his coming to the isle, to keep the lamp of religion alight, Danish raids and massacres notwithstanding, and to send forth missionaries and found monasteries, and Alessandria was one of those planted by the Irish Prince's followers.

In their island homes at least, and perhaps beyond the confines of its shores, but always in communion with their Irish mother-church, they kept a separate calendar, and had a curious tonsure, shaving the front of the head from ear to ear, and leaving their hair to grow behind this line. Their habitations were the little dome-shaped stone houses still to be seen in parts of Ireland, and on the Holy Isles off the coast of Lorne. They were somewhat like the Esquimaux houses, but instead of the snow-blocks flat stones were chosen, and each course was made to encroach on the circle, until the walls met at a height of over seven feet, when a space was left for the smoke of a small fire lit in the centre to escape. The first church was probably a larger structure of the same kind, but may have been of the ordinary parallelogram type retained till the Middle Ages. Then a cruciform cathedral was built, with a short nave and square tower, which still exists. There was also, as in the Irish churches, a separate campanile, or bell-tower, but it is still a puzzle where they rung the bells, as these towers are usually closed at the top with a conical cap.

It must certainly have been from communication with their monks in Italy that the Irish and Iona parent churches received the knotted patterns now

From a photograph.

DUNSTAFFNAGE.

The Old Scots Castle, of which the Dukes of Argyll are Hereditary Keepers.

called Celtic. Italy received them from the Coptic churches of the East. The same designs are found at Cairo and at Iona. Many are identical. Others have been a little changed. Rope work and basket work gave the idea in most cases, and plants in others. I have specimens in brass from Syria and Egypt, which give the origin of all the best sculptures of the West of Scotland. San Ambrogio itself is full of them. One sees many of them also in Rome.

The journeyings of the missionaries encouraged commerce. They helped the people around them to engage in some industries besides those of fishing and hunting. An implement made of part of the bone of a whale for arranging the woollen threads on a loom has been found in Tyree, an island which was called the Granary of Iona, for it was from thence they got most of their barley. In Tyree, and on the Ross of Mull near Iona, bronze pots have been found, bronze pins and needles and brooches and rings, all probably got by commerce with the south. Phœnician glass beads and necklaces of polished jet beads have also been discovered. But the natives of the Hebrides had cattle and fish and corn to give; and the vessels even of the earliest times, when only constructed of skins fitted over light wooden frames, made wonderfully long voyages, and may have taken grain. Tyree has a most fertile though scanty soil, for there is much lime in the sea-shells of which it is largely composed.

There is a wonderfully full account given of the life of Columba in Latin by Adamnan, who wrote when men could remember the founder of the Iona Church. I give here an attempt to translate the spirit of one of the hymns Columba composed.

COLUMBA'S HYMN

(From the Gaelic)

How delightful for me on Udalen to be!
  From the brow of the rock summit there
To be oft looking down on the waves of the sea!
  The world is their course, as they onward fare,
To their father chanting their music, and free
  They sing as they go, and their psalms rise in air.

How delightful to walk on the smooth, sparkling strand,
  And there to hear wonderful song
From the source of delight, from the birds' swift band,
  When the crowding waves roar long
On the rocks and the capes of the sandy land,
  And their sound near the church is strong!

How pleasant to look on Thy creatures, O Lord,
  That arise from the ocean deep!
To watch the ebb and the flood Thou hast stored,
  While my mystical name I keep.
Oh, "Cul-ri-Erinn!"[1] contrition accord
  As my sins to my memory leap!

That I may for ever bless Him who upholds
  All things that are great, or are small;
Who all the bright glories of Heaven unfolds
  Whose voice in the sound of the sea doth call,
Whose are the mountains, and shores and wolds,
  God, the Creator, Preserver of all!

[1] "My back to Ireland."

Columba's Hymn

What joy on this island to Heaven to bend
   And gratefully psalms to Jehovah to sing,
And hours to devout meditation to lend,
   And think on my Saviour, the Holy King!
How joyous my way, when to work I wend,—
   To the toil for my God, all comforting!

At times to be fishing, or plucking dulse weed
   From the rocks, or in prayer, be alone;
At times giving food to the poor in their need,
   To me by God's mercy made known.
Vouchsafed in the presence of Him whom I need
   Is the wisdom I call not mine own.
My God and my king, Thy servant am I—
   He lets none deceive me—my God throned on high!

CHAPTER XXXI

Isle of Mull.—Loch "Baa," or the Lake of "Life and Beauty," was rather a discovery for "my people." They never went there during the first years after their marriage. Their attention was called to it by a letter from Lord Ellesmere, the brother of the Duke of Sutherland. He had taken the name of Egerton on inheriting the Bridgewater property in Lancashire. He wrote thus to my grandmother, his sister-in-law:

August 1, 1856.

MY DEAR HARRIET,

Loch Sunart is the inlet from which I date my letter, while yachting.

The scene depicted above, in my pen-and-ink sketch, is not Loch Sunart, but Loch Baa, in the Island of Mull, a water Paradise, the one shore of which and both ends belong to Argyll, and one side of the lake to Lord Strathallan, individuals possibly of merit in their way, but apparently insensible of the immense superiority of their possession to the rest of the habitable world! I have spent upon its bosom three days of unalloyed happiness, such as Seyed, King of Ethiopia, endeavoured in vain to secure. I lighted in an odd way, while seeking for dependants of the Argyll Dynasty, on the tenant of the opposite bank, a widowed lady, much like what Ellen, in Scott's "Lady of the Lake," might have been if Malcolm had taken in the romance to drinking, and had died young and left her in possession of Loch Katrine, with a right of fishing and a turn for hospitality. I became a child of the family, and was put under the charge of a brother-in-law, a Mr. Gordon, a near cousin of the Lochs, a man of Australian experiences, very agreeable, and an inveterate fly-fisherman. Since the days when I used to leave Dunrobin for school under a fire of injunctions to make up for lost time by severe study, I have never left a place with so much regret.

   Your affectionate—E.E. no longer,
  but B.B., which signifies Blighted Being,
  happiness away from Loch Baa being out
  of the question.

The dome-shaped hill in the centre of the sketch beyond is Ben Tallagh, unenviable as having been ascended in squalls of rain by my wife and daughter and a guide, a walk of some twelve miles, much of it perpendicular, and a river or two to be crossed.

The letter awoke curiosity, and Loch Baa was visited and admired so much that visits became almost annual. There is an old house about a mile from the lake, and only a quarter of a mile from the sea loch, called by the Norsemen Loch Scaffort, and by the old Irish Celts Loch na Keal. This opens, broad-bosomed, to the west; on the left is the great range of mountains culminating in Ben More, 3,200 feet high, and on the right the lower swelling hills, that look down from their other slope on the Sound of Mull. Seaward there is a rocky isle called Eorsa, blocking the entrance to the outer ocean, and further towards the straits the green, comparatively flat island of Inchkenneth. Further again on the right is Ulva, the rocky home of Dr. Livingstone's father. A pretty little river, full of trout and grilze, escapes from the lake, and wanders, after a long tortuous course that gives fishing for two miles, instead of the quarter of a mile, by a straight line its waters have not been clever enough to find, into the salt-water loch.

I have added greatly to Knock House, which has now accommodation for a large party, and the deer-stalkers come each year to kill stags on the range behind it. The valleys pasture many cattle. In the sea are low rocks, bearing on their smooth surfaces fresh-looking scratches and grooves, the marks of the ancient glaciers that were pushed from the glens of old into the sea. Many seals constantly bask in the sun on these rocks, or look still happier when there is not much sun.

Between Knock House and the sea there is an ancient burial-place, long disused. Some years ago I had travelled straight from Osborne to Knock, and, wishing to see if amid the grass-grown "place of peace" there were any carved stones, I wandered there, and, standing on a flat slab, began with my foot to remove the long grass that quite covered the inscription. I was startled, when I had succeeded in this, to see at my feet the inscription: "Captain D. Campbell, 74th Regt., and his wife Maria Blachford, of Osborne House, Isle of Wight." It seemed as if the dead woman now lying there had wished to send me a message, and had made me visit her tomb because I had only some hours before left the place, hundreds of miles away, where her childhood had been spent! It was from the family of Blachford that the property was purchased by the Queen, at the instance of the Prince Consort. Captain Campbell had been quartered at Carisbrook, and had evidently thence made the acquaintance of the Blachford family. Knock was one of a class of old houses tenanted by gentleman farmers who had usually served in the army, and very poor farmers they were. The army pay was, of course, insufficient to keep them and the farms going, and family after family became ruined, their place being taken by humbler folk, whose youth had not been occupied with thoughts of manœuvring alone, and who could attend better to the business of agriculture or cattle-keeping, and were not above sending their children into business in the towns.

Now let us take a boat on the shore of the salt-water loch, and row out past the seal rocks, and watch how seals flop into the water as we get near them. They are cunning animals, and will now only show for a while the tip of their noses above the surface, to get air, and then go down again. You may sometimes see them swimming in the clear tide under the boat, and mark how swiftly they pass. It makes one understand how deadly they are for the fish at the mouth of a salmon river, and why it is necessary to keep down their numbers if you want to keep your lake and river well stocked. Further out we see the crest of Benmore in the clear air, quite free from the clouds that have loved to rest upon it, and even on this warm day there is a great snow wreath lying at the base of the precipice which falls away abruptly on the southern side of the highest ridge.

Now it is time to put out the fishing-lines, and white and yellow flies, three to each line; and the pollock whiting and coal fish, here called lythe and seith, begin at once to take. I have caught with friends, in one boat, over a hundred in an hour. Some of them, as we get into greater depths, are fine big fish, three or four pounds in weight, and make a capital fight before they are hauled in. There is no better fish for the table than lythe, if fresh. It is too delicate to keep long, or be sent away unless salted, and then it is no better than others.

We pass the rough rocks and rugged slopes of Eorsa, and the keeper tells us of a hind who swam from the Mull mainland to the isle, a distance of a quarter of a mile, that she might calve there. She brought up her young one most successfully, and then it became time, in her opinion, to return to her friends on the shore she had left. But the fawn did not at first understand the benefit of leaving its nursery, and the mother had to take it down to the water's edge, and take short swims and come back to encourage it. Finally she thought she had done enough in the way of lessons, so she pushed the fawn into the sea, confident that what she could do her fawn could do also—and with reason, for her little one followed by her side, she encouraging it, until both mother and fawn stood happily under the frowning precipice of Trap Rock, that guards the shore looking down on Eorsa Isle.

Here the water becomes very deep, and there is excellent lobster-fishing. On each side of the steep cliffs there are many shallow bays, half hidden by ice-polished rocks, which retain the sea-water in basins, forming ideal places for the cultivation of oysters. Our Governments have, however, never yet seen the wisdom of the French, who encourage by all means in their power the formation of oyster-parks. and derive a great revenue from them, while the oysters form a mainstay for the support of many fishermen along the coast.

When the Headland of Gribun is passed, the outer ocean opens to us, though we are still under the shelter that Inchkenneth gives. On this low green island, with its white sandy shore, Dr. Johnson was entertained. We land also, and look at the beautifully carved stones in the little green chapel enclosure.

Where is Iona? can we see it yet? Yes, there it is, low down in the west, with white sand gleaming along its shores. "We were now treading," said Johnson, "that illustrious island whence roving bands and rude barbarians received the benefits of knowledge and the blessings of religion." The colours along the coast are often so intense, when the sun shines, that I have heard them compared to those seen along the shores of the Red Sea. The purity of the white of the sand, composed almost entirely of broken shells, the blue-green of the water of the sea, as it flows over these sands, the brightness of the hue of the turf, over which larks are constantly singing, the sparkle of glittering lines of waves, the many colours of the shore boulders, and the variegated granites and marbles of the rocks, all promote a blending of strong colours one would not expect to see so far to the north. But we must be content with a distant view through our glasses of the hoary cathedral, and imagine that we can at another time see the island on which no snake has ever dared to venture, and where the fiercest storms provide a fountain by means of a cave which has in its roof an orifice, which spouts, like the nostril of a whale, a great jet of water heavenwards whenever the breakers crash with a sullen roar into the cave.

Dr. Johnson made also an expedition thence to a famous cave beyond Gribun. This cavern is called Mackinnon's Cave, and can only be reached, by a man on foot, at low water. At flood tide it is necessary to have a boat to reach it. As we have a boat, we go on, knowing that we can enter, no matter what the state of the tide. Dr. Johnson went at low tide on foot, and said, "We climbed neither very nimbly, nor very securely," over great boulders, which strew the shore at this point. The cave entrance is in a great cliff, of beautifully coloured sandstone. It has a grand portal, finer than that of any temple. Various ferns, grasses, and flowers find footing on the ledges on each side. The roof is at first about seventy feet high, and then narrows down to a vast doorway. The floor of the entrance ascends between the over-arching rock, and is strewn with lovely pebbles of blue and green and white, and then near the actual aperture which forms the gateway a sandy slope takes the place of the pebbles, and we pass the inner entrance and find it necessary to have lights to see the full extent of the fine hall we have entered. The sides have opened back, and the roof has risen, and we are in a place that would easily hold six hundred persons, the sandy floor still sloping up before us in a gentle incline, to a low ridge, whereon is a great flat stone.

Twice some children who have been with me in this hall have declared that they have seen an old man with a white beard sitting on that stone as we approached. On one of these occasions two dogs that were with us, and had shown no sign of excitement until we got near the stone, then fled back to the sunlit entrance we had left behind us. I never saw anything, but the children wondered I had not, and when I called to the dogs to come back they shook their heads in proper disapproval of the proposition made to them!

Be there or not an old man haunting the place, he was perhaps only taking a lunch on this natural table, which we have found useful for the same purpose. Beyond this table stone, the roof again comes down and the sides get together until there is only a space of about twenty feet overhead, and a corridor leads on about eighty yards to another room, but a small one, and then there occurs a fall of rock from the roof, barring all further progress. The view from the big stone seawards through the entrance shows the wonderful Isle of Staffa, the gem made of basaltic black columns, with green turf on the top of the superincumbent rocks, floating on the sea about ten miles off, and the cavern front exactly frames this beautiful vision of bright water and the blue islet in the distance.

There is no sign anywhere of man's habitation, although in old days this splendid natural house must have sheltered the old savages. But we have been told that traces have been found not far off, and we ask where? Oh, just down by the shore near Gribun; and we resolve to see what can be seen here. The plough of a farmer had struck on a stone, which turned out to be the top of a sepulchre. We all determined to call upon this perhaps prehistoric man; and getting spades and pickaxes at the farm, which was soon reached after re-embarking, we went with the farmer to the place. There was a lovely slope of greensward above the sandy bay.

Soon we found the place where the plough had struck, and dug. Yes, there was a flat stone, and another, and the spades were at work, and we gazed at last on an ancient grave that might have been in Egypt, so like was the mode of sepulchre to that of the early men in Egypt before the pyramid-building race had come to the Nile from the East. There was the same ring of rough stones placed round the skeleton, which had been buried in the sand, with its knees drawn up to its chin. There was the same pot, or one very like the Egyptian pots, placed by his side. There was the same flint spear, or large arrow flint blade on one side of him, that he might have some food on his eternal journey, and some chance of killing spirit game with the stone weapon as he passed onward through the shades of the new world. The bones crumbled. The skull showed a man of fairly developed brain. The pot was rudely fashioned of baked clay, with herringbone pattern, slashed by a sharpened stone in the clay before baking. The arrow-head was well fashioned. One would give a good deal to have pictures, or some delineation of their manners, to bring the life of these distant ancestors of ours before our eyes. But these men of the Stone Age have nowhere left pictures of their lives, as did the later Egyptians.

Such graves are found in Brittany, and all along the coasts. There are a number of similar graves in the Ross of Mull. At the time they hunted and fished here, the country was probably covered with forest. Even where the sea-breezes blow strongly, there is often a growth in places where the sheep have not grazed and been able to destroy the vegetation; a growth of willow, birch, holly, alder, and oak. Wherever we find the word Darroch, or Derry, an oak forest stood. Much was burnt for fuel, much destroyed by sheep. What gives one a fair idea of the scarcity of the old population is that more forest was not destroyed by them. You find in the peat mosses considerable trees of oak and other kinds which have fallen where they grew, and been engulfed in the peat and never used. They have seldom any mark of tools on them. It must indeed have been a difficult job, with flint tools, to cut down an oak. But by fire they could be ringed round so as to be made to fall, that the boughs at all events might be more easily reached and be broken up.

But now we must leave, and stop theorising for the time, for the sail must be attended to, and with a good breeze from the west we sweep back towards Knock, and landing, go to the house, the windows of which look towards the sea loch and across the river and meadows to the woods of Gruline. There is a charming old garden near it; and a hill and a rising plantation shelter it, with sycamores a hundred years old.

The inland expeditions from this place are just as fascinating as are those to seaward. There is a shooting-lodge at the fresh-water Loch Baa, looking out on copse-covered ridges dipping sharply into the water, and burns that come tumbling in white foam from precipitous crags, and as we again take boat—but this time upon the fresh-water lake, to try for trout—stories are told of *Salmo ferox*, and kelpies, and wild-duck shooting, and magnificent heads of stags. The average weight last season of twenty-five stags killed was eighteen stone. A good billiard-table at the lodge puts us all in hopeful temper, and we are prepared to believe that there is no hart under twenty stone.

But the fishing at first was only remarkable for the fat sticklebacks caught. This minute fish always seemed to have too much food in Loch Baa, for its belly was always like a balloon. It appeared that this was a stickleback weakness which did not denote good health; and if they always took flies as large as themselves, their disease of stoutness was easily accounted for. But off the wooded slope that jutted into the lake beyond the home bay we caught two grilse of 5 and 7 lb., and further on two more, the heaviest being 9 lb. The fish do not run large; I have never caught one weighing more than 11 lb. But they fight well, and there are also heavy trout of 10 lb., which are more sluggish when played. Lunch is taken on shore near the end of the lake, three miles away; and at the spot chosen there are old birches, and oaks, two and three feet in diameter, though not rising to tall trees. There is a most lovely view of Glen Clachig, a deep rift in the mountains to the left. A great peak, like a sharp pyramid, lifts its point so high that it seems higher than Ben More itself, and the glen, bordered on the south by a steep grassy descent, is in the north broken by copses and a great ravine down which pours a charming cascade as it enters the woods.

Away up on the summit level is an interesting place over which the ancient track leading from Iona and the Ross of Mull must have brought the Irish monks on their pilgrimages to convert the heathen Picts. On the top of the ridge, by the side of the pathway, are two cairns of stones at a little distance the one from the other, and the one is called Cul-ri-Erin, and the other Cul-ri-Alban. Alban was the old name for the land of the Picts, Erin for Ireland. Cul-ri means the "back towards." So the old wayfarers, when they passed from the lands settled by the Gaels from Ireland, over to Pictland, or Alban, called the western cairn the "Back to Erin," and the Erinach or Western Gaels, as they passed from our side to the Irish-settled shore, called the eastern cairn the "Back to Alban."

That evening we were all very stiff and tired, and told stories which nobody believed to be anything but travesties on Highland character and manners. An ignorant Southerner, for instance, said he knew a gentleman who called on a laird, and found him not at home. On returning in the evening the laird asked his servant what became of his visitor when he found there was nobody in the house.

"Oh, sir," the man replied, "he just went from ta door into the middle of the road and swore at large."

A Highlander having some grievances was persuaded by his friends that he ought to go up to London to see the King, and get redress. He resolved to do so, and went up to town, having received many commissions from his friends, charging him to do various things for them. On arriving in town, he was much disappointed at not being allowed to see the King, and at getting no satisfactory answers from any of the officials. He went back much mortified, but his pride made him resolve not to show how neglectfully he had been treated.

"Weel, Geordie," said his friends, "did ye get

what ye wanted? and what did the King say to our petitions?"

He answered, "I have na got all yet, but maybe it will not be long before we get what we want."

"Not long, did ye say? But what did King George say?"

"Ooo, he just say to me—says he—'Ye see, Geordie, I'm sorry that I cannot ask ye to dine to-night, but I'll see to your case, and I'm sorry I cannot ask ye to-morry, for ye ken, Geordie, it's Charlotte's (the Queen's) washing day.'"

A Mull man was told to bring the postbag down a glen as fast as he could, and was provided with a horse for the purpose. He arrived later than he had ever been before, and on being asked why he was so late, he said, "Oh, I would have been in much better time, had I not been sair hampered with a horse."

Highland devotion to an employer was shown characteristically when a keeper said to a shooting-tenant who had lost a contested election, "Well, sir, I just wish I had the head of your opponent to hang up in the hall, with the heads of the other beasts."

Of Highland ghost stories we had none. Highland ghosts do not now haunt shooting-lodges. They are bad for the nerves of the shooting-tenants. Being gentlemanly or ladylike ghosts, they preserve the traditional courtesy of the Highland character and do not come unless they are asked. But a

An Authentic Ghost

Lowland lady gave us her own personal experience of a place where she had lived seventeen years before she saw the family ghost. It was in this wise: A spirit of her own sex called Green Mary haunted her castle in the past. The present lady of the castle didn't believe it. But she believes it now, although it is nearly sixteen years since she has been convinced of the truth of the apparition's becoming visible "noos ad thans," or now and then. When she saw it she was coming back after dark from a smoking-room where some repairs were being made. It was a room to reach which she had to pass through a larger chamber, and it was in this larger room that she perceived, by the strong firelight, a figure advancing to her, but with the face turned away, so that she saw only the side of its cheek. She felt that the ghost wanted to make her look at itself, and never thought that it was anything odd until it came close, when she heard the rustle of the dress, but no footfall, and the shawl over its head was queerly disposed, as a sort of high-placed snood. It passed her still turning its face away, went across to a corner of the room, and there seemed to enter the wall. One of her sons and another person in the house saw it the same week, and were much alarmed. It was then seen in other rooms—once in a passage, when it was holding a lamp, and showed its face, and once with the face averted and without the lamp. The lady said she could not have been mistaken, and was not a bit nervous; she had just left the carpenter, where he was working, and a corridor beyond was brilliantly lit, so there was nothing but the odd presence of this silent gliding figure to make her feel nervous.

Knock, Aros, Mull.—To-day I am quite stiff after an excursion to see the golden eagle's nest, although I rode part of the way. We left the pony at the crossing of the burn in the glen, and walked up the path to the "Coll." This track is almost obliterated at the top, by landslips. We turned on the ridge, looking down to Glenmore, and kept along the top of the precipice fronting Glen Clachaig, until we could go down the ravine, between the rock and the peak of Benmore. The "talus," at the foot of the rock, where an overhanging ledge has made a good nesting-place for the eagles, is steep; but one can, with a little trouble, get up to the sheltered ledge on which the young are, and even, if one chooses, to the eyry itself. I contented myself with getting within six or seven yards. The mother sailed away placidly, looking very handsome, when we came round the corner.

"There is not a hare within a mile of the nest," McIntyre said, "although the hares are abundant everywhere else on the hills. They take almost only hares," he continued; when what did I see? Just at his feet, the leg of a lamb!

"Oh yes," said McIntyre, "just the leg of one lamb, but they hardly ever take a grouse."

So he went on, and creeping along the ledge arrived at the nest, I behind him.

" What bird is that, McIntyre—that bird plucked close to the nest ? "

"Oh, just one grouse," he answered, and took it up. It had been so neatly plucked and so lately killed that it looked as if prepared by some London cook for the eaglets. These two little monsters sidled and crouched, looking like grey gulls ; and when McIntyre was putting his hand alongside them, one of them rose indignantly, and then both turned their rumps on him and sat down again. Sulky dignity could not have been better expressed. It was the attitude of passive protest against unwarrantable intrusion. The old bird never came near us, evidently considering us hopeless nuisances. The nest smelled, and I scrambled back, after taking a rough sketch. The position chosen is perfect for shelter against all winds but one—a very rare wind here—coming directly up Glen Clachaig. Last year on a ledge on Ben Goar, the eyry was carelessly placed, and water came into the nest, killing the young. A waterspout could flow over this place, and the projecting ledges above it would make it harmless. We got down the ravine, and came back along the green bottom of the stream side.

CHAPTER XXXII

Kintyre, or Head of the Land.—I make no apology for speaking of Kintyre—for there one can have the most varied shore, the most varied golf links, the best cheese, the best air, the best farming and farmhouses, the best view of Ireland in any district in Scotland! What can man wish for more? Communication with the outside world? Yes, the quickest. It is the wireless telegraph station for America. One immense steel mast is put up here, the other, which receives or sends messages, is on the shore of the American continent, and Kintyre gets the first news from the New World, and transmits anything worth recording from the Old. Sport? Yes, one "shooting tenant" out of many there had four thousand grouse, six hundred sea-trout, and ten salmon in a short autumn season. Sea-fishing? Yes, the creeks near by afford the greatest herring catches now obtained anywhere near the coast, and off Southend the line-fishing for amusement from boats is wonderfully good. Mushrooms? Yes, any number! You may swallow anything in, or about Kintyre!

It was to its harbour that the Stone of Destiny, the crowning stone of the Irish kings, and ever since the Coronation Stone of the kings of Scotland and of Great Britain, was first brought. Some say that it was Jacob's pillow; and if this be true, Jacob must have been a hard-headed man. Kinloch was the old name for Campbeltown, the head of the Loch. There is but one harbour for a voyager from Ireland, and hither came the stone, and thence it was taken after many years to Dunadd, near the Crinan Canal, and so on to Dunstaffnage, then to Scone, and thence to Westminster—a strangely rolling stone that may yet have much history to witness!

Southend, Kintyre.—The finest golf course I know is at Southend, in the Peninsula of Kintyre. A steamer from Greenock takes one to Campbeltown, passing the lovely Island of Arran, and making a voyage which is a delight if the great Firth and wonderful mountains can be seen in fair weather. From Campbeltown, coaches and motors take the tourist either to Machrihanish Links or to Southend. Both give the perfect sod for golf; but at Machrihanish one cannot have the fine views which spread out before the eyes of the golf-player at Southend, where from every "hole" and "tee" the panorama of the varied coastline at one's feet, with the old Dun of Dunaverty, the rocky promontory of Kiel, the hills of the Moil, the beautiful outline of the Isle of Sanda lying out in the Atlantic a few miles away, and the cosy village and inn, seemed specially designed by nature to heal the wounds inflicted on the spirit by the misfortunes attendant on golf when one gets into a bunker. But the obstacles on the course here—which is a most "sporting course"—are chiefly natural. The sod is not so constant as at Machrihanish, though of the same quality where it shows its cuplike hollows and little green plains. But hillocks have to be "negotiated," and one has more of the excitement of possible failure than one can experience where artificial earth-walls are banked up in orderly array to catch balls before arriving on the greens.

Far away over the sea the coast of Ireland is clearly visible, and the lighthouse on the point near Belfast flashes over the waters in response to the tower placed on the Kintyre bold headland to the right of the visitor. It was at the Dun in the centre of the view that an old castle stood on a site formerly fortified by the Picts. This is the place where the MacDonalds made their last stand in the seventeenth century, and where their garrison of 300 men were refused quarter because they had been guilty of burning alive the people of a glen in Lorne. Leslie found he could not control his men in this matter; and though commanding the Clansmen who had marched down with him from Inveraray, he and the Marquis of Argyll experienced the impossibility of stopping the retribution which victorious soldiers, infuriated by an enemy's cruelty, often exact. It is said that they both were away riding in Glen Breckery when the slaughter occurred. That only one person, with a child, escaped seems certain.

About sixty years ago skulls occasionally appeared, washed out of the sands at the foot of the rock where the fort stood. The war was followed by the "plantation" of Kintyre by men from Ayrshire, who turned the desert into a garden by introducing good agriculture. Great sums of money were spent by the successors of the Marquis of Argyll in draining and making all kinds of improvements. In the time of Charles II. a coal-mine was opened, which has continued its work ever since; and although the coal is not of the best quality, it gives a very useful fuel, and the mines are being extended, and a light railway connects them with Campbeltown Harbour. Glen Breckery, running up into the hills at the back of the Moil, is a charming valley, contrasting strongly with the neighbouring shore of sand and rock and open ocean at Southend. For it is like a vale in Cumberland, with soft green sloping hills on each side, getting sterner towards the head of the glen, where a path leads over a steep ascent to let the traveller find he has to climb down rough ground to a broken coast where are a whole series of most picturesque sea-caves. It is well worth the climb to visit them, and if any one prefer society to nature, he should make the acquaintance of the farmers and their families in the admirable farmhouses near the village, where he will find ample scope for instruction for himself in the best mode of farming, of cheese-making, and see a yeomanry, the very ideal of an agricultural community, holding their own in spite of foreign competition favoured by the doctrines of the day, and equal in resource, vigour of intellect, and of body to any of the rural population of the Old or New World. There are some remarkable standing monoliths near the village, and their purpose is more mysterious here than anywhere, for they stand sometimes on hillsides, sometimes on the low grounds, and are seemingly neither marks of meeting-places, nor of sepulchres, nor of worship.

In the plain behind Campbeltown very fine specimens have been found of the bronze leaf-shaped swords, with scabbards of the same metal about eight inches long, and designed to receive the points of the weapons, the upper part of the scabbard having been apparently only of leather or wood now decayed. Bronze spear-heads have been found lying with these, as though some soldier had placed his treasure of arms hidden in a thicket at the side of an old tarn or small lake that existed until not long ago, for old maps show it as existing in the seventeenth century. It was drained in comparatively late years. On most of these shallow lakes, as in Ireland, there were pile-dwellings, huts on platforms on poles driven into the bottom. The boats were coracles, or cow-hides stretched over a light framework of oak or ash saplings. For killing birds the sling was a favourite weapon. Both coracles and "dugouts" were used till the seventeenth century, as were the lake dwellings.

One of the delights of these shores for children is the quantity of little cornelians and agates to be found in almost every heap of gravel on the beach. You find the purest sand, with cowrie shells which can be strung into lovely necklaces, and then bits of stone which are as bright as those that the Egyptian queens used to love to have beaded round their necks. Somewhere in the sea between Ireland and Scotland there must be a treasure reef of these half-precious stones, sacred to the jewel-cases of the mermaids. If these pebbles be taken and cut into beads, with a silver bead between each, a charming ornament is fashioned. It is curious how little we have of the German aptitude to make use in rural districts of the smaller industries. There is, for instance, a soapstone in Kintyre that might be made into cups and carvings of all sorts. Why do we leave it to the Germans to make the little china mugs with local views on them for local sales? The big shops would not kill local cleverness in manufacture if children's fancy were drawn to making original things from the materials at hand. Technical colleges are excellent, but we might begin technical training almost in the nursery, and so evolve some local taste for useful contrivances of originality. Still more possible would it be to inculcate neatness and cleanliness of packing the ordinary products of the farm—eggs, vegetables, and other foods.

CHAPTER XXXIII

An Armada Wreck.—The modern theory that a minority must suffer is a very old Campbell doctrine. It may shock holders of the theory of the rights of man, and sticklers for equality before the law, but present-day official announcements are even more cogent than were the theories of feudal supremacy. It is only in form that these maxims change. The wonder lies not so much in the fact that mankind have in all ages given the majority power, but that the mastery so obtained has been delegated to one man by the conquering crowd. Thus the institution of chiefship derived from the undoubted historic fatherhood of one ancient ancestor, and sanctified and continued vicariously in the person of his eldest descendant in each generation, was a Celtic form of assertion of the maxim quoted above, which remained for a surprisingly long time.

It was surprising because in many cases the chief thus elevated and maintained in his elevation was in his own person a case of the minority—namely, himself—causing some suffering to the majority—that is, to all his clansmen. I give an instance—namely, that it was not uncommon, when a daughter of the chief married, that the dowry should be provided for her by the clansmen. Is not this a case of "the majority must suffer" becoming a tenet of faith among the Celts? "Fines" in England, "Casualties" in Scotland—namely, the payment of a year's rent, or other extra burden, being imposed under given circumstances, for the benefit of the "Superior"—give other cases, where the majority was weak, and the one man who must necessarily have been the numerical minority had it all his own way! But perhaps this was only the result of the topsy-turvydom coincident with Irish descent. In any case these customs were kept among our people; and of course when Norman usages came to mix with the Celtic patriarchal taxes, these exactions, or dues, or duties, were systematised as giving all the dignity which the full setting forth in black ink and parchment of deeds and charters could give to them.

Only lately I recovered rights of salmon-fishing in a river—rights which had been clean forgotten, but had been clearly written in a charter given by King Robert the Bruce; and the innocent gentlemen who imagined that they had all legal security for the exercise of the salmon-killing they had so long exercised without any question being asked, were told that they were unconscious poachers, and must give up the pleasures of illegal sport to which they had been so long accustomed, if they did not pay their rent to the right man!

Rights to minerals on other men's land, rights to hunting over other men's forests, rights of fishing on other men's river banks, rights of getting other men to provide your daughters' dowries—all these were the reward of patriotism in the days when the world, or at least Scotland, was very young and innocent. The highest cultivation is probably shown when a majority respects the exercise by a minority of power to possess that which has been honestly won; and when full value shall be made to the minority for anything the majority takes for itself, or for other individuals. Now, among the rights given to worthy men in the past is the right which is called that of "Admiralty." When a misguided public opinion put up lighthouses and diminished the number of wrecks upon the coasts, it was not thought necessary to compensate the owners of Rights of Admiralty, although all flotsam and jetsam—that is, all that was cast on the shore in the form of wreck was legally theirs. Seriously speaking, this was of course an exceptional case.

In old days the majority was the people on shore, and the minority those at sea, and if the minority suffered it was all right. Now when commerce makes it the interest of the majority to protect their cargoes at sea, and lighthouses prevent shipwrecks, the majority are willing to damage themselves only slightly; and in the manner of insurance against evil, they make common cause with the mariner, save him, and make the minority suffer in the persons of those who can no longer get booty from wrecks.

Centuries ago we used to have our cellars well filled with wine from wrecks. The chief wealth of the peasantry on some parts of the coasts came from wrecks. But there is still balm in Gilead, and any wreck by law belongs to those who hold the Admiralty rights. Government officers may claim on the part of the Crown; but the Crown itself, through the people, gave away its powers. Thus when the Spanish ships, with whose masters the Scottish nation was at peace, came round Cape Wrath in the galleons which escaped the Channel battle, and took refuge, or were cast ashore by storms, they were well received, and were taken possession of, they and their ships, as flotsam and jetsam, by the chiefs having Charters of Admiralty.

It was on the strength of such a document that in 1670 my predecessor began operations with a diving-bell on the wreck of a vessel which had been blown up in Tobermory Harbour. The Government in London, in the person of the Duke of York, afterwards James II., thinking that he ought to have the right, as Lord High Admiral, remonstrated. There was a lawsuit, and the Earl of Argyll won it, but we do not know what he got. The work was probably interrupted by the troubles of the time.

I found a map showing the position of the "Spanish Wrack," in 1875, and sent a diver down. But he had a bad equipment, and after bringing up a brass stanchion and some wood, he had to desist. There came a report that a Norwegian ship had brought up on her anchor a gold coin. This was related to us by an old man. A few gentlemen in Glasgow subscribed money, and "dove" in 1904-5, obtaining the compasses of the captain, a bronze breech-loading cannon, a part of another piece of ordnance, many cannon-balls, a silver candlestick, swords, dollars, arquebuses, and other small articles; and now we know that the name of the captain of the *Florencia*, this vessel furnished by Tuscany for the Armada, was Pereira.

On a plate recovered in 1906 was a mark graven on the margin, but much worn and damaged by over-cleaning at a Glasgow silversmith's to whom it had been sent. After a scrutiny under magnifying glasses, the design seemed to be a Saltire cross under a coronet. Below the Saltire, or St. Andrew's cross, is a disc, or holy wafer, with rays falling from it. Inquiry among Portuguese coats-of-arms showed that the Pereira family had a Saltire cross on their shield. It is, then, apparently a piece of the commander's plate, which has been raised from the plate-closet of Tobermory Harbour after more than three hundred years. The vessel was always said to have taken a Portuguese crew on board at Vigo.

A curious thing in connection with this last search

is that the man employed to locate the metal declared that he could do so with the divining rod, so much employed for water-finding. His powers were put to the test before he went to Tobermory, by the gentlemen interested. Bars of copper were put down in three places in the bottom of the Gareloch, at a depth of a little less than ten fathoms. The metal-finder was rowed over the line of these deposits, and located all three places correctly. This could hardly have been chance, or "thought-reading." His belief in metal lying at the bottom of Tobermory Harbour was to some extent justified by the number of cannon-balls found.

CHAPTER XXXIV

During the early and mid-Victorian times it was a matter of course that peers and ministers should each have their well-appointed coach, with coachman and footmen in gorgeous liveries of the family colours. The coachman wore a short white wig and three-cornered hat, and the footmen had staves in their hands, and cocked hats, worn as in the days of Napoleon, with the pointed ends not " fore and aft," but to each side. These are familiar now to the London public only through the " turn-out" of the Lord Mayor, and a few others who keep to old custom. Even when there was no ceremony many people drove about in high yellow coaches, which were only reached by steps which folded up and formed an inner bulwark to the door. No one could get out or get in without the manipulation of this folding flight of cloth-covered steps.

The carriage was really a survival of the time when the roads were rough and when the seats of the carriage and the cover were placed so as to rest wholly on long suspension bands with plenty of space between the wheels and the body of the carriage, to allow plenty of swing, and to give stability. In travelling, this form was valuable; and a private posting carriage was a little world in itself, with complete outfit for lighting, reading, eating, and sleeping. The boxes that held all travelling clothes and toilette gear were made of leather to match the carriage itself, and were often adorned, like the panels of the doors, with the painted coat-of-arms of the owners. The convenient " brougham " only came into fashion with the peer of that name, whom many now alive can remember. Postillions were always employed in the country, usually with four horses. In these cases the family arms were worn on their left arms, on a silver oval plate; and short blue or black jackets, white breeches, and cockaded "beaver" hat and boots completed their equipment.

CHAPTER XXXV

The Founding of British East Africa.—The regions over which the British flag is hoisted have had no addition made to them during the last five years, unless we call the raising of our standard over some Arctic lands or islands along the North-west Passage a fresh acquisition. As the whole of the Arctic area is undoubtedly rising slowly, and will in the course of a million years be again a warm continent, the acquisition may become valuable to " our race "—as every one now calls the people among whom he lives, even although that " race " be compounded of many races. As Greenland bears proof in its coal of a hot climate, we are perhaps yet in good time in annexing promptly all present icefields for the fuel our descendants may need, supposing the warming process may be as slow as has hitherto been the gradual upheaval, of which there are manifest signs. Just as in Asia the salt Caspian and Euxine are the remains of an ancient ocean covering part of Siberia, so it is probable that James and Hudson Bays are portions of a sea that covered the North American and

Canadian low prairie country. In the north, near the line of the Saskatchewan River, you may see lakes full of alkali salts, and marshes that have all the appearance of slow desiccation or drying. This is probably the case with the continent of Australia also. It is only where the great mountains of Central Asia rise predominant over all the ranges of the world that there has probably been little change in the height of land since man was first brought into being on their western slope.

It is said that the first mother of us all called our first father "Union Jack"; but we have not yet seen his flag flying over the primal paradise, and there are reasons against any attempt to erect a mere flag as a memento of our earliest traditions. Quite sufficient unto us at present is the Empire we have inherited, and enlarged.

The last big enlargement was the act of a company, just as so many other lands in former centuries had been acquired by private and commercial action. These companies were looked at with aversion by some of the old Governments in England who feared responsibility. So it was in the last case. The Liberal party then in office could not bear the idea of the acquisition of the coast opposite the big Island of Mombasa on the east central shore of Africa. To build a railway to the great lake which was held to be the chief source of the Nile was called a "wild cat" scheme. Yet the company, telling its shareholders, before they subscribed at all, that any dividends would probably have to be "taken in philanthropy," got the necessary money, planted the flag from the River Juba to the Kenia mountain in the south, and pushed an expedition, under that most distinguished and intrepid officer Sir Edward Lugard, up over the "Mau Plateau" on to the Victoria Nyanza Lake; made Mwanga, the king, a vassal of our Empire; put down slavery and bloodshed; and, turning the most warlike of the tribes met on the way, namely, the Masai, into excellent policemen, caused the "Pax Britannica" to be a reality among the swarming and often quarrelling black tribes of the centre of Africa.

This country of British East Africa has proved to be a great and important addition to our influence in Africa.

Mr. Cecil Rhodes' scheme of a railway from the Cape to Cairo may come to pass. The making of railways on a great continent like that of Africa is more likely to proceed first in the direction of railways taking more or less the lines of latitude, instead of those of longitude. As soon as the white man makes a lodgment in the interior or on the coast, he desires to get from the centre to the sea, or *vice versa*, and to lay down a line which shall "tap the interior." So it has been in America, even though the Missouri and Mississippi take the place of the Nile in Africa and run partly north and south. The rivers are always the first avenues of approach to an interior, for boats for travel, and fish for eating give facilities for exploration, and a ready highway. But when waters fail, the land trails are usually by latitude. So it has been with the work of the opening up of Africa. Where the Congo and the Niger serve, there the waters make the avenue of approach. Where the streams have taken men to an interior remote from the ocean on either side of the continent, caravan routes gradually become railway routes from east to west. Thus now that we have established ourselves at Khartoum on the Upper Nile we have a new line of rails to Port Sudan on the Red Sea, thus securing our position in Nubia and making it immeasurably better than before. From Khartoum we control the Nile after the junction of the " White " and the " Blue " tributaries to its wonderful stream. We can reinforce our garrison from India and by the sea, which we control, and provide such a force in Nubia that Egypt is practically at our mercy. She could not live a day without the Nile, whose waters we could turn. It is not in the case of Egypt an affair like that of the tale told in Swabia of a youth who stuck his cap into the spring that supplies the first trickle of water that flows to make the Danube, and cried, " How they will cry out in Vienna when they see I have stopped the Danube ! " That Swabian should go to Khartoum, where he really could stop, by a barrage, the Nile flowing past Cairo, because there is not a known drop of water flowing into the Nile for a thousand miles after it has received the currents sent down by the Blue and the White Niles. While the Danube has tributaries at every mile, the Nile has none for over a thousand miles.

Nor is this rail to the Red Sea from Khartoum the only line which will fortify the possessions secured on the Nile. The Bahr-el-Ghazel, the country to the west of Khartoum, is also to be granted a line.

This will bring in many pilgrims to Mecca, much fibre and gums, and the hundred products of the hot but moist interior country. Now, the problem is how to link up the British in Nubia with the British in Uganda, the country at the north end of the great Victoria Nyanza Lake. From Uganda caravans already find their way to the Niger British territory to the west. But the country is difficult, and is partly infested by that terrible scourge the smaller tsetse fly, which carries with it the " sleeping sickness," a plague which has come from Nigeria and threatens to decimate the Uganda kingdom, wherever the land lies low, near water. At a height of two hundred or three hundred feet the fly is unknown.

There is healthy highland to the east of this lake, and it is probable that the best line of the railway will be one that shall start from some station on the Mau Plateau line already made, and working satisfactorily, and go by the elevated country toward Abyssinia, meeting the line which is also already in operation at some point between Port Sudan and Khartoum.

The Nile makes "such a mess" by flowing into gigantic swamps covered with the "sud" or floating vegetation, when it emerges from the hilly country to the north of Nyanza, that it will probably be difficult to carry it directly north, and a roundabout way will have to be taken to avoid the basin, which seems to be the bed of an old inland fresh-water sea. The glorious forests and scenery along a northeast route would make such a line even more popular for tourists than is already the Mau Plateau line to Mombasa from Kampalla. The same wonderful variety of game, from giraffes to the tiny gazelles, would be seen from the carriage windows, and a revenue could be got from shooting licences alone.

February 3, 1891.

MY DEAR MR. GOSCHEN,

With reference to the conversation Sir William Mackinnon and I had the pleasure of having with you, now some time ago, may I remind you that it is very essential for us to know soon if we can continue our operations for opening up the territories of British East Africa, backed by a solid guarantee, such as will enable us to raise money in the London market?

I do not disguise from myself that others must take our place unless the promises of the Brussels Conference are fulfilled, for we are already outrunning our financial tether.

A three-per-cent. guarantee seems to me, from

all I have heard in the city as to the feeling in regard to Africa, to be necessary.

KENSINGTON,
March 7, 1891.

MY DEAR SIR WILLIAM MACKINNON,

No news as yet from the Treasury. If the silence is prolonged, I must go to see if they have fallen asleep.

The Italian demands, and Foreign Office letter will have been mailed to you yesterday. We are to have a Court on Tuesday, by which time your views will be communicated. It looks on the maps as if a line might be possible as the frontier between us and the Italians (supposing they give us Kismayu to ourselves), taking the tributary of the Juba that runs from Lake Abbala and then taking a line of latitude due westward until it joins the longitude line 35. This to be followed north. The 35 longitude would keep them far enough from the main course of the Blue Nile, and would give them the major proportion of Kaffa, which I grudge them, but Kismayu may be worth something if we can have it entirely to ourselves.

I think we should go in for a small Zambesi flotilla Co. Two light draught wheel steamers, with an attendant barge for each, would be enough to begin with to make the experiment; but it is a traffic that is sure to grow greatly.

Captain Hodgkinson think that the *Aska* would be the best boat to take the Zambesi-Zanzibar monthly service, and that we can't profitably go further up than just inside the bar to a place called Foot Point, the sandbanks being so shifting between Foot Point and Chindi.

March 10, 1890.—The Court did not like the notion of fixing on a lake and tributary to the Juba, which may or may not exist, and preferred to draw the frontier line at degrees of latitude and longitude that would as nearly as possible represent the same idea as to what we should claim or leave. It was therefore decided that we should ask to have Kismayu to ourselves, and all the right bank of the Juba, but that, in face of the F.O. opinion, it would not be well to insist on the little tract on the left bank. That the frontier should follow the Juba to a point where the river meets the 6th degree latitude and should follow that 6th degree westward to the 35th longitude, and then follow the 35th longitude up to the place where the Blue Nile intersects it, after which we get parts claimed by Egypt.

A letter is to be written, to embody these views, to the F.O., and the matter of the four northern points is also to be mentioned, namely, that any reversion of them should make them fall to us.

March 16.—I went to consult Sir John Fowler. He recommends a certain Mr. Bakewell, as being a first-rate surveyor, accustomed to hot climates, in which he is represented to luxuriate, and this evening Sir John Fowler came to me to announce that

Mr. Bakewell would be willing to go, and that soon. Sir John Fowler is confident he would make as good speed as any man, and give a basis on which to proceed in the construction of a metre line—other smaller gauges being "toy things." The Court are in favour of sending him, and meanwhile Sir Donald Stewart is to substantiate as far as he can, by Indian Railway Department opinion at the India Office, our contention that the line can be made for £2,500 per mile. Sir John Fowler thinks it will cost more than that, and that we shall be lucky if we reach the Lake Victoria Nyanza under £2,000,000. But he is pleased at the account of the "woodiness" of the country, as affording sleepers, an advantage he had not when he wanted to make a line to Khartoum.

We shall have very uphill work in getting three-quarters of a million, or even half a million, beyond the Government guarantee. I think the line should as far as possible be a "bee" line. If we can only see the lake we shall see daylight.

KENSINGTON,
April 10, 1891.

MY DEAR MR. GOSCHEN,

I enclose for your information the estimate made by Sir John Fowler for a railway between Mombasa and Victoria Nyanza. You will observe that the estimates are for a good line with a good broad gauge, and that the amount would be about £1,800,000.

You may agree in view of the obligations the Government entered into at Brussels in reference to steamers that you may make the amount of your guarantee £1,500,000, on condition that we place two steamers on the lake, thereby fulfilling that part of the Government obligation.

The Court of the Imperial East African Company hopes that with the Estimate in your hands—an Estimate that will be supplemented in a few days by one from the Railway Department of the India Office—you will now be able to let us proceed in the raising of money, and in our Administration work, by the introduction of a Bill into Parliament during this Session.

The India Office Estimate will probably not amount to the sum mentioned by Sir John Fowler.

KENSINGTON,
June 13, 1891.

MY DEAR HARCOURT,

If you were not so busy, I would come to bully you about East Africa, and wish I could expound to you at Dalchenna, or somewhere in the Highlands, that the East African business has nothing whatever to do with Rhodes' or Randolph's enterprise. It was told the few shareholders, at their first meeting, that their "dividends must be taken out in philanthropy" and already between 4,000 and 5,000 slaves have received freedom. The railway to the lake cuts the only caravan routes used now for slaves in East Africa, so that when it is made there can be no slave-running except to the shore of the Red Sea, or to Morocco. This matter is not like the Suakin Campaigns, which were regarded as a lamentable waste of men and money, but this enterprise is to be undertaken with a golden bayonet and influences of which you would altogether approve. Other European Powers are in complete accord with us, so that the "responsibilities of Empire" are minimised to the lowest point compatible with the safeguarding of commerce and the already partially established coast trading interests which we do guard by flotillas, the expense of which will be lessened by any railroad that would make the coast traffic increase, and stop the slave-running.

Please bring a non-combative consideration to these points, for this is no Jingo affair, but a sober, economical, and necessary business.

July 16, 1891.

My dear Sir William Mackinnon,

The proposed vote is very insufficient, but it may help us in the money market, as indicating the honesty of the Government intention to help us. We must economise strictly meanwhile. The legality of the Certificate plan, *à la* Suez Canal, should now be definitely arranged for.

I do not know whether we or the Government are to do the survey. No time should be lost in getting Bakewell, or whosoever you think best, engaged. Then the main effort should be made from Dagoreti, and that as soon as possible. The route up to Machakos may well be surveyed more expeditiously and more roughly.

What is wanted is a certainty on which the Government may ask the House for a vote next year.

Aug. 26, 1891.—Had an interview at the Treasury with Sir Reginald Welby this morning. They appoint a Royal Engineer named Macdonald. He is expected now at Aden, and is telegraphed to come home, and to state what assistant he prefers. If he answers that he has none, we can look out for one he will approve of. With regard to the escort, I fear we must trust to the Askaris. The Admiralty won't allow any force to be detached from gunboats, which might release our Indian police at Witu for the service.

The Indian Government won't detach a force from India. We could enlist there, and may do so, but that is a work of time, and we want the men now.

The F.O. must therefore be asked to prevail on the Zanzibar Sultan to let us have Askaris, which force may, later on, be supported by Indian police. These are, however, expensive. The F.O. want the survey party to be supported by Lugard's force, withdrawn from Uganda. The matter of cutting down expenditure by withdrawing from the smaller places should at once be faced. We should be able to tell our shareholders that we have done all we can to retrench.

Sept. 20, 1891.—I do hope the sending of the steamers will be managed, and the Uganda enterprise insisted on.

The steamer would form the strongest base for any continuance. In my opinion, the steamers armed would be sufficient for the present, to show that we are " all there." I do not believe in sufficient money being now procurable to continue internal operations, unless M'Wanga with Lugard has a very decisive victory, in which case Uganda might be made tributary to the upkeep of a force there. Otherwise the expense would be too great, for we must remember that during railway construction there may be difficulties with natives, and all the force we can command must guard the railway as it progresses. Make one step at a time, and make that step firm, as the Romans did, who never had expeditions *en l'air*, but had each conquest made like a telescope, the last joint but an emanation from the first joint!

March 22, 1892.—I feel inclined to hold on to our steamer and to send her out. She may be the only tangible thing we may possess in the interior, if Gladstone comes in. She will be an argument the more in helping to get public opinion in our favour ; and when it is demonstrated by the Germans and ourselves that much can be got from the

Nyanza littoral, it will seem absurd to everybody that the intermediate space should not be bridged by a railway.

I am glad to hear of the C.N.S. offer. With the Stanley Boat Fund, we should have £12,000, and if the Government would give £5,000 the thing could be done. All the missionary people would be on our side. So I would go ahead with our already formed plans.

April 3, 1892.—A. C. much interested in the last scraps of news from Uganda. I told him I wanted the Government to go ahead. He said: "Ah, not with the railroad, that's quite impossible—we could never pass it. The Opposition would do all they possibly could to delay it, and it would not be practicable." About the steamer, he appeared to think the case was different;—and we must try to get that.

May 8, 1892.—Had a talk with Lord Salisbury. I told him that we should have to send him a letter this week on the subject of the necessity of retirement from the interior owing to the cost of an extended Administration, and the difficulties in the way of raising more money. He replied, "From the interior—yes," and was evidently loth to say anything. I emphasised the statements so often made, that we had undertaken a national work. "Yes," he said, "I do not think Sir William knew how much he was undertaking," and went on to say that the end might likely be that East Africa might become a Crown Colony. "Well," Lord Salisbury said, "I think Portal would be glad to take over the whole affair."

On the subject of taxation of people in the Sultan's Suzerainty, *i.e.* the Shore Strip, Lord Salisbury said there must be observance of treaties, and that the Germans had done themselves no good by imposing the taxation they had attempted; that we could tax all exports, and that five per cent. should be enough for the present. Sir Francis De Winton, who was present, said that the great object was to encourage people to take up "Shambas," and that taxation should be very sparingly resorted to. Indeed, he did not know what could well be taxed without making more trouble than the little money was worth. Sir F. at the same time said that he did not think we were yet at the end of our resources, and that there was too much expense in the London Management. But the last are vague generalities. The important matter is that the impression gathered by me is that we should put clearly forward the necessity, in case of no assistance being given, of handing over to the Crown our position and rights in E. Africa.

July 8, 1892.—At Bradford I got a considerable majority of English and Scots votes, but 1,100 Irish votes decided the contest against me. Among the business men in the Exchange Ward we were two to one. I am glad I fought the fight, as it put heart into our fellows.

It's a pity the Government won't go on with the through-steamer plan from London to Zanzibar. I suppose we should tender for one vessel at £11,000 or £12,000 to do the Aden-Zanzibar business.

July 12, 1892.—Now that the election is going against the Government, we must make up our minds to the inevitable hostility, in regard to E. Africa, of their successors. Shaw Lefevre, at Bradford, was as uncompromising in his hostility as are Vernon Harcourt and Gladstone.

Mr. G. Mackenzie has written a memo. suggesting the raising of money by debentures on E. African assets; but he puts in the forefront a railway guarantee as an asset, which the new men will not give. We must act as if there were no chance of this, and cut our cloth according. The expenditure must be based only on what will pay, and we cannot go on paying for other people's (the nation's) responsibilities. If any Government goes on with the railway so much the better, but we have not only no right to calculate upon it, but it would be wrong to do so.

Oct. 20, 1892 (Edinburgh).—I presided at a meeting (dinner) of the Scottish Geographical Society to-night, at Mr. Bruce's request, and the most healthy feeling was shown by F.C. and all.

Bruce says the Moderator of the F.C. will head a Deputation to Rosebery, and I met his son (who is a Unionist) to-night.

I met to-night a young man, Kelvin, who has

spent some years in Uganda; you know him as one of those anxious to get up the Emin Relief Expedition. He will do all he can. We must all work at the "stye brae" for the next two months, and get good men to back Lugard's representation.

Oct. 29, 1892.—What is wanted is to show repeatedly to the public what we have done in the short space of our rule in the actual emancipation of slavery. We can be judged by our works, which are good.

The Government will probably proceed upon the lines of purchase of our interests which B. advocates, and will try to buy them at "Prairie Value." What I am anxious about is that we shall not so spend our money as to put us at the mercy of those who desire to buy us out for nothing. If we spend all we have, we cannot, as beggars, be choosers. We must cut down now, so as to be in a position to go on as Coastguardsmen if nothing else, and be able, as an unambitious but still solvent Company, to have some voice in the proposed changes.

Personally I should be glad to see any solution that would keep the Hinterland in British hands. I am convinced that the Company, without the Hinterland, cannot beget sufficient interest to make people support it. I am also convinced that the Company cannot work the Hinterland without Government aid, because people will not take out "dividends in philanthropy" nowadays to any great extent.

Your requests to the Government for aid are more than they will give, but there is no harm in asking. If the occupation of Uganda be continued, the completion of a railroad to the lake at no distant date is a certainty; but it is probable that Harcourt, Gladstone, Morley, and Co. will have their way in blocking the railway project for the present, and I notice in yesterday's papers that the Government people in London are saying that there is no Cabinet discussion about Uganda, and that the evacuation is to take place in the three months stipulated.

We must cut our cloth according to this intention of evacuation (as far as our financial affairs are concerned), and be in a position, by retrenchment, to go on as mere Coastguardsmen; or, as a solvent Company, to make terms for our places being taken by the British Government.

Nov. 26, 1892.—I hear it said that E. Africa will now be governed "through Zanzibar," which looks as if they meant to make use of Portal. But I doubt their sending him personally up-country.

Harcourt's line was to say that we ought to be very grateful to have a burden taken off our shoulders. Rhodes' line was to say that the route to the coast was useless, as the country is such a wretchedly poor one; that only a hundred miles or so of railway would be required to connect the water tributes of Tanganyika and Victoria; and that the line due south of the Great Lake is the line to take to get commerce along a route—that Uganda should be held—but got at by this cheaper route.

Harcourt says : " Here is a man who will govern three times your area, at one-third of the cost, etc."

I believe the Commission is very much a dodge to send people to sleep.

Nov. 13, 1892.—Harcourt called to-day, and after much chaffing the following points appeared worth noting :

(1) He poured contempt on the railroad. Said it would never pay, and that Mr. Rhodes laughed at it also.

(2) He said that what he wanted to know was, " What is to be done during the four years before a railroad could reach Uganda ? "

I replied : "Administer the country with £40,000 expenditure."

He said Mr. Rhodes offered to do it for £26,000 and scoffed at wishing to administer " all the countries beyond." He said you had told him Lugard was doing wholly unauthorised things in going further than Uganda.

(3) I asked if he meant the Government to make the railroad or that we should do it, when he again repeated that the railroad was useless, and that there was nothing for it to carry. It was thus doubtful what he meant by the inquiry about a four years' interval until the railway was made, but he protested

that a *modus vivendi* for the present was all that he could think of, that in four years he hoped to have nothing more to do with affairs!

He asked if I would be in favour of continuing with the Company working the interior, provided "there were no question of money"; and I said, "Yes, personally I should be in favour of continuing if all expenses were paid, but I could not tell what the others desired who were of our Board."

Nov. 21, 1892.—Harcourt wants to "shirk out of Uganda." "You have made the difficulty; if we pay you for a time, you are bound to get out of it," he says.

I say: "The situation was made by us only at the instigation of the Government, and by the invitation of Mwanga himself to Jackson. We, the Company, tell you, the Government, on what terms we know, from experience, continued occupation can be ensured. Continued occupation for a term precluding the idea of retirement, which would be ruinous there and disgraceful here, is the only basis on which the Company can continue. All difficulties would be tenfold enhanced, were a mere 'hand to mouth' feeling adopted, and our enemies in Uganda encouraged to believe that the occupation is only temporary.

"It is only by the length of the term proposed now for occupation that men will judge whether Britain means to keep Uganda, or to 'scuttle.'

"We are responsible, as a Company, for occupation while our money lasts. When that is gone, the Government, which we as a chartered Company represent, becomes responsible."

Dec. 13, 1892.—Had a talk with the present Home Secretary about Africa, and find he is full of the idea that has been put into several of the heads of the Government by Rhodes, and by others who desire to shirk the expense of the Mombasa-Nyanza Railway. Their idea is of course that it is best to wait until arrangements can be made with the German Government for the through transit by lake and rail to the Zambesi.

Of course this is nonsense. There would be endless "breaking of bulk"—endless difficulty with the Germans and the Congo State—endless delays in not having the traffic over lines under our own control. But there is so much ignorance that anything which looks like an alternative plan does no damage. It is therefore important to make as many converts as possible among ministers, and A. tells me that he will be very glad to see Captain Pringle and Mr. Twining after the 12th, and to talk over with them the "difficulties" of the route they traversed.

Feb. 8, 1893.—I do not think that the Uganda debate in the House has brought any damage to the African cause, although it may not have specially benefited the Company. Coutts' speech, which consisted mainly of a rebuttal of the charge against the Company, was well received, as you will probably have heard from Mackenzie, who was in the House to hear the debate. One thing is certain, and that is that the Conservatives and Unionists are now definitely committed to the making of the railroad. The Kismayu fighting is most unfortunate. I think we should tell the Government that although in peace we can administer the Coast Ports, it is not to be expected that we can wage war against the Somalis or others if they attack in force. That we have not lost our right, as British subjects, to protection because we have a Charter. That, on the contrary, the Charter makes us the servants and representatives of the nation, and that we rely on the aid of imperial power to back our position, whenever menaced by overpowering numbers. That we have spent about £150,000 in enforcing imperial wishes strengthens our claim, in the same degree that it weakens us in the power of fulfilling our hopes of maintaining ourselves under all circumstances elsewhere.

March 6, 1893.—The death of the Sultan of Zanzibar opens a fresh opportunity to the Foreign Office to snub us, and curtail us of the anticipated privileges. The worst of it is that we are very helpless against the Government. We had the country on our side when it became a question of the country reaping the fruits of our exertions, in the retention of Uganda; but we shall not have the country with us when we occupy the position of people lying in wait at the coast to tax British goods in transit. The Foreign Office seems to dispute our claim to commute the revenue hitherto paid to the Sultan. At Brussels a friend of ours found that the opinion was held that although five per cent. could only be levied on imports under the Brussels Conference rules, and that money could be taken for slave trade repression, it is competent to levy export duties on goods leaving the East African Coasts.

This may be, but we have no money to carry on expensive lawsuits.

April 12, 1893.—Mr. Stanley is here, and I communicated to him the contents of Mr. Mackenzie's letter, announcing that it had been settled that Sir William remains a Director, but resigns the Presidency. Sir Arnold Kemball will do the work excellently well in negotiating with the Government the terms on which they will assume the responsibility of carrying on the good work. We must all feel that the British Government, even if it choose to call itself the " Zanzibar State," is a better power, with greater authority and means to carry on the Administration than a company can be, especially if that company be hampered rather than aided at home.

If the Government can be got to practically carry on our work, we shall feel that our mission is accomplished, though not exactly in the way we wanted. But what is ever accomplished exactly in the way man desires?

CHAPTER XXXVI

Uganda.—That the result of our work in obtaining possession of the East African Central Littoral, and of Uganda, has not realised the dismal prophecies of our opponents, but is bearing good fruit, may be judged by the statements made by Sir Frederick Lugard, Sir Clement Hill, and Bishop Tucker, on January 16, 1907, as to the railway traffic from the lake to the eastern sea.

Within the last two years the imports of East Africa have doubled, the exports have more than doubled, and the receipts of the Uganda railway have increased from £124,503 in 1904 and £165,135 in 1905 to £222,164 in 1906. The Uganda Protectorate has doubled its imports and exports within some three years. Mr. Wilson gave just praise to the mission agencies, which have done an enormous work in Uganda, and which in particular have relieved the administration of the great problem of education, having taken it upon their shoulders with the most marvellous results.

Sir Clement Hill said that a point that should not be overlooked was that England had succeeded in putting down the slave trade, and slavery had practically died out in East Africa. This they owed to those great pioneers of civilisation, who, like Sir Frederick Lugard, had risked their lives in our service and given us the best of their days.

Bishop Tucker spoke of the progress of Church missions, and after some further discussion the meeting ended with votes of thanks to the lecturer and the chairman.

When it is remembered that these results have already been achieved, despite the unlooked-for and terrible visitation of the sleeping fever, a disease brought by caravans from the west coast, and wholly unknown in Uganda when our Company undertook the acquisition of the country, it must be confessed that the opposition to our scheme was a mistake. If Dr. Koch, the German savant, and the investigations of the British medical men, be successful in discovering an antidote to this plague, the full fruition of our hopes will be attained. The fly which carries the germ, and inoculates man with its poison, never leaves the low and marshy country. Mr. Hayes Sadler, who has for a considerable time been the British Resident at Intebwe, considers that a very slight altitude is sufficient to guard against its attacks.

There are great riches to be developed in various species of rubber, and in the fibrous leaves of a plant which grows "like a weed." It was owing to the patriotic instigation of Sir William Mackinnon, a native of Campbelltown, Argyllshire, that Britain was not left out of the competition among the leading European nations for a place in the central regions of Africa. He carried his work through, against the opposition of the "Small Englanders," who were fearful on this occasion, as ever, of responsibility, and anxious to limit all national effort to what they could themselves smell and touch without leaving their armchair. We have the same over-cautious gentlemen cropping up at all times. But it is more difficult to find an antidote for their sleeping sickness than to discover one that repels the attacks of the smaller disease.

The following shows part of the success achieved, as reported this year by the Government Blue Book.

"The development of traffic on the railway has been one of the most encouraging features of the progress of the Protectorate during the period under review. The net receipts, which were £2,639 in 1904-5, rose to £56,678 in 1905-6, and to £76,150 for 1906-7; and this although the rates on most grains and seeds have been lowered to the very small figure of ½d. per ton-mile in order to encourage the agricultural development of the Protectorate. In connection with the railway I may mention that the steamship *Clement Hill* has now been completed and will shortly be running on the lake, and a cargo steamer, the *Nyanza*, has been constructed in this country, and is on its way to the Protectorate. Increased wharf accommodation is being provided at Kilindini and Port Florence at an estimated cost of £55,000 and £10,000 respectively.

"Turning to native affairs; the settlement of the Masai on their reserves has been satisfactorily completed, and a large tract in the Rift Valley has thus been opened to European settlement. Disturbances in the Sotik, Nandi, and Embo countries have necessitated the despatch of armed forces to those regions; and, in the result, after comparatively little loss of life, the tribes concerned have submitted to our rule, and civilised government is now being introduced in their countries. I am glad to note that the majority of the natives welcome the change, as is demonstrated by their willing payment of hut-tax, the receipts from which are estimated at £74,263 for 1907-8 as against £43,604 in 1905-6. A small sum has been provided on the current Estimates for encouraging the technical education of the natives by grants to the Mission Schools. The regulation and protection of native labourers is a matter of great importance, for which, at your suggestion, provision will be made this year by the appointment of a Secretary for Native Affairs, with three assistants."

CHAPTER XXXVII

Country-House Acting

ALTHOUGH the Scottish Horse Regiment and the Regiment of Scouts now prove that Highlanders can ride, such was not their ancient reputation. When performing an important service requiring quick communications a Highland rider is reported to have excused himself for being late, because he "had been sair tackled by having a horse to ride." But riding was taught at some country houses.

There exists at Inveraray a great hall, one hundred and twenty feet long, and fifty broad, which was used as a riding-school, and occasionally as a theatre. Here Sheridan and Monk Lewis and Tom Campbell used to take part in plays, or instruct those who were to do so, and original pieces were performed. Probably these were not of the best, but we have programmes still existing of the performances, which could not have been given before any very critical audiences, except when the house party were not themselves among the actors. Even then there was probably much leniency of judgment. For that leniency I appeal when the following production is submitted, and its chief virtue lies in the fact that the chief character was taken from life, and that the songs were sung by singers as untrained in their art as the writer was in his.

THE COACH AND SIX

A BRIEF COMEDY

DRAMATIS PERSONÆ

OLD MISS SMYTH (dressed in upper part of person like a man).
YOUNG MISS SMITH.
SQUIRE THATCHBRIDGE.
STUBBS.
MARY (Innkeeper's niece doing maid's duty).
HOUSEKEEPER.
OSTLER (a good-looking one).
SERVANT.

SCENE I.—*Old English wayside Inn.*
SCENE II.—*Interior of Thatchbridge House.*
SCENE III.—*The Inn hall.*

BALLET OF CRICKETERS AND THEIR RUSTIC GIRL FRIENDS OUTSIDE THATCHBRIDGE ARMS

Before action begins of play in Scene I

(*Rustic cricketers and their girl friends come on stage*)

BATSMAN. I'm the champion village bat!
What do you say, my girls, to that?
Don't we know the cricket chat?
I'm the champion village bat!
Ranji—singi—right you are!
Slip, and cut, and bowl, Houp-la!
Ne'er a stroke will your bowling bar!
Score, as you toe the crease! Houp-la!

CHORUS. Right you are! Right you are!
Don't be too particular!
Crikey! I'm a cricket star!
Right you are! Right you are!

BOWLER.	No great bat—but what of that?
	Three bats bowled! The prize, a hat!
CHORUS.	He's won a hat, and "Darn" and "Drat"
	Were words he drew from a famous bat!
BOWLERS.	We're the bowlers that afar
	Place the fields a stroke to mar!
	Would you like a good twistar?
	Right you are! Right you are!
CHORUS.	Right you are! Right you are!
	Don't be too particular!
	Crikey, I'm a cricket star!
	Right you are! Right you are!

(GIRL *with cricket ball sings*.)

        I'm the bowler bowls the lad!
        Be he old or undergrad.
        Truth to tell, 'tis rather sad!
        All admire, and say "Egad"!

(*Throws ball at one who catches and returns it.*)

        Hit me! block me! that's not bad!
        Why, I'll bowl you off your pad!
        Won't I beat you, and, bedad,
        Fix you through your favourite fad!

CHORUS.	Won't she make the stoutest bat
	Palpitate and pit-a-pat?
	Won't he feel an awful flat
	When he hears her cry "How's that"?
CHORUS.	Right you are! right you are!
	Don't be too particular!
	Crikey! she's the cricket star!
	Right you are! Right you are!

(*Some drink beer and others go to Inn or disperse.*)

SCENE I

Outside of Thatchbridge Arms Inn. Coach standing ready for horses to be put to (made of papered canvas. Wheels a little sunk behind rising cobble-stone pavement painted on canvas. Coach need not be full size, if sunk in roadway between bank).
Note: MARY's *part can be spoken in any local dialect;* OLD MISS SMYTH'S *by a man dressed as a gaunt lady.*

The Coach and Six

OSTLER'S *Song.*

(OSTLER *sings outside Inn at opening of Curtain.*)

OSTLER. If you've got stables, and tin beside,
    On a racing 'oss you may place your pride,
        And, rubbing him down (*hisses in time*),
        Bet your last crown
        He'll land you a fortune on Epsom Down!

If you've got money, nor care to count,
On a hunting 'oss you'll have your mount,
    And first in the chase (*hisses in time*)
    Know how to face
    The brook and the fences that bar the race!
But I've less money, by fortune sent!
So with roadsters good I am content:
    Yet you're no dunce! (*hisses in time*)
    You'll know at once!
    Sometimes I race, sometimes I hunts.

MARY *puts head out of window and sings after* OSTLER.

MARY'S *Song.*

MARY. Oh, who would a maid at a bar not be?
    At a wayside inn with a sign at swing—
All guests to see, in a way so free,—
    At times to work, and at times to sing,—
And bound to all men all things to be!
Oh, I am the maid of the hostelry!

Oh, I am the maid with the bunch of keys,
    And hearts and doors on stairs and floors,
Are opened wide with a turn of these!
    So memory soars from the world of bores,
To secrets of life that no one sees!
Oh, I am the maid with the bunch of keys!

But what of the Inn, if it ancient be?
    'Tis all for the best if the maid be young!
Her youth and her looks give her novelty!
    The guest who would grumble deserves to be hung,
For clean and sweet must the Inn well be,
Where I am the maid of the hostelry!

OSTLER *and* MARY *together*.

An old English way we have, they say!
    But where's a better? You'll find there's none!
Our horses and girls know how to stay!
    If the foreigner run, he finds he's done!
Then hurrah! for the land we love and know,
That on old and young can her love bestow!

Enter MARY *from Inn.*

MARY. Squire going to drive himself again to-day?

OSTLER. Yes, of course he is. Nothing will suit the gents now but to drive 'emselves. Why don't they do ostler? That would show them a thing or two. How can you know about a hoss by only cracking a whip over him, and feelin' his mouth a mile off?

MARY. Well, they do do it beautiful.

OSTLER. Of course if a gent won't employ real talent, amatoors can get themselves up to look like the real thing, but it's the professional who puts them straight. I say, Miss Mary, give us a tip. Who is he sweet on? There's some'un a-tooling of him while he tools the 'osses. Who is it now?

MARY. You didn't give me the straight tip last Derby. Why, I lost ever so much. I'd rather take Squire's opinion than yours, any day.

OSTLER. You know I made it up to you, and only put you wrong to get heavier odds around here against the 'oss that won, and you know I'd pay you more any day than you lost. Don't you now?

MARY. I thought you was an honest man. You don't even know your own business. Do you think I am going to tell you of other people's?

OSTLER. Now, don't take on, Miss Mary. But who is to sit beside the Squire to-day, eh?

MARY. I'll tell you who I'd like to see sit beside him, and that's me.

OSTLER. No, no; he'll look for rank and money.

MARY. Money? He says money's nothing to him.

OSTLER. Why, who told you that?

MARY. Why, the lawyer—the handsome Mr. Stubbs that come with the coach. He told me—he's my lawyer!

OSTLER. Your lawyer, Miss Mary! He won't undertake your case.

MARY. How do you know that? He'd do anything for me.

OSTLER. Well, you are made much of by every one. There's our young mistress as fond of you as though you were her sister. And then there's this visitor—well, I never! When did he come?

MARY. Why, yesterday.

OSTLER. And he's liked by you already. He ought to be ashamed of himself. If his name was Studs, now, instead of Stubbs, there might be something in him.

MARY. P'raps I knew him before.

OSTLER. Well, I'm not to be trotted out, miss, by you or any one. When do you take your tubs?

MARY. Tubs?

OSTLER. Stubbs or Tubs—he won't wash, or Tubs would be best.

MARY. No use joking over your betters, John. Why, here he comes!

(*Enter* STUBBS.)

STUBBS. Morning, Miss Mary; how are you this morning?

OSTLER (*aside*). Got to Marying her already, eh? Well, he's rushing his fences, but I'll put a barbed wire in—specially as I shan't hurt no horse if I lame him.

MARY. Good morning, sir. Hope you found your room comfortable?

STUBBS. Oh, very. Fine fresh air here. I say (*to* OSTLER), just go, my good man, and get me a cigar—don't see any other servants about. (*Exit* OSTLER.) Well, Miss Mary, I was asking you some things last night and I want to know more to-day. I told you I was a lawyer, so you won't mind a little cross-examination?

MARY. Oh no, sir, if you are not cross for long.

STUBBS. Yesterday I asked you all about yourself. Now the next most interesting thing is to know all about the place where you live. I know Squire Thatchbridge, but I have never been here or to his place before. I was at school with him. He was an elder son and succeeded to the property;

I was a younger son and had to work for money. But now I'm richer than the Squire. Squires don't like arguing, and it's arguing that makes money. How far is the house from here?

MARY. Only twenty minutes' walk, and there's an old church and carved tombs, and the lake and the ducks, and the farm, and the pigs that got the first prize, and the school and the scholards, and the big elm and——

STUBBS. Ugh!—nothing so dull as country park—flat country—fat cow, chewing cud under elm-tree. I never have lived a rural, a truly rural, life, with a fat cow under a tree. I'd rather stay at home with you, Mary, than make acquaintance with all these agitating objects. But the Squire will remember me, and if I can leave you a short time, Mary, it will be to find him. Has he horses down here? Is there any hunt near this? Any guests with him at present? I want all the news, you see.

MARY. Squire's got lots of horses. He drives that coach there himself, twenty miles away and back, and likes to take company on the coach. But they say that he's going to have lots of company when the repairs is done to the Manor. They talk of a ball.

(*Enter* OSTLER *with cigars.*)

STUBBS. Thanks. Can you tell me (*to* OSTLER) how many horses the Squire has?

OSTLER. I know all about 'im 'cos my aunt is his housekeeper. He's got everything under repair, so she tells me. Don't know about 'is 'osses now. When 'is 'ouse is full we get our best guests taken away, for Squire, as soon as he 'ears of any one here he would like to see, asks him up to the Manor. But now he don't want no one, so they says, 'cos there's repairs a-going on.

STUBBS. Oh, but he'll wish to see me.

MARY. No, sir. At least, I mean, he has *no* one with him now, and he has not taken anybody lately away from the inn.

OSTLER. No, sir—at least, we are not under repairs. Squire is. I can get you a good hack for a ride, sir—see the neighbourhood. Like that cigar, sir? 'Twasn't grown here, but we sells them good. I does the waiter, and gets a little profit on them. You'll take a dozen, won't you, sir?—or perhaps a box—couldn't get better, sir.

MARY. Oh, that's a secret!

STUBBS. Can you keep one? So can I! I've got a big one!

MARY. What is it? Do tell?

STUBBS. Lawyers never tell secrets. It's their arguing that tells.

MARY. Well, I won't tell you mine, although it's much more interesting than yours.

STUBBS. How do you know? Mine's all about you!

MARY. About me! Do tell!

STUBBS. All about your people, about the Squire, and the Inn, and Thatchbridge Hall.

MARY. So is mine all about the people of the Inn. Oh, such a grand secret!

STUBBS. What—a jolly one?

MARY. My eye! yes.

STUBBS. Oh, mine isn't jolly.

MARY. Then I don't want to hear it. Oh yes, I do! Do tell!

STUBBS. Tit for tat, you know! Now you begin!

MARY. Oh, mine's a fortune in itself. But I won't tell.

STUBBS. Mine's misfortune in itself. But I won't tell.

MARY. All I know is that some one's got a fortune!

STUBBS. And I'm to get no change out of that? Tell me what it is you know, and I'll go partner with you. A penny for your thoughts!

MARY. Oh, nothing.

STUBBS. Well, tell me who is staying here.

MARY. No one but a young lady and her brother. She came three days ago and I'm already a great friend of hers. Then there are the people who came on the coach with yourself.

STUBBS. Now, you are not an ordinary innkeeper's servant. You are a friend of the family that keeps the place. You manage the place as much as its mistress does, I'm told, and there's nothing she would not do for you. Tell me your secret and I'll go partner with you!

MARY. Oh, sir!

OSTLER. Why, he's made you an offer—and if I don't break his head! May I ask, sir, if your business is with the Squire, or the hosses, or the missus?

STUBBS. My business is in London, not here. Your business is with the 'orses, not with me!

MARY. London! Oh, how can you live there?

STUBBS. It's a nice place to get away from, and when there you hear so much talk of money that you think you have it, or if you have not, that you ought to have it—makes you feel yourself meritorious. (*Sits down.*)

MARY. Is it true that some of the streets are paved with gold?

STUBBS. Well, it's true you see lots of gold hair on the streets—on ladies' heads of course—quite as common in London as brown eyes—suits very well with the brown eyes.

OSTLER. Why, they must be piebalds! Like to see a pair of them down here in the country.

STUBBS. Well, Londoners are not decidedly averse to pairing. And you can get uncoupled there, too—there's nothing you can't get there. Why, you've only one Squire here. If you listen to them in London they'll tell you that they have hundreds of "squires" (*squares*) in their town, and there's a council there to take care of the "squires," which is quite right.

MARY. Our Squire don't need no taking care of.

STUBBS. You know nothing about his affairs, then. But tell me, he's not going to marry any one, is he?

MARY. Oh, I don't say that; but tell me of London. Is it not too big to be pleasant?

STUBBS. No; you would never be unpleasant, however much of you there might be.

OSTLER (*aside*). Curse him! how he turns things round. (*To* STUBBS) But it's not such good air as here.

STUBBS. Isn't it, though! A little fog in winter—very rare—that's what keeps the town so healthy, because people don't see each other when they are ill, and so don't catch things which they would catch if they saw each other ill. By the time the spring comes everybody's all right again.

OSTLER. I'd rather keep sound all the year round.

STUBBS. Why, so we do in London. It's the healthiest, grandest, pleasantest city in the world. You can be out-of-doors more days in the year than in any other capital in the universe. Its people are the most good-natured, large-minded, and patriotic people that God ever made come together.

OSTLER. Gum together? By gum! We have some gumption here, too.

STUBBS. Come together, stupid, I said. It is a big place. Why I have left it now, and I don't believe they've missed me!

MARY. But won't they find you out?

STUBBS. When they do we shall find the whole town coming after me, so we'll make the best of our quiet time now we're alone!

OSTLER. I can't stand this no more! (*Exit.*)

(*Enter* YOUNG MISS SMYTH.)

(*Sings* SONG.)

MISS S. I'm a little short-sighted, you know!
    Don't see people clearly, and so
        Mistakes here and there
        Must occur, I declare,
    When a glance through my glasses I throw!

    Show you can't help it, and then
    'Tisn't rude to stare straight at the men
        If one make reply,
        With a glass in his eye,
    Why, *I* need not answer "Amen!"

    Cold, or caressing, or coy,
    You are safe with the glass as a toy.
        You've only to say,
        "What? When? Yesterday?
    Oh, how could I see you, my boy?"

    The fault in my eyes doesn't show!
    Can't see without glasses, and so
        Excuse me if I
        Now pass you all by,
    I'm a little short-sighted, you know!

STUBBS (*rising and bowing*). Good morning, Miss Smyth.

MISS S. Oh, who's that? I did not see you. Good morning. Mary, now tell me about the arrivals. Have you seen anything of the ladies who came this morning?

STUBBS. Don't let me interfere with your arrangements.

(*Enters house.*)

MARY. Oh yes, miss. But let me talk of Mr. Stubbs first. He says he's a lawyer, but I think he must be an orficer, and he's a friend of the Squire's, and he likes hunting.

MISS S. Yes, yes; we'll know all about him in time—but what of the others who came?

MARY. There was only a commercial traveller, and the lady whose name is the same as yours.

MISS S. Yes, but no relation of mine!

MARY. No; the lady told me she was not. Who would ever have thought she could be? You are so beautiful—and she——

MISS S. I have hardly seen her—at least I did not use my glasses; but there are varieties of Smyth. We mostly spell ourselves with a "y" to escape being Smith. And we are never related, if we can help it.

(*Re-enter* STUBBS.)

STUBBS. Mary, you have a capital cook. Who is the lady that came yesterday?

MARY. Miss Smyth.

STUBBS. You don't mean to say so?

MISS S. Miss *Melpomene* Smyth.

STUBBS. What? Same name—you are not related?

MISS S. No, no!

STUBBS. No relation?

MISS S. Why, Smyths never are related.

STUBBS. No, you're right. I've noticed that.

  To vary life, Smith changed to Smyth,
  Disowning Smith as kin or kith;
  Yet Smith's old i kept asking y
  All Smiths and Smyths told lies and myths.
  For men of pith, if Smiths or Smyths,
  Are judged herewith,

If they are y's, or see with i's,
That Smith in Smyth apparent lies.

MARY (*aside*). Did you ever hear any one so clever?

STUBBS. I say, didn't you tell me that the Squire was at home? When can I see him, do you think?

MISS S. I'm told the Squire will be coming soon to drive the coach, and that he's a splendid whip, and he takes a party most afternoons. He takes any one that likes to go. When he's not hunting, that's one of his amusements.

STUBBS. Shall you go to-day, Miss Smyth?

MISS S. Perhaps, if he asks me.

STUBBS. And your namesake, is she going?

MISS S. I don't know. Perhaps if you want to know you might ask her yourself.

STUBBS. Will she stay here long, do you think?

MISS S. How can I know?

STUBBS. You won't, I suppose (*to* MARY)?

MARY. Really, sir, if this is an Inn, it's not an Innquiry shop! no one is obliged to give answers to all questions. You won't find answers on the Bill of Fare.

STUBBS. You know it's in my profession to ask questions, and find out about things. I suppose I can't help it. You won't think me indiscreet (*to* MISS SMYTH)?

MISS S. I've heard that questions are not indiscreet, but answers may be.

STUBBS (*aside*). Clever girl!

MISS S. (*aside*). Good-looking man, but awfully impudent. Well, I don't like 'em too modest. (*Aloud*) I'm going to Thatchbridge Hall. Shall I tell the Squire you are here?

STUBBS. No, no—for heaven's sake. We were friends at school, but he doesn't know all my luck since then. But he'll remember me. I shall call on him now, if he does not come. (*Aside*) He'll see enough of me whether he likes it or not, but I won't let him make her acquaintance if I can help it. Never mind his house being under repairs. If people don't propose themselves, they are often not asked at all, and I like to come down on my friends. It's a pleasant surprise for them. (*Aloud*) Who comes here? Tell me quick, before she hears what we say.

MISS S. (*low in his ear*). That's Miss Smyth.

(*Enter* OLD MISS SMYTH, *sees them with heads together.*)

OLD MISS S. Oh, I beg pardon.

YOUNG MISS S. (*hurriedly*). Not at all, not at all, Miss Smyth. I was only telling Mr. Stubbs what you told me—that you are anxious to see the neighbourhood; and as he was saying that he'd like to assist you, I was telling him of you, and I am sure he would wish to escort you! Miss Smyth, Mr. Stubbs—Mr. Stubbs, Miss Smyth (*introducing them*). Now I must go, but Mr. Stubbs will tell you everything, and show you all you wish to see, I'm sure. (*Exit.*)

STUBBS (*aside*). That beats everything. "Tres femme," as the French say, which can't be translated, but means much.

OLD MISS S. (*aside*). Whispering to himself now that he is not whispering to her. Good day, sir; I confess I'm glad to find a gentleman who is a good guide.

STUBBS. Assure you, never did guide any one. Most unfortunate that I'm engaged to go to Squire Thatchbridge.

OLD MISS S. Thatchbridge Manor! Just where I want to go to. I'm a most resolute tourist, Mr. Snubs.

STUBBS. Stubbs, madam, if you please.

OLD MISS S. Mr. Stubbs—beg pardon—I'll put you in my diary. You know some of my books of travel? I thought so. I sketch and write, and nothing escapes me. Where do you think I've just come from?

STUBBS. From the Inn, I think, madam. Excuse me, the Squire will be waiting for me.

OLD MISS S. No, he's coming here. They said so. Yes, sir, from the Rocky Mountains. What do you think of that? I'll show you my notes and sketches.

STUBBS. Oh, Lord!

OLD MISS S. Yes, you may be surprised, but I was with the hairy men in the Japanese Islands last year; and this year, where do you think I'm going to?—you'll never guess.

STUBBS. Thatchbridge Manor you said, madam.

OLD MISS S. You need not be so formal with me who have seen the world. Thibet! Nothing can stop me.

STUBBS. They say beauty and modesty go far.

OLD MISS S. I've got a number of subscribers down already

for my next volume. I have no doubt that it will sell in London and Pekin, for the interest of the narrative will centre in Russian-Chinese-Siamese-Franco-Germanic-Britannic difficulties. Before again daring uncivilised regions, I take strength from my native land and store my memory with old England's best scenes. I ride and sketch on horseback, most accurately I assure you, although of course finish must be added when I'm dismounted. I hope it won't shock you to know I ride in the old fashion. Side position twists the body, which should be straight. I don't shock you, do I?

STUBBS. Oh no, I'm too far gone.

OLD MISS S. But I go much further. I've had my nose, my toes, my cheek, frost-bitten.

STUBBS. There's a good deal of cheek left!

OLD MISS S. And I've got a medal I wear on my left breast.

STUBBS. Where?

OLD MISS S. Here! It was given for saving life. A Patagonian was upset in his canoe in coming alongside the ship. I was in my cabin, and I tied two spare petticoats together, and they were long enough to reach down from the port to the water. The next wave saw him hanging on to my skirts. But the porthole was between us. My arm is strong, but the strain was great, until they let a rope down from the deck. I then recovered my garment. It is that which I now wear.

STUBBS. Ugh! Most interesting!

OLD MISS S. I quote Tennyson, though I have gone further than have penetrated his writings, "My arm is strong because my heart is pure." That was said by a knight in armour. But I've worn armour too.

STUBBS (*aside*). Brazen person!

OLD MISS S. Yes, in the South Seas. Quilted armour against poisoned arrows, for I feared lockjaw.

STUBBS. What a blessed result!

OLD MISS S. Yes, they told me I looked well, and after Thibet I may face the African forests and the poisoned arrows there. African travellers have written some good books, but they don't sufficiently describe the ethnological, botanical, geological, and zoological configuration of the country through which they go. I can stand sun as well as cold, though I have had one sunstroke, and still feel a little queer sometimes.

STUBBS. Excuse me, I must be off. Bad luck to it, here comes the Squire.

(*Enter* SQUIRE, *to whom* OLD MISS SMYTH *immediately advances.*)

OLD MISS S. I think I have the pleasure of speaking to Squire Thatchbridge. I am a tourist, anxious to describe the homes and happiness of England's squires. Those who had —what does Mrs. Hemans say? "Stately homes of England," was it?—no, stately establishments of Great Britain before the conquest—are to have separate chapters giving the most minute circumstances showing their daily movements, indoors and out-of-doors. There lives will be mirrored. The public shall, through these paragraphs, look in upon them as through their windows, and admire all they do, hear all they say. The noble confidences between man and wife, the interchange of confidential views on politics, the social life around them, and their intimate family relations shall all be exhibited for the admiration of an expectant public, whose right as well as whose pleasure it is to drink their fill of domestic details. I was cradled myself, you may like to know, at Babycombe.

SQUIRE. Baby come? ugh!

OLD MISS S. That's in the sweet west. I am nothing if not geographical. I was cradled at Babycombe.

SQUIRE (*aside*). Sweet baby! (*Aloud*) Bless me, madam, I see an acquaintance there. How are you, Stubbs? Haven't met you for an age. University match, five years ago, last time, I think. (*Aside*) Who is this awful female you've got hold of?

STUBBS. I got hold of her! It's all t'other way. (*Aside*) I was going to call on you. I don't know anything about her, but I was going to warn you that she's in the neighbourhood. She's called by some absurd classical name.

SQUIRE (*aside*). What a nuisance! Stubbs was nuisance enough. At school we used to call him "mad Stubbs." Wonder what brings him here! (*Aloud*) Madam, I'll send you an answer. My friend and I will retire now to talk over old times. May I ask whom I have the honour of addressing?

OLD MISS S. Selections from my works are, of course, made for the public, that the chief attraction of the neighbourhood, Thatchbridge Hall, may be viewed by them. My name is Melpomene! I knew you would ask it. It has a charm, has it not, Squire? I will tell you more when I see you at home.

SQUIRE. My house is under repair. I have no guests there now, Miss Melpom—(*aside*) I can't get round the name.

OLD MISS S. But the beautiful exterior, and the internal architecture that can delight an eye accustomed to crave for quaintness, and pining for the proportions of the spacious days of great Elizabeth?

STUBBS. Truly, I was going to propose a visit myself. Since we were at school we have hardly seen each other.

SQUIRE. Wish I had a room fit for you, old man. But the workmen and I are the only people who find the place habitable now.

STUBBS (*aside*). I'll find it habitable enough for myself soon. It won't be so for him long!

OLD MISS S. Grant me permission, Squire Thatchbridge. Your courtesy shall not be abused. I can give you valuable hints as to the placing of your furniture—and your landscape gardening. The chief charms of some places come from my inspiration. At one place a lake was made by my advice. The owner drowned himself in it—why I do not know, but it may have been because of my absence. Memory changes not, even if your best hayfield is changed to water. I wrote his epitaph.

STUBBS. I'll have to come to you—(*aside*) if only to defend you from this literary fury. I know her ways will be too much for you. If alone she will overpower you! You were always too good-natured.

SQUIRE. Another time I hope I shall see you at my house. Now, I should be ashamed of letting you sleep there, for I have given my servants holiday, and all is in confusion. Let me show you some of the neighbourhood. I take the coach out, with any one who likes to come.

OLD MISS S. I'll gladly go. May I have the box-seat, Squire, that you may tell me about the country? (*Seats herself at a table at door of Inn.*)

SQUIRE. We'll arrange all that when we see who comes.

Who has come to the Inn? Only a few, I suppose; our season has hardly begun.

(YOUNG MISS SMYTH *at window, which she throws open.*)

YOUNG MISS S. (*Sings*).

    A while in town, a while away—
        A time for your home and your travel!
    A season for quiet, a season to stray,
    One day to be pensive, another be gay;
        So may we life's troubles unravel!

    I joy in sunlight's sparkling glance,
        As green in the woodland it quivers,
    When far through the leaves I would ever advance
    Where heat with the cool of the earth has a dance,
        And mists are afloat on the rivers!

    I joy in town, its streets, and glare,
        Where life is a race, never-ending,
    And no one has ever a moment to spare;
    Yes, oh, how I love the old Vanity Fair,
        Its buying, and racket, and spending!

    Give change to me, come weal or woe;
        I'll sift, like a miner, life's gravel!
    Sometimes 'tis but sand, sometimes it may glow
    All golden, all sweet with—oh, how should I know?
        Some changes debar one from travel!

SQUIRE. What a charming voice!—who is it?

STUBBS. Oh, only a tourist. I think I know the man who has probably engaged her to sing at the next town. You can hardly ask her up to your house. (*Aside*) Damn me if I don't tell her that he's not worth a button!

SQUIRE. Can't I, though!

(*Enter* YOUNG MISS SMYTH.)

YOUNG MISS S. (*aside*). Oh dear, I did not know these gentlemen were here. Gentlemen are always where they should not be. When wanted one can't find them—when not wanted they are listening to what you say! (*Seeing* OLD MISS SMYTH) Dear me, what a strange-looking man!

STUBBS. I hope you slept well, Miss Smyth (*to* YOUNG MISS SMYTH).

OLD MISS S. I don't talk of sleeping before gentlemen. But I can sleep anywhere. I have slept on the top of Chimborazo—that's a mountain.

YOUNG MISS S. (*aside*). A good lie, I should say. Who are these friends of yours (*to* STUBBS)? That one at the table seems an extraordinary person. Who is he?

STUBBS. He? He! he! Why, you introduced "him" yourself to me. "He's" got a new hat on; but "he" is otherwise much as "he" was. He? He! he! oh, he's a a person who has been everywhere—knows everything. Don't you recognise my friend?

OLD MISS S. (*without rising—bowing stiffly*). I hope now they won't mistake us for each other!

YOUNG MISS S. (*to* STUBBS.) Where are my glasses? Of course I know the voice. I hope you enjoyed her society?

OLD MISS S. I've got the box-seat!

SQUIRE. May I ask you to drive with me? We'll be back by lunch if we go in the morning, and by tea-time if we go in the afternoon.

YOUNG MISS S. Certainly, but I had rather that creature did not sit near me.

SQUIRE (*laughing*). Oh, she must take a back seat when you're on board.

STUBBS (*aside*). Hope he won't be smitten by her!

OSTLER (*from Inn*). When do you start, sir?

SQUIRE. At once, if the company desire.

THE OTHERS. Oh, at once, at once!

OLD MISS S. Mary, tell the others. We'll go and get our hats and cloaks. (*All go to Inn,* OLD MISS S. *last.*) I'll take notes and write poems during the trip, that precious time be not lost.

(*Enter* OSTLER *and* MARY. OSTLER *looks to coach—*STUBBS *and* SQUIRE *walk up and down.*)

SQUIRE. I fear that virago will come, but no one need speak to her. You and Miss Smyth, and Mary if she likes to come, will take the front seats, and young Smyth, her brother, and the old termagant can go behind. Lord, what a woman! "Mulled Pomery" I think she called herself! Ugh, how horrid!

STUBBS. Oh yes, make her take a back seat and sit upon some one—young Smyth. He's young, he can stand it. He's not bound to speak to her either. Besides, she'll be quite happy doing all the talking herself, and the groom may answer her questions. We will see and hear nothing of her. We won't ask her name. It will probably be worse than her looks.

OSTLER. That's all right now, Miss Mary. Get that young gent to help with the steps, will you? while I just sees to these straps. (MARY *gets steps with* YOUNG SMYTH *and places them against coach*.) Lord, that old woman! Not as I mind Smyths when they're young and hearty and pretty; but when they are old—bah! they're not goldsmiths, nor yet jewellers—are they, my jewel?

MARY. Don't talk so to me, John. Here they come, and I'll have a ride too.

(OLD MISS SMYTH *storms the steps, but* OSTLER *makes them slip, and she falls.* "*Not hurt?*" "*Oh dear, no, I'm not easily hurt.*" *Then* "*Come along, then,*" *and they replace steps at back, get her up, and before she can clamber over coach to get to front, other steps have let* YOUNG MISS SMYTH, MISS MARY, *and the* SQUIRE *and* MR. STUBBS *mount, and they occupy the front.* SQUIRE *shouts,* "*The youngster will tell you, with the groom, all about the things they have heard,*" *and the Curtain comes down as the* SQUIRE *cracks his whip for a start, with a shout of* "*Let them go now!*")

CURTAIN

SCENE II

Interior of Thatchbridge Hall. House is under repair, and brown holland covers part of room and ceiling. A chimneypiece and a fine room with armour, pictures, etc., showing except where ceiling covered and part of wall.

HOUSEKEEPER. There's that impertinent Mr. Stubbs insisted on coming here, when he was told that he was in the way. Leastwise the Squire seems to think he can't say "No," but he told him as much as that he was not wanted, and all Mr. Stubbs said was that they were at school together—as if this was a school, and them still schoolboys! If it were, I'd give Master Stubbs a birching, that I would. His face is the most impudent I've seen. He's a lawyer, I know, but what I don't know is why the judges allow the lawyers to be so impudent. Why can't they stop 'em, if they are judges of character? And he's been a-prying round, and lifting this cloth and that cloth to see what's underneath, just as curious as a magpie. Pretends he's fond of old furniture. Old fiddlesticks! though I'm fond of pretty things too when I can show them to tourists. He ought to be a tourist, and pay for what he sees, like a gentleman. Now I showed that tapestry in the dining-room, and told him it was a Goblin Room, and he laughed and said it was the best French he had heard for many a day. But a compliment isn't coin, and what's the use of a man admiring the leg of a table if he can't hand a tip, or knowing that a bit of carved brass is invaluable if he's not worth a brass farthing himself? He said that picture was a Ferrati, and I wanted to tell him that I didn't believe that any one called himself by that name, but he deserved to be called Ferret.

> Responsible persons in our situations,
> Officially bound to make no revelations,
> Can do a great deal by the merest expression,
> To leave upon all a most sterling impression.
> But 'tis hard—wery hard—if folks pull us up short,
> We want, as good servants, the fullest support.
> We all have our trials, our worries, temptations,
> Distractions surround us with insinuations.
> Yet we must keep up all the family credit,
> Yes, all who have watched us, sincerely have said it,
> But 'tis hard, very hard, while we're holding the fort,
> The public don't give us the fullest support.
> And mind, if my song be a little bit wrong,
>   Or halt in its phrase or its metre,
> I'm always a pattern to every slattern—
>   I work to make everything neater!
> The interest I take in the family makes
>   Their circle selecter—completer!
>
> (*Folds her arms over bosom proudly.*)

(*Enter* SQUIRE THATCHBRIDGE.)

SQUIRE. Good-day, Mrs. Hardy. We must have done with these fellows, the painters and plumbers and carpenters, else we'll never get 'em out of the house. There's Mr. Stubbs; I would not have had him, but I can't help it. He's got some business to talk to me about—no pleasant business either. I think these workmen are dawdling—don't you, Mrs. Hardy? And the painter who is doing that ceiling, why, he's ever so long about it (*pointing up to covered ceiling*).

HOUSEKEEPER. They do say that they works so long, they can't do the work. Why, the plumber says the drains are not all he'd like 'em to be; and although every woman always is offended when the drains of her house are found fault with, yet I thought you'd like to be on the safe side, so I did not scold him so much as I ought. Then the carpenter, he said that, good as the house was, the want of ventilation had introduced dry rot (beg pardon for using such bad words to you, sir), and unless some of the floors were looked to, a man of your weight and position might go through, and I thought it best you should be on the safe side, sir. And then the head painter, he said that each coat wanted drying, especially with the colours you ordered, sir, and that he could satisfy you with a tint that would prevent you having green paper, which is always poison, and he'd send again to London, so I let him because I thought you would like to be on the safe side, sir. Now I would like to ask your instructions, sir. Do you wish Mr. Stubbs to see everything in the house, and hear about everything, for if you do I'll do my best to satisfy his curiosity, but without that leave I would not answer every question. Will you tell me your wishes? because I like to be on the safe side, sir.

SQUIRE. Stubbs? Well—no—yes—no, of course he need not see any rooms you want closed. You can lock the doors and say nothing about it.

HOUSEKEEPER. But he gets in when the workmen come out for their dinner. He knows all the rooms, I do believe, already, and he's making what he calls rubbings of the patterns on the furniture. Oh, sir, he's a rubber that climbs in at the back doors.

(*Enter* STUBBS.)

SQUIRE (*to* HOUSEKEEPER). Never mind now. I'll see about it. (*To* STUBBS) Like to have a ride to-day, Stubbs? Fine morning!

STUBBS. Quite happy at home or anywhere. Can always amuse myself in the house. I've been overhauling some of your treasures, and I assure you I am filled with admiration for lots of things. May I ask where you got that—— (*A knock at the door, and boy enters with letter and gives it to* HOUSEKEEPER). Oh, there's a letter. What time does your post come? That's not come by post, I think—I don't see a stamp on it. Perhaps one of your passengers by the coach—eh, Squire?

HOUSEKEEPER *gives the letter to* SQUIRE, *saying*—It's addressed to him (*with a jerk of her head towards* STUBBS).

SQUIRE. It's addressed to you. I am not so fortunate as to have correspondence (except by post) here.

STUBBS (*opening and reading letter*). I guessed right. It does come from one of your fair passengers. She asks if she may bring her wish to your knowledge that she would like so much to see the house. Here's the letter.

SQUIRE. From the lovely Miss Smyth! (STUBBS *laughs.*) Why does she write to you, you rascal, when she was sitting near me yesterday, and might have asked me then? Oh, do kindly go and see if the boy hasn't yet gone, while I write a note in reply. Why, of course I shall be delighted to take down all the curl-papers in the house for her, and show her anything that pleases her. Do go and see if you can stop the boy, if he has gone. He may be waiting outside for the answer (*exit* STUBBS). (*To* HOUSEKEEPER) Now, I must get rid of my friend there, if only for an hour or two. There is no company. What can I do?

HOUSEKEEPER. I might show him into a room I could tell him he has not yet seen, and lock him up there—by accident?

SQUIRE. No, no, I must not be discourteous. He would suspect a trick there at once.

HOUSEKEEPER. But, as an old servant, may I ask who is this lady?

SQUIRE. She is the most beautiful, the most adorable creature in the world. She is so charming that every man, woman, and child must like her. The voice and looks of an angel!

HOUSEKEEPER. But is she well-born, sir?

SQUIRE. Well-born? I should think so. Saxon origin, I believe, mixed with the best Norman blood. Looks as if all her ancestors had fed on roses and pearls, and lilies and peonies, and snowdrops and blushes—but I must write immediately.

HOUSEKEEPER (*aside*). Lord! hope she's not a gardener's daughter. (*Aloud*) Here's paper and ink in the drawer of this table, sir, and blotting-paper. Now, dear young master, do take care as you write, and act with thought, as if your poor dear mother and father was a-looking at you.

SQUIRE. Get along, you old silly. (*Writes.*)

(*Re-enter* STUBBS.)

STUBBS. All right, old boy, messenger waiting. Can't I do anything for you?

SQUIRE. Yes; I have made arrangements for you, too. If you don't mind giving this note to the boy, on your way to the stable—for I've got a capital horse for you, and this morning I want you to try him as a special favour to me, because you will be able to appreciate him more to-morrow. To-morrow's meet is, I hear, to be at a place not far from this, and you and I will see a good run together, I trust. Be back for lunch or not, as you like, but make the most of the sun in the morning and enjoy yourself. The groom has orders to show you the horse, and I hope you will try his jumping powers—splendid jumper, by Jove!

STUBBS. Thanks—thanks. (*Aside*) Won't I lead him over a bit of difficult country—and he'll never find out, for I know the lie of the land hereabouts pretty well now, and can lay a pretty good drag! (*Aloud*) Thank you. You always were an unselfish chap. (*Aside*) Damme, there are some things one must be selfish about. Sport and love are two of them, and I can't keep up the humbug of treating him long as if all these things really belonged to him, instead of to his creditors who sent me here. (*Aloud*) Ye-es, confoundedly unselfish.

Nice horse—good scent. Yes—er—er—do you know, I don't like leaving you all to yourself, when we have not met for so long. Let's take a stroll together, and talk of hunting and of old days at school. Do you remember the fight you had with Mad Thomson, when I was your second, and you licked his head off although you were only half his size? (*Aside*) Confound him, if he cuts me out with that girl, I'll kill him. But I'll soon convince her he's a bankrupt.

SQUIRE. My dear fellow, I remember nothing now, but that I want you to enjoy yourself, that I have made all arrangements for that purpose. Don't think of me.

STUBBS. Oh, Thatchbridge, don't think of me! I like to loaf around a country house. A little amuses me.

SQUIRE. All in good time, Stubbs. I'll see you further first—that is, I want you to appreciate the country around before you see the details about here. Never miss fine weather. The house will do for a rainy day—you'll disappoint my grooms. You look pale. Too much desk and chamber work. I mean to send you back strong and rosy—never mind me. (*Aside*) Damn him! He's a worse leech than most lawyers, or than any doctor. (*Aloud*) I'll take no denial. I won't be selfish. But you'll excuse me coming with you, as I have some important estate business.

STUBBS. Oh, I could help you in that—judicial opinion, you know, might indeed be necessary, considering (*with meaning*) all I know of your affairs.

SQUIRE. You can't indeed. My land-steward's waiting—so is your horse.

STUBBS. I'll accept your kind offer. I was only hesitating a moment, not liking to tempt you away to the hunting-field, when you would otherwise have the pleasure of again driving the fair ladies at your hostelry. All right, though, just as you wish—only I would not that you leave better company for my sake. I'll take the letter. (*Exit* STUBBS.)

SQUIRE. Now, he'll be away some time at all events. Good Mrs. Hardy, I'll let you judge yourself of the young lady's attractions. You shall look out for me and come and tell me as soon as she is near, and then go and bring her yourself to this room. As she only asked to see the house she might consider me as misinterpreting her intentions if

I appeared at once, but you can take her through the Hall to this room, where I shall be as though accidentally. Lord, I don't know why it is, but I feel as shy as a schoolboy. Were it not for my recent financial troubles I would have more nerve. D—— bad thing for nerves is worry.

HOUSEKEEPER. I'll do what you wish, sir, but do remember to behave as though your dear mother and father was a-looking down on you. (*Exit.*)

SQUIRE. She never gave me any warning of this happiness. Just like her sweet nature—her girlish modesty. But why write to that damned ass, Stubbs?—that's what puzzles me. Of course he was staying at the Inn with her, and may have had some talk with her on the journey—but can't have had much. I hope it's the last time she won't ask anything straight from me—at all events I'll tell her so. Wish that mare would break Stubbs's neck—fear there's no chance of that. How long she is in coming! What is Stubbs doing, I wonder? Surely he can't have taken my letter himself— no, no, but I was a fool to give it him. No, he's a mile off now. Hope he won't injure her. Beautiful beast she is. Oh, that sweet modesty, that graceful form! Blest if I don't think I had best give him another, and take her myself. The groom's a careful man and won't let her do too much. Ah, there she comes—Lord, how my heart beats!

(*Enter* HOUSEKEEPER.)

HOUSEKEEPER. I thought I would just come in and tell you, sir, that I see a lady coming down the avenue, and wanted to get your last orders, sir. Is there anything else I can do for you, sir? Did you say I was to bring her at once to this apartment? Wouldn't the Yeller *H*ante-room be more appropriate than your own room, sir?

SQUIRE. No—no, do as I tell you, Hardy. Mind you don't keep her waiting. You can tell her to come here. *Here*, mind, and show her in yourself. Am I tidy, Hardy?

HOUSEKEEPER. Tidy?—no, sir, I can't say you are. Why, your necktie is not as straight as it might be. You don't look quite so neat as I would like to see your poor dear mother's son.

SQUIRE. Bless me, I must go and repair damages, etc.,

HARDY. Well, I won't be long. Now go your way, and I'll go mine. Bless me, I'll just give my hair another brush.

(*Enter* SERVANT.)

SERVANT. The man from the stable, sir, says your best horse is very ill—took quite sudden—begs you'll come at once—and a message from the Inn says one of the coach team is ill—looks like poison, sir.

SQUIRE. Damn! Go, Hardy—I'll be back in a moment. Make the lady take a seat. Curse the horses, curse my wig!

HOUSEKEEPER. Now, my nephew, as is at the head of the Inn stables, though they call him ostler only, will be sure to put him right. Let my nephew see him, Squire!

(*Exeunt* HOUSEKEEPER *and* SQUIRE *by different doors.*)

SERVANT. Well, if Mr. Stubbs gets me into trouble, he's promised to pay me handsomely for it. I'm tired of this sitivation, and shall be glad to go to London with him. He says as this whole house really belongs to him! (*Exit.*)

(*Enter* HOUSEKEEPER *with* OLD MISS SMYTH.)

HOUSEKEEPER. There's some mistake—you say you have an appointment with the Squire. Nonsense, he's got no place vacant. Why, he's expecting a young lady, and when I seed you coming down the avenue, I told him she was coming—thinking her's you—and now that she's not come I can't waste time on you, for she'll be here soon,—so you must say what you want. If you want a sitivation this is not the time to apply. You have almost forced your way in, and I won't be responsible—indeed I won't—for your ways. Nothing but the Squire's own handwriting in your hand there would have let you get so far—no, not if I had died in trying to put you back. I can't complain of your language, but I do of your pushing. Fancy an old servant of the family like me pushed aside!

OLD MISS S. Leave your master to me, my good woman. See if I don't master him. Now, you have said quite enough. I will recommend your zeal to him—a good thing, zeal, when there's not too much of it! Then shall I read you part of his letter to convince you that I don't want any situation but one free from your excellent intentions? " Mr. Thatchbridge presents his compliments to Miss Smyth, and hearing that she and her party desire to visit the Hall and Park, encloses an order, of which he hopes she will be so good as to make use at any time convenient to her."

HOUSEKEEPER. Well, I suppose I ought to beg pardon; any way, I'll offer you a seat, and go and tell the Squire of your arrival. (*Aside*) Well, I never—a "new woman," I suppose. Well, if they are none of them newer than that—and civiller—I'd sooner have a sweetheart among the older ones, if that be possible, if I were a gentleman, as I am in feeling! (*Exit.*)

OLD MISS S. Now that old thing's gone I may take a seat. Sitting is conducive to meditation. Calm and thought are good when circumstances are agitating. I will sit down. All things come to her who knows how to wait—and sit down. (*Takes chair with back to door* SQUIRE *left by.*) A fine place. When will it be properly arranged? When an intelligent mistress knows how to set things in order. I will uncover a picture and meditate. (*Does so, and reseats herself so that hat and feathers and back of head only seen above chair back.*)

(*Enter* SQUIRE *softly.*)

SQUIRE (*advancing very slowly to chair on seeing it occupied*). What luck to come upon her so—in maiden meditation! Let me look at her for a moment, while yet she does not know I am here. Happy chair! She likes that picture. By Jove! what a fortunate fellow I am!

(MISS SMYTH *here rises to look closer at picture.*)

Lord! what's that? There is some hideous mistake.

(*Enter* HOUSEKEEPER.)

HOUSEKEEPER. There's the young lady, sir, you have been expecting.

(OLD MISS SMYTH *turns.*)

OLD MISS S. Most kind of you, Squire Thatchbridge, to send me such a kind note. I assure you I shall keep it. You have not forgotten that a note in your handwriting is even better than a message, but another time you will give me your autograph in my Birthday Book. Ah, birthdays are sweet things to remember! No? Oh, then I won't press you this time.

SQUIRE (*falling back into a seat—faintly*). I suppose Mr. Stubbs gave you my note. It was intended——

OLD MISS S. Of course it was kindly intended. Most courteous. I am accustomed to courtesy, but appreciate yours. Although I had not a chance of entertaining you with any stories of my travels yesterday, I shall be able now to devote my time to you, and will not, I assure you, give it all to your curios and pictures. I am told that the owners of Thatchbridge have always been famous for their hospitality. I knew I should not be disappointed in you. Nor can you be with me.

SQUIRE (*to* HOUSEKEEPER *aside—groaning*). This is some dreadful mistake, brought about by that cursed Stubbs.

HOUSEKEEPER. I thought he'd be a wiper in your buzum, sir.

SQUIRE. And here's a boa constrictor here. Oh, do get me a glass of port wine. (*To* OLD MISS SMYTH) Excuse me, I was only telling the housekeeper to get some refreshment. I do not feel well. (*Exit* HOUSEKEEPER.)

OLD MISS S. Not feel well? Not faint? Let me take care of you. (*Advances.* SQUIRE *makes desperate leap and puts table between them.*) Oh, you have had some refreshment already. I don't want any now, but if it comes will drink one little glass to the health of the proprietor of much that is beautiful, and which should be enjoyed in better health (*sits down in* SQUIRE'S *armchair*). Do you often drink port in the morning? I never do—an occasional cigarette, perhaps. Let me offer you one that I bought after the ascent of the great Pyramid. (*Enter* HOUSEKEEPER *with wine*). (SQUIRE *offers a glass to* OLD MISS SMYTH.) No, thank you, principles before pleasure. (SQUIRE *refuses cigarette with a bow.*) I smoke all over my little house. It's the only way to prevent any bad smell, and to let people enjoy the good smells.

SQUIRE. What did the note you received say?

OLD MISS S. Just what I knew you would say, that you would be delighted to show me your house, and all within it. Now I claim my rights. When did your mother die, and your father? How many beds can you make up in the house?—sweet quiet home for literary person. Let me read your good heart.

SQUIRE. I'll let you do anything—I'll tell you if you will follow the housekeeper into that room. I'll join you in a moment. (*Exeunt* OLD MISS SMYTH *and* HOUSEKEEPER—SQUIRE *nearly empties caraffe of port, and pours it down his throat.*) Won't I give it to that scoundrel! But I suppose I must show her the place; it would not be like a gentleman to show her only the door.

OLD MISS S. (*voice heard at door*). Now, Squire, all the pictures and the house, and the grounds, and Park—I must see all. We'll take the surroundings first, please. Then when tired, sit in the rooms and see the pretty things at ease.

SQUIRE. Heaven help me, I suppose I must become Bear-leader for the time. When shall I get rid of her—and who is she—and why does she come here? Oh that villain Stubbs! (*Exit.*)

(*Enter* HOUSEKEEPER.)

HOUSEKEEPER. Well, I never! I believe now she wants to make a sitivation! But there must be some good in her, for she asked after his dear father and mother!

(*Exit* HOUSEKEEPER, *enter* STUBBS *and* YOUNG MISS SMYTH.)

STUBBS. The Squire has deputed me to show you his house. He is *so* sorry that he is engaged himself, or he would be here. Fact is, between you and me, he is much taken up with a young lady who called on him.

YOUNG MISS S. Oh, really, how kind of him to let you come! My brother heard that he would certainly allow us to see his grounds and house, and I thank you, Mr. Stubbs, for writing for me.

STUBBS. Well, the Squire is attending to another lady, to tell you the truth—a lady to whom I think he is much attached, so we had best not try to find him. What good luck for me to fulfil the desire I have had to be of use to you, Miss Smyth! Your brother has been taken to the stable—

that will interest him. The Squire wanted me to go to the stable, but I had an idea that you might be coming, and I gave up my ride in hopes of meeting you.

YOUNG MISS S. I am so fond of pictures. What is that one?

STUBBS. Most remarkable picture. Glad I am with you, because to tell you the truth—and I know you won't repeat what I say—the Squire doesn't know anything about the pictures he calls his. That's by a famous Italian—slightly retouched, I fear. The School of Bologna—getting dark. They tempt picture-restorers. I've been telling the housekeeper all they want is a wet sponge. I'm fond of sponging—on my friends' pictures, you know, I mean—makes them show up so well.

YOUNG MISS S. You have been smoking. I do so like the smell of a cigarette.

STUBBS. Yes, but the Squire doesn't in his rooms. May I offer you some wine? The Squire has drunk nearly all. He's always drinking sadly in the mornings—and in the afternoons too. Sad thing, Miss Smyth, because he has talents.

YOUNG MISS S. I am sure he does not take too much. How beautifully he drove yesterday!

STUBBS. Yes, but the horses are carefully trained for him. Allow me to offer you a seat. No wine?

YOUNG MISS S. Oh no, not for me. I'll sit a moment, but then you must take me all through the rooms. Oh, what a rich man the owner of this house must be!

STUBBS. No, head-over-ears in debt. The mortgagees are going to take it all from him now, because he has such fearful debts. Do you know he lost £4,000 to me at billiards last night? I happen to be the lawyer sent down by his creditors—of course this is in confidence—and I have not told him yet—but I am instructed to take possession of all he has as soon as possible. I'm one of the chief creditors. The place practically belongs to me already!

YOUNG MISS S. How very dreadful! Then you are the rich one of the two friends. But you must not tell me so much about your friend, else I shall think he's not worthy of your friendship.

STUBBS. But I try to look after him, to steady him. Of course I only keep what I win from him to save it for him.

YOUNG MISS S. How generous of you! Of course, as you are a lawyer, you can help him a great deal.

STUBBS. Yes, that's just it. We are accustomed to defend people. The most desperate character can be sure to have all that can be said for him stated in the best way. I know he's not safe without me. That's why I came here. But his estate is past saving—the sale won't give half what he owes.

YOUNG MISS S. (*rising*). You make me feel quite sad. I wish that I could help him. It is so melancholy to see a good-looking man in want of help.

STUBBS. Yes, but, believe me, this requires a man. A woman can do nothing in these cases—believe me—nothing at all. A man with knowledge of law and of the world is what is necessary.

YOUNG MISS S. Such a house, with so many beautiful things in danger!

STUBBS. Yes, there are no end of beautiful things. Now let me show you the next room. We'll go all through the rooms and then I'll show you the garden—but the house will take us some time. How good of you to come! You more than relieve any sadness I feel at my friend's mistakes and misfortunes.

YOUNG MISS S. Oh, do show me everything. (*Exeunt.*)

(*Enter* HOUSEKEEPER.)

HOUSEKEEPER. Where are they now? I ought to be looking after them, for I've an opinion that she's as artful as that Mr. Stubbs. Tastes differ, but I'm old-fashioned, and I mistrust young women who don't shake hands in the old way. I never have done what I see them doing, lifting up their hands as though they were ringing a little hand-bell or stealing a blossom from a climbing gerryanums, giving their wrist and fingers a little flourish in the air at the height of their own roguish eyes. No—no, a handshake used to be a handshake, and not a twist as though they were shaking a handkerchief above their heads out of a high window. No, I've known some different styles too, in my day. To be sure my poor dear husband that's gone, he used to be too limp when he said "How d'ye do?" He gave his hand quietly-like, but it was too much like the fin of a dead fish. Then there was our dear bishop, him that always talked about his "disease" and how he did travel all over it, going to every parish, as he said, in his disease—poor dear Lord Bishop! He died of it, sure enough, but he gave a good lift of his hand when he met you, but the lift was from below, and then he raised you up as he did in religion—indeed he did—and then brought your hand down again. It was no pump-handling, for the waters of affection came with one up and down—they did—once up, once down, that was our bishop's way. He did not expect your hand to meet him in the clouds, he didn't— leastways not on earth—when he shook hands. And I've known some that just gave one silent squeeze to your fingers that forced your marriage ring into your flesh, and made you feel crushed and affectionate-like afterwards, with all your fingers pressed together in one loving mass, just like sticks of the toffee I made in old days for the Squire, when he and I was young. Oh, Lord, the memories that come to me! And then there was our old rector, who seemed not to like to shake hands, and put his fingers out, and shrank back as soon as they touched another's, for his mind was delicate and tender, and he was so retiring. Then there was the dear old Squire. Lord, he never shook your hand, but he genteelly stretched out his own with the forefinger held downwards, and you took that, and felt—oh, my! so grateful at his condescension! And last, but in course not least in my sad memories, my poor dear love that was before my poor dear husband—how loving was his handshake! for it was like few others when he took hold of my hand, as if he never could leave go again, and gave my hand a pull towards his poor self that nearly pulled me over on the top of him, for he was shorter than me. Do you think any of these dear departed would have shown the true affection to me that so aggravated my affliction if I had seemed only to wave my hand to them with a pocket-handkerchief—the pocket-handkerchief, moreover, left out? No, indeed; why should they? And it makes my feelings about Mr. Stubbs none the less acute that he should be taken in and follow that 'ere hand-bell ringer; and as to my young Squire taking to her, Lord preserve us!—but strange things do happen, and even old servants must be civil sometimes. It's as much as their place is worth. (*Exit.*)

(*Enter* SQUIRE *and* OLD MISS SMYTH.)

OLD MISS S. We have yet more to see, I know—you have more to show. I could stay here for ever—walking on and on through these treasures. And I feel with you, Squire—no unnecessary talk comes from you. You just say what is right—no more. It is a true expression of happiness when silence comes with companionship. No loud protestations, but the silent sympathy of understanding natures—is it not so, I say? We feel it, we know it.

SQUIRE (*aside*). By Jove! she'll kill me. But I won't speak, then she'll go. (*Aloud*) Pardon me, I have bad news from the stables—my horse is ill.

OLD MISS S. I will go with you, I will prescribe. Tell me the symptoms.

SQUIRE. No, I fear he may infect you. What should I do if you got ill here? (*Aside*) Oh Lord!

OLD MISS S. The veterinary science, my dear Squire, must be studied. Do not fear, I shall catch no harm. I appreciate your tenderness. But the veterinary science——
(*Goes out, talking loudly with* SQUIRE.)

(*Enter* STUBBS *and* YOUNG MISS SMYTH.)

STUBBS. We'll pass this way to the other side of the grounds. I must show you my favourite view. With you in the foreground it will be perfect.

YOUNG MISS S. Really, Mr. Stubbs (*pleased*) how can you talk such nonsense!

STUBBS. Ah, the most lovely scenes without some one to share them are ugly. I must consult you—the Squire wanted me to consult you—about removing a tree. Let us sit at a window and settle together the fate of that tree. Ah, Miss Smyth, the hopes of more than the life of a tree may depend on your word. (*Exeunt.*)

(*Enter* SQUIRE *and* OLD MISS SMYTH.)

OLD MISS S. You are quite right to think twice before going to the stables. A true doctor knows the pace kills.

Quack prescriptions increase illness. You are already becoming like me, slow but sure.

SQUIRE. Madam, your kindness kills me. Sit down here till I am back.

OLD MISS S. No, I go with you. (*Exeunt.*)

(*Enter* STUBBS *and* YOUNG MISS SMYTH.)

YOUNG MISS S. You will be kind and merciful if you have power here—if he is ruined—won't you?

STUBBS. If mercy be crowned by love, let mercy crown my—wig!

YOUNG MISS S. How can you joke?

STUBBS. Only to veil anxiety—the anxiety of waiting for an answer.

YOUNG MISS S. Let us go into the garden again.
(*Exeunt.*)

(*Enter* HOUSEKEEPER.)

HOUSEKEEPER. Now, I must take away that wine. (*As she goes with tray to door,* SQUIRE *comes in hastily, bumping against her.*) Lord, Squire, what a hurry you are in! You have just missed your friend and the young lady.

SQUIRE. Friend and young lady! Confound it! Where are they? But what friend? You don't mean Mr. Stubbs, I hope?

HOUSEKEEPER. Yes—who else, sir?—with a young lady with fair hair and blue eyes.

SQUIRE. Where are they? Why did you allow them in? Where are they? Can't you speak?

HOUSEKEEPER. Heavens! Don't be angry. I think they are somewhere in the house. I thought they had your permission.

SQUIRE. In the house? He has seen his last day here!
(*Exit hastily.*)

(*Enter* STUBBS *and* YOUNG MISS SMYTH *from grounds.*)

STUBBS. Your walk has made you more beautiful than ever.

YOUNG MISS S. It's all very well for you to talk nonsense, but if we had kept to the walks instead of going through that wood, I wouldn't have torn my dress—just look at it now. Doesn't it look disgraceful?

STUBBS (*falling on knees*). Let me pin it up, Miss Smyth. It will never show. (*Standing up*) Oh, there's the housekeeper. Mrs. Hardy, you can help Miss Smyth.

YOUNG MISS S. Oh, do, dear Mrs. Hardy. Here's such a tear.

HOUSEKEEPER. Come with me, miss (*stiffly*). It is much better that I should attend to it than Mr. Stubbs there.

YOUNG MISS S. I know you'll do it beautifully. (*Exit with* HOUSEKEEPER.)

STUBBS. Wonder why it is I am so modest, so diffident. There I was on my knees intending to do it, and I didn't. Shyness has been my bane through life. I find out things that may be of use to me, and then hesitation lets another take advantage of the information I have gathered—all comes from being too good-natured. I don't ask enough. I don't complain enough. The art of complaint is a decoration to life. (*Sings.*)

>You asked me, friend, what I was doing,
>If rich and busy, wed or wooing?
>I said I was in nothing needing,
>A lawyer lived, haranguing, pleading.
>
>" I'm glad to hear it," he replied,
>For reading at the Bar implied
>With me much fun, but little feeding,
>And, anything, bar legal reading.

Now I must look again at that suit. May be able to assure the Squire it's false. Good for him to know the worst. Not bad armour. Very old! Probably made in Germany about the end of the month of January last year. Now if I pull the string I may see more of the panelling of the room. Dark oak. Decidedly gloomy. Makes room like inside of a coffin with brass handles. Well, financially he's in his coffin already. Is that ceiling good? Must get a bit uncovered. Hullo! (*Has pulled string which brings down on him large sheet covering ceiling. He is completely covered, and struggles up and down.*) Goodness! There's some one coming. I'll lie low.

(*Enter* SQUIRE *with* YOUNG MISS SMYTH *and* HOUSEKEEPER.)

SQUIRE. Ah, what is this? Here's some one pulled the ceiling-cloth down. (STUBBS *lies low so as not to be seen.*) Who has done this, and what's that? Lucky I have my stick with me. There's a thief hiding under the cloth. Excuse me, Miss Smyth, but I must arrest him. I'm a magistrate, you and Mrs. Hardy are witnesses. Come out, you rascal! (*Cloth moves—muffled voice says,* "*I can't, I will, I can't.*") Come out, I tell you—take that, and that, and that. (*Cudgels him with the stick. He bobs about and howls.*) Wait! Do you think I'd wait, while you are robbing me?

HOUSEKEEPER and YOUNG MISS SMITH. Oh Squire! It's Mr. Stubbs!

SQUIRE. Stubbs! Impossible. He's riding. (*Falls on him again with stick.*)

STUBBS. Stop, Squire, stop—it's I—it's Stubbs. (*Emerges covered with dust and white, and dishevelled and ridiculous.* YOUNG MISS SMYTH *laughs at him,* HOUSEKEEPER *also.*)

SQUIRE. 'Pon my word, beg pardon, Stubbs, but I had a thief in here last year, and I thought you were another. Hope I haven't hurt you. Come, let's get you cleaned. Devilish sorry, I'm sure. (*Turns away laughing.*) Thought you were miles away. Had to show ladies the house, you know, and glad to show one of my treasures in you.

HOUSEKEEPER (*grinning*). Want a basin of water, sir?

YOUNG MISS S. Oh, let me pin you up, Mr. Stubbs (*laughing*). But the housekeeper repaired damages for me so well, that I'm sure she will be able to understand what you want.

HOUSEKEEPER. I know what you want, sir (*stiffly*). Best come with me.

STUBBS (*with melancholy grin*). Most amusing, I'm sure. (*Aside*) He'll have no mercy from me, now!

(*Exit with* HOUSEKEEPER.)

SQUIRE. Now, my dear Miss Smyth, I've lots more to show you (*gives his arm and leaves with* YOUNG MISS SMYTH *by opposite entrance. Curtain falls.*)

Before action begins of play in Scene III

Thatchbridge Arms Hall. Enter racing men and women

MEN.	How-d'ye-do! How-d'ye-do!
	Come to see the Race! Have you?
	Gad—but that's a lovely view (*going to window*)!
	Have my glass to see it through?
WOMEN.	Landscapes of our England true!
	Richest greens to dreamy blue!
	Lands from whence our fathers drew
	Blood that nerves the wide world through!
ALL.	We're come from Town in cloak and gown
	With glance and glass for Epsom Down!
	Passing jokes with Peer and clown,
	Happier far than King with Crown!
MEN.	What'll you bet? I'll give you odds!
WOMEN.	Oh, my cue I'll take from you!
MEN.	Why, I'll ask the gallery gods!
	Don't they know a thing or two!
CHORUS.	Thank you, thank you, that will do!
	Don't they know a thing or two!
	Keep it dark 'twixt me and you!
	Thank you, thank you, that will do!
WOMEN.	I betted with you, but you see me through!
	Nor make me pay, for I hardly knew!
MAN.	I fancy I did, but our talking grew—
WOMAN.	A little haphazard 'twixt me and you!
	Tell me, Jack, and don't be cross,
	How to bet, nor pay a loss!
MEN.	"Cheat-em-well's" a lovely horse.
	There's the bell to clear the course (*dinner-bell rings*).
	Songs will end as all things do.
	Pour me draughts of Thatchbridge brew!
	Freshen me with Irish stew!
	Tip me winks from eyes so blue!
	Come what may from out the ruck,
	Loss is loss, and luck is luck!

The Coach and Six

  Aye to him who has the pluck
  Love shall come, and flags be struck!
  They're off! in varied colours, fleet!
  Red's first—strung out in a grassy street!
  White's first—ah no—the favourite's beat!
  Wager me now for another heat!
  Lead to paddock the victor sleek!
  There'll be another Epsom week!
  Luck may turn, for luck's a freak!
  Love from you's the luck I seek!

    (*Dinner-bell rings again.*)

WOMAN. Thank you, thank you, that will do!
    Keep it dark 'twixt me and you!
MAN.   Don't she know a thing or two!
    Eat and drink! The stew and brew!
MAN.   Love! don't you agree? you do!
WOMAN. There's the bell for Irish stew!
CHORUS. Thank you, thank you, that will do!
    Don't they know a thing or two!
    Keep it dark 'twixt me and you!
    Thank you, thank you! That will do!
          [*Exeunt.*

SCENE III

Thatchbridge Arms Inn. The Hall of the Inn

(*Enter* MARY.)

MARY. If I want to know a secret, can't I let it be?
    No! I can't, for it's a worry, not to peep and see!
  If a secret be a pleasure for but two or three,
    It is selfish not to share it; 'specially with me!

  If a secret be a secret, I would never pry,
    Only watch, for 'tis so tempting! Yes; with half an eye!

      (*Holds up letter to eye.*)

  No! I'll leave it still a secret,—shall I tell you why?
    Wait! a secret's oft a worry!—Wait, till by-and-by!

(*Holding letter in her hand*) I can't be wrong in giving a letter to the person whose name stands on the cover, can I? Of course I can't open the letter—although I should like to do so, but I'm English and I'm honest—and there's nothing to be seen by holding it up to the light. He will be glad to please her, though she is not so pretty as the young one—no (*laughing*). I'm sure he would wish me to think he has a good heart, so I'll give it to Miss Smyth, as the letter is addressed to her. Why not?

(*Enter* OLD MISS SMYTH.)

OLD MISS S. I heard you asking after me. Any more messages for me from the Hall. I expect quite a heavy correspondence with the Squire now. I have opened up to him several lines of thought. I have correspondence with many notable persons in many parts of the world.

MARY. There's one letter addressed to you, and it comes from the Hall. (*Gives the letter.*)

OLD MISS S. (*looking at cover*). The Squire's hand! I know his hand—saw his autograph under a portrait—I have a good memory, I never forget. But it may be from Mr. Stubbs. (*Breaks open letter*). Do I know the hand? He does not sign himself—except as——oh, I mustn't say—I feel myself blushing.

MARY (*anxiously*). Why, one would think it's a proposal by the way you speak.

OLD MISS S. It would not be right to violate the secrets of a susceptible heart—but I may tell you that I would not accept a man who proposed after only a few days' acquaintance.

MARY. Oh, of course you would not—no one would. (*Aside*) Wouldn't I, though, if it came from Mr. Stubbs! (*Aloud*) Are you sure it's not a proposal? You look so pleased. How sad if I may not congratulate you!

OLD MISS S. I don't intend to write my autobiography yet, but when I do I'll send you a copy. To-day will be a most interesting incident in that most interesting volume. Indeed, Mary, the days spent at your house will always be most pleasing to me. There's nothing like old England after all. The vigour of her young men and their enterprise is most astonishing.

MARY (*aside*). What on earth can he have said? I must find out another time. (*Aloud*) If you want pen and ink, you know where to find them in the parlour. (*Exit.*)

OLD MISS S. Now I can read it again in the rapt silence of an ancient inn. (*Unfolds letter with delight and reads.*)

"MY DEAR MISS SMYTH,

"Let me tell you how hurt I was that our pleasant interview was cut short. But, believe me, I shall always look back to our meeting with feelings too deep for expression, and with hope too ardent for words, that more time may be given me under more favourable circumstances. Pray command me in any way you wish. As I am somewhat lame, owing to a slight sprained ankle, I am not able to ride, but may be walking in the grounds about noon near that curious old summer-house that is so well worth seeing. Would that I could hope that your walk may take you in that direction! and let me remain, ever, dear Miss Smyth, your admirer."

I knew it would come, I knew that I had inspired him A noble-minded man!

All comes to her who waits!
    Oh yes! How long?
Although the parish parson states
My birth a little backward dates,
Most wise is she who latest mates:
    I'm young! I'm strong!

All comes to her who waits!
    I know that song!
I've kept my billet-doux in crates!
Their name is legion! nor abates
My lovers' ardour! yet the Fates
    Might do me wrong!

All comes to her who waits!
    Oh yes! How long?
Most bless'd is she whose nature hates
To give much pain, and who abates
A little of her pride, and states
    She's "kyind," if strong!

(*Enter* YOUNG MISS SMYTH.)

But it would be cruel to give him hopes. He must consume himself with impatience for a time. I must have quiet to reflect. (*Goes out dancing with joy.*)

YOUNG MISS S. I wonder what that strange woman was doing. I saw her skipping about just now, like a lamb. She must be mad. I must ask Mary about her. She must be somebody supposed to be respectable, for the Squire was taking her about before we met him yesterday. Oh, that poor Mr. Stubbs! I wonder how he is this morning. Did one ever see any one look so ridiculous? (*Laughing*) I wish my brother could have seen. He did laugh so when I described what happened. But I ought not to have laughed, because he was very kind to me, though he did get my new frock torn. How on earth did he get under that furniture-cloth? He must have meant to play us some joke. How sorry the Squire must be to have beaten his old friend! But I don't think Mr. Stubbs likes the Squire. I do—yes—that I do!

(*Enter* SQUIRE.)

SQUIRE. You here, Miss Smyth! what a pleasure! It is what I had hoped might be. Since yesterday, I have been longing to ask you to drive with me again. Will you? Or will you let me give you a mount—your brother also—of course, for the meet next time you both are within reach? I was to have gone to-day, but put it off in hopes of being of further service to you. Stubbs, poor fellow, declares he's got a sprained ankle and could not go. He took his misfortunes yesterday very well—ha! ha! But I don't think he's quite pleased with me. Do you know that I have kept the letter you wrote to me next my heart—no, in my desk it is just now—but I have kept it where I thought it safest and esteem it my greatest treasure.

YOUNG MISS S. I had a very pleasant visit to Thatchbridge House—but what letter, Squire? I never wrote any letter; what letter can you mean?

SQUIRE. Oh, it's all very well to make a joke of it, and try to get out of it that way! But I assure you it is a talisman to me—a charm. I feel my luck's made so long as I keep it safe. Dear Miss Smyth, don't be unkind. Now do be kind, and tell me it won't be the last letter you will send to me!

YOUNG MISS S. There must be some mistake—you are most kind—but I don't know what you mean by my letter, because I never wrote one—never—to you, that is—never. Indeed I did not. [*Exit*.

(*Enter* OLD MISS SMYTH.)

OLD MISS S. Good-day, good-day, dear Squire Thatchbridge. I shall ever remember with gratitude your kindness. The note Mr. Stubbs brought to me on the morning after my arrival here in your own fine firm hand is already pasted in my book, and ranks among the most beautiful poems I have enshrined in its pages.

SQUIRE (*aside*). Confound that woman! (*Aloud*) Madam, you do me too much honour. If my hand be bold, I make bold to say I never troubled you with it. (*Aside*) "Bold hand" indeed! I believe she'll propose for my "bold hand" next. (*Aloud*) Mr. Stubbs gave you a letter from me, do you say? When?

OLD MISS S. Oh, Squire, you know all about it. After we arrived. Such a nice note, and I did not thank you expressly for it yesterday, but I do now. It won't leave my journal. It is the record of a distinctly interesting morning. If it were not in my journal that contains so many private remarks, and such a good opinion of you, sir, I would show it you. But, believe me, it is embalmed in its most precious pages.

SQUIRE. Am I mad, or are you—slightly mistaken, madam? I never wrote you a line.

OLD MISS S. Was not Mr. Stubbs your messenger—your own best friend? How good of you to send so trusted a messenger with it!

SQUIRE. I give you my word of honour—Stubbs must have made a mistake. (*Aside*) Oh, the villain! (*Aloud*) Where's the Maid Mary, she may set this right—I can't explain it. Mary! (*Enter* MARY) Did Mr. Stubbs ask for Miss Smyth to give her a letter from the Squire?

MARY. Yes, miss, and I think he gave it to you, miss (*turning to* OLD MISS SMYTH).

OLD MISS S. Of course he did.

SQUIRE. And may I inquire (*to* OLD MISS SMYTH), madam, why it was that you appear to have almost asked or the letter, and, if I may believe my ears, to have opened the letter and, if I am not mistaken, madam, to have read the letter, and, if I am not doing you an injustice, madam, to have taken the contents as though addressed to yourself, and, if my righteous annoyance does not lead me astray, madam, to have acted as though those words were addressed to you, instead of to another? (*Paces angrily up and down with hands behind coat tails.*)

OLD MISS S. Squire Thatchbridge, how can you speak like that? (*pleadingly*). You know you wrote to me. You know you did. Honourable as you are, you would not take away my copyright.

SQUIRE. Copyright, madam—copybook indeed! You are, madam, no longer a child to talk of copybooks. If it were not ungentlemanlike, I'd use strong language. Give me the letter.

OLD MISS S. How can you? Your heart, if not your magisterial knowledge, would tell you that the ownership of a letter, once delivered, resides in the person to whom it is addressed. I know you are making believe to try me. But I have a temper that has withstood the vicissitudes of all climates.

SQUIRE. Can you deny that my letter was addressed to Miss Smyth?

OLD MISS S. It was, Squire. You are coming round.

SQUIRE. Coming round indeed! Please give me my letter.

OLD MISS S. The letter is in the pocket of the dress of the addressee. Oh, Squire, don't turn your back on me— on me, Honoria Eurydice Euphrosyne Melpomene Smyth.

SQUIRE. What? Is your name Miss Smyth? Heavens! I see it now. But you are not related to the beautiful young Miss Smyth?

OLD MISS S. Beautiful! Young! indeed! No, I am not related to that lady. Do I look like her? Am I not taller, statelier?

MARY. I'm sure, sir, that Mr. Stubbs did only what was

right. I told Mr. Stubbs myself what room Miss Smyth had, and he delivered the letter when she came out.

(*Enter* STUBBS.)

STUBBS. Did I hear some one say I only did what was right? Never was truer word spoken, and I think it was Miss Mary who said it.

MARY. Yes, sir; I'm sure Mr. Stubbs would not give a wrong message for worlds. He asked John if Miss Smyth was in. I'll call him—John! John!

(*Enter* YOUNG MISS SMYTH, *then enter* OSTLER.)

MARY. Didn't Mr. Stubbs ask you for Miss Smyth, and you said she was in, when Mr. Stubbs brought a letter?

OSTLER. Yes, that he did, and I pointed out where the biggest of the two was, thinking the Squire would only write to big people.

YOUNG MISS S. (*to* SQUIRE). Oh, didn't you know that this tall lady was called Miss Smyth?

SQUIRE. Know? How should I know that any one but yourself bore that blessed name? Are you sure she can be? I should not have thought it possible that you could have been named in the same day with her, much less with the same sound. She called herself Melpo—Melpo Melpominia, Melancholy Mania, or some such rubbish.

OLD MISS S. I have travelled much, and yet never felt so fatigued and faint as now!

SQUIRE. Excuse me (*to* YOUNG MISS SMYTH), how could I know? What a horrid accident! Of course my letter was for you. How rude you must have thought me not to write.

YOUNG MISS S. I'm sure I did not. I could not think you rude.

STUBBS. It's not my fault. Now let me have a little private business talk with the Squire. (*The others retire to back of stage.*) Squire, you think you have got the better of me. You have not. I had some feeling for you. You had none for me. I come down here, the agent professionally engaged of those who hold your mortgages, with orders to foreclose. They know you can't pay them the interest owing. I thought I might serve you, but I shall not. My report on the value of your land will be adverse. You are a ruined man, for the state of your affairs is fully known to me and you cannot borrow another farthing. Thatchbridge will now belong to my principals.

SQUIRE. Good God, Stubbs! What an infamous thing! (*To the others*) My friends, I must leave you. Excuse me, I have had bad news.

OTHERS. What is it? What is it?

SQUIRE. I'm a ruined man. My creditors take my estate and house in security for my debts. Stubbs truly says there is no one who will lend me money.

STUBBS. Very sorry! My principals have decided to call up their money; and as the place may be a little improved, and cut up for building lots, they take possession.

YOUNG MISS S. Now for my secret!

MARY. Oh law, yes, now for the secret. It will pop out now at the right time!

YOUNG MISS S. Mr. Stubbs, you are wrong. I will pay off the mortgages. I would do so were they three times the sum that they can be now. I have a secret which I have managed to keep—I'm sure I don't know how—for some days. My uncle in Australia died recently leaving me with more money than I know what to do with. I am sorry to disappoint Mr. Stubbs, but he probably has enough of his own without taking the Squire's beautiful house, which I hope he may long possess, and be ever loth to leave.

OLD MISS S. (*to* YOUNG MISS S.). Are you a suffragist? No? Well, I am. It's only suffragists who can propose in a manly way. Squire Thatchbridge, I will give you all my literary property. It's worth hundreds on hundreds of thousands. You are a free man—I'm a free woman. Henceforth we'll write journals together.

SQUIRE. Please go.

OLD MISS S. Yes, I'll go on. You with me!

SQUIRE (*to* YOUNG MISS S.), I have only one way of paying my load of debt and gratitude—and that is by asking Miss Smyth not to leave this place.

OLD MISS S. Me, you mean. I won't!

SQUIRE. Yes, you will!

YOUNG MISS S. I leave that to be discussed later. Mary

has been so good a friend to me that she shall share my fortune, and I'll give her £500 a year at once.

(OSTLER *whistles part of his old song. Goes to* MARY, *who with him goes to front of stage, others a little back.*)

MARY. Oh! dear mistress! How can I ever thank you!

OSTLER. "Ostleralia," did she say?

MARY. No, stupid! Australia. Where there's new guineas, and kangaroos, and bushmen, and roughriders, and any number of gallant men and beautiful women—and cockatoos!

OSTLER. Oh cocky! Long way off, isn't it?

MARY. Beneath your feet.

OSTLER. Why, my head's not been above my feet since last May day! Lots of money! She'll make me head of her stables, won't she? Are we all going down to below our feet, where the uncle with the money lived? Are people there attached to their money?

MARY. Not when dead, I believe.

OSTLER. Then it will come here, and we'll all be ever so rich. Lord, here's my aunt, the Squire's housekeeper, a-coming.

HOUSEKEEPER (*to* STUBBS). What have you been a-saying and a-doing?

STUBBS. By Jove, £500 a year's not to be despised. I'll make Mary a serious proposal. She's managed a house well—and I'm clever enough to manage her. If she's not of my rank, she's five hundred golden reasons a year to make me forget that. What a world it is! I came here to do executioner, and I am led out to the slaughter myself! Damme, any one can marry a Smith, but few can pluck such a rose as my rose, Mary. I hope it won't be rosemary and rue! No, no—I'll do it. By Jove, I do love her. She shall have a silk gown next week, though I may wait years for mine! (*To the others*) I knew there would be some possibility of misunderstanding. But it's not my fault. It's all the fault of that enlarged edition of the Smyth Series—too large to be easily moved, as I think, by anything. (*A heavy groan is heard. All look round and find that* OLD MISS SMYTH *has swooned and has fallen against* MARY, *who can hardly support the weight.* STUBBS *rushes forward, embracing both, and supporting* OLD MISS SMYTH *to sofa, where she lies unconscious—there is much commotion.*) Miss Mary and I will chafe her hands and feet. Bring some water. (*Others hurry out and in with sponge, water, etc.* STUBBS *goes on rubbing on hand of* OLD MISS SMYTH *and* MARY *on the other side. As they rub the hands they gradually relax efforts, and begin to take each other's hands, as though by mistake. When they have done this, they say they are tired—will others take their place?* STUBBS *and* MARY *then retire to corner of room and make love, and their place at both sides of the body are taken by* SQUIRE *and* YOUNG MISS SMYTH, *whose conduct gradually assimilates to that of last couple. Then* JOHN *and* HOUSEKEEPER *rub away at the old lady's hands, until they also get tired of doing anything but talk to each other—yet all this time all brokenly encourage each other to awaken the old lady. When they have paired off around her*, MARY *and* STUBBS *sing the song as below.*)

(*While this is going on* MARY *sings.*)

MARY. All have got some little trouble,
                    Very true!
Life, they say, is but a bubble,
Few there are see rainbows double,
Oftener storm and snow, oftener pain and woe.
                    Very true!
Yet if we have pecks of sorrow,
Still a grain of joy we'll borrow,
Hoping for a bright to-morrow (*turning to prostrate*
                    MISS S.)
                How d'ye do?

STUBBS. They are fools who make a bother (*pointing at old*
                    MISS S.)
                  Very true!
Knock one down; if comes another
Hit him too! He'll join his brother!
       So let none complain,
        Come the sun, or rain,
                    We'll pull through!
If the world a while be dreary,
If sometimes at eve we weary,
While we live, good hearts, be cheery.
(*To* OLD MISS S.) How d'ye do?

(*Long pause of silence while rubbing still goes on.*)

OLD MISS S. (*suddenly sitting up, and in sepulchral voice*).

Where am I? Why are these nurses and doctors in pairs?

SQUIRE. I knew our exertions would make you all right again.

STUBBS. You see you are so magnetic that you have had a great attraction for all of us.

OLD MISS S. Don't speak to me, sir!

> It falls upon my ear with a bubble and a squeak,
> And a thrill and a sobbing in the air,
> And I know, and I feel, though I try in vain to speak.
> By the weight on my chest, IT is there!
> And I vow I will move, but I cannot move at all,
> Though my limbs do not seem to know why,
> And I yearn to call out, but I cannot, cannot call,
> And I long, but I cannot, to die!
> The weight keeps on increasing, oh, how I must perspire!
> And I think in misery "oh don't!"
> And yelling in the lightest possible attire!
> I suddenly spring up with a voluble "I won't!"

(*They hold her down.*)

> And I know it's all a dream, though amidships I am queer,
> And my knees are no more what they were;
> And I give one awful sigh, feeling older by a year,
> And solemnly declare, "What a horrible nightmare!"

(*They all shrink away.*)

(*Enter* HOUSEKEEPER.)

HOUSEKEEPER. Mr. Stubbs, I have brought your scarf-pin. I found it under a cloth torn down in the drawing-room. How it came there I don't know. But there it is. It is yourn, sir, I think? Dear me, what's wrong? Oh, let me give the poor lady salts. (*Goes to her with bottle and stands behind her.*) Now you feel better, don't you? Lord, that such a dear strong thing should look faint!

SQUIRE.   I hope you'll join one more excursion,
          And on my coach take your diversion,
          This lady here will change her name,
          Yet always be to me the same.

YOUNG MISS S.   If Smyth has proved a name magnetic,

(*To* O. MISS S.)   Don't make its triumphs too pathetic.

(*To* AUDIENCE).   I hope you'll wish us joy, and more—
          You won't despise our coach and four.

STUBBS.   Old Thatchbridge Manor nearly killed me,
          But Thatchbridge Inn with joy has filled me.
          Australia's uncle's charming niece,
          Your maid's the best part of the piece!

MARY.   I know not what at Squire's befell you;
          My love confess and gladly tell you.

(*To* O. MISS S).   Mistakes in giving letters may
          Produce the best parts of the play.

HOUSEKEEPER.   I do not know what they are after;
          'Tis not a time, or place, for laughter.
          Oh what are we all coming to?
          I like Propriety—I do!

(*Pointing to* OLD MISS SMYTH, *who is sitting up dolefully.*)

JOHN.   I hope you'll tip me each a fiver,
          And give her some good corpse-reviver,
          And make her Whip; though Fortune kicks.

(*Pointing to* HOUSEKEEPER)

          'Tis she's made up our Coach and Six!
          If I'm not luckiest—please to note
          I have alone an antidote!

ALL.   As advertised " Life's best Elixir "
          We'll find in this 'ere " Coach and Sixer "!
          We'll hope to gain a decent wage,
          And drive it over many a stage.
          Ye passengers from country, city,—
          Those not in Love's gay harness, pity,—

The Coach and Six

> Excuse the one who's just awoke,
> And she who cannot see our joke!

(*The couples take each other's hands,* YOUNG MISS SMYTH *and* SQUIRE *holding theirs at level of head.*)

HOUSEKEEPER (*to* OLD MISS SMYTH). Take some more salts. It's just as well you are out of it.

OLD MISS S. Out of salts?

HOUSEKEEPER. Out of sorts, no—out of this coach and six. Though you drove them!

ALL *but* HOUSEKEEPER (*to* OLD MISS SMYTH, *who is sitting up dolefully.*) Hope you are better, miss. We all fell in love over you!

> She's not among the " might have beens,"
> She lives to grace all comic scenes.
> We hope she'll wed a man of means,—
> A Smyth to rear sweet Smythereens!

OLD MISS S. Go along!

(*Holding hands, they all make their bow to* OLD MISS SMYTH, *back to audience, bowing very low. Then turn and bow to* AUDIENCE *only when curtain rises again; the two pairs in front, others behind them.*

CURTAIN FALLS

Finis

The following Opera was performed at Covent Garden, at Manchester, Liverpool, and Glasgow, Mr. Hamish McCunn being the composer.

DIARMID

DRAMATIS PERSONÆ

DIARMID (a hero of the Feinne)	*Tenor.*
FIONN (King of the Feinne)	*Baritone.*
ERAGON (King of the Norse)	*Bass.*
GRANIA (Fionn's Queen)	*Soprano.*
EILA (Fionn's Daughter—Grania's step-daughter)	*Mezzo-Soprano.*
FREYA (Norse Goddess of Love)	*Contralto.*
FIRST MESSENGER	*Bass.*
A PRISONER	*Bass.*

Shades of the Immortals, Freya's attendant Maidens, Scottish Soldiers, Norse Warriors, Vikings, Chiefs, Attendants, Hunters, Messengers, People, Gnomes, Hobgoblins, Sprites, and Fairies.

Scene.—ERIN OR SCOTIA.   *Period.*—2nd CENTURY.

ACT I

(SCENE —*A " Broch," Fort, or " Dun." Evening. Sentries. Ground sloping, shows outer walls on lower level beyond. Intermediate space has beehive-like stone huts. Distant sea. Hills. Woods. Moors.*)

PROCESSION AND CHORUS OF SCOTTISH SOLDIERS

(*Some soldiers are occupied in piling great stones on the walls to strengthen the fortifications.*)

SOLDIERS.   Norway's dread warriors come to assail us;
　　　　　　Beaten, they fled, but return with their Monarch.
　　　　　　Here watch we their fleets, and hear songs of their
　　　　　　　　oarsmen—
　　　　　　Watch from the mountains, as eagles for fishes:
　　　　　　Our beacons flash warning from headland to
　　　　　　　　headland.

Diarmid

CHIEFS (*making rounds*).
  We have watched and have laboured, our bulwarks are stronger—
  Watch yet with care! The invader will strike like the stormbolt!   [*Exeunt.*

SOLDIERS. We have watched, and they come not. Sleep!
Rest and refreshment!
What shall avail us long watching?
Fear falls on the strangers!
Sleep! The woods and walls conceal us!
Rest! our heavy task is done!
Never by the sword of stranger
Was a Scottish province won!
  Sleep and rest!

(*They lie down, and the Sentries also leave the walls. Fires glow in the little stone huts. Evening draws on.* DIARMID *enters, fatigued, and his face lined with care; looking excited and exhausted; carrying great stone.*)

DIARMID. Asleep! while Eragon's great host draws near!
Awake! awake!

SOLDIERS. Sleep! and rest. We have no fear!
Diarmid, rest, for thou art overwrought—
To-morrow watch; to-night no fight is sought.

DIARMID. Awake! awake! I have toiled from day unto day.
Pile stones yet higher on the walls!
Rest not to-night, when danger calls!

(EILA *enters from Fort.*)

EILA. Diarmid's voice I heard! a warning sound!
 Voice, wonted summoner to gallant games!
Voice that has made my heart in love abound—
 Diarmid, dearest of our bravest names.

  SONG.—(EILA.)

Heavy thy burden, Diarmid,
 Rest from thy toil awhile!
Watching are sentries, seaward—
 Watching o'er mount and isle.

        Hearken my words, beloved;—
          Birds fly to sleep on shore,
        Calling " good night " to ocean,
          "Good night," for day is o'er!

        Clouds have been lifted gently,
          Leaving the hill-top clear;
        Dew-mists along the lowland
          Herald night's silence near.

        Listen! for love's more peaceful,
          Sweeter than aught beside:
        Now round thee night is bringing
          Love's peace from land and tide!

DIARMID (*pointing to distant promontories and nearer headlands, where fires of beacon-fires appear, and laying hand on* EILA'*s arm.*)

    See how the beacon-fires spring forth to answer
      thee!
    To-morrow eve the Norsemen must be fought!
    The warning lights are sparkling o'er the sea
      Where dragon-ships its tides and storms have
      fought.
    Away! and tell thy father Fionn—rouse the chiefs!

EILA.   Nay, let me stay with thee!

DIARMID.   Away! this is no time for love! Away!
                            (*Exit* EILA.)
    Wake! Better than meat is care for our land!
      Stronger than food is the hope of renown;
    The metal that's purest the deepest can strike!
      How shall man forge for his lifetime a crown?
    By giving his comrades and country his all,
    His name shall be honoured in hut and in hall!
    Forsaken, now I toil alone;
    Let me seek light from Heaven's throne.

    Immortals! for your aid I cry,
    Who stride in mists of glory by!

Oh give me of the strength that streams
   Through all your elements of air,
Fierce purity of fiery gleams,
   The peace that only power can bear.
(*Distant thunder.*)

The strength that curbs the breakers' roar
Gives calm to mountain and to shore,
Clears for the sun the paths of day,
And makes the tides the moon obey!
Strength! strength! I faint; let me implore
The gods to grant me strength to swing
My sword in battle's inmost ring!

(*A flash of lightning, loud thunder. A vision of Immortal Heroes appears in the clouds.* DIARMID *kneels down, and, as the song of enchantment proceeds, covers his face with his mantle, leaning on the great stone he had carried.*)

SHADES OF THE IMMORTALS.

   Youth! we have trodden the path thou desirest!
      Our bliss thou shalt gain,
   If proof 'gainst temptation and peril the direst
      Thou faithful remain!

   Thine be a gift by our benison granted!
      In one place alone
   Shall thy body feel Death; for thou art enchanted!
      Arise! and begone!

(*They vanish. Distant lightning and thunder. The moon breaks through the rolling clouds, and shines over the sea.* DIARMID *slowly rises, looking younger and more beautiful.*)

DIARMID. No dream was the vision! No sense of bereavement,
   No toil weights the heart the Immortals make gay!
No weapons, though launched by the arms that are strongest,
   Can sap the brave blood that my pulses obey.

Yet feel I the spell! 'Twas as water poured o'er me,
But reached not my foot. Glad am I that still
Communion I have with the mother that bore me,
With comrades and kinsfolk! If magic can kill
(*doubtingly*) The love of the women—ye gods! then restore me
The weakness you took by the curse of your will!

(*He seats himself, reclining, on the stone, and falls to sleep. FREYA, with attendant maidens, appears in the air near him, her arms extended towards him.*)

FREYA. Diarmid, upon thee now Freya has power!
In sleep as thou liest, Love's dream be upon thee!
Sleep! Never is vanquished in bosom of mortals
The dream thou beholdest!
Now, whether it harm thee,
Or, if it bless thee,
I give thee enchantment!
All women who see thee
Shall straight be enamoured;
The lock on thy forehead,
Whenever thou bar'st it,
Shall be like the torch-fire!
Great Freya hath spoken—
Her doom be upon thee!

ATTENDANTS.
Strong are our youths, but the hero before us
  Hath the limbs and the locks of enchantment and gold!
We love him, and weep for the Northland that bore us—
  Her foe hath the might of enchantment and gold!

FREYA (*turning from him, frowning; to audience*).
Now have I triumphed!
Now, if he conquer,
Yet through the women there shall be vengeance!
If o'er my country,
If over Norway
He shall be victor,
Doom shall be on him!

ATTENDANTS.
>Strong are our youths, etc.

FREYA *and* ATTENDANTS.
>Dream of great Freya!
>Youth only measures
>Freya's sweet treasures!
>Hail to great Freya!
>>Hail!

(*Curtain falls slowly as* FREYA *and* MAIDENS *slowly disappear, and* DIARMID *remains in a deep sleep.*)

END OF ACT I

ACT II

SCENE I

(*A wood. Morning.* FIONN *and his young wife,* GRANIA FIONN, *brooding in melancholy.*)

GRANIA (*derisively*).
>Thus lonely is thy regal state, so soon, O King!
>Thou takest to the woods, like otter chased
>From stream and shore! I thought I was a Queen,
>And wedded to a King who met his foes!

FIONN.
>Grania, have patience. Soon will come my friends,
>And we shall chase the Norsemen to the sea—
>Have patience still, and all shall yet be well.

GRANIA.
>All well! nay, nought is well. They come for spoil;
>Thou must send treasure ere they quit their hold.

FIONN.
>How purchase peace from men who are like wolves?

GRANIA.
>By sending treasure, by a hostage borne.

FIONN.
>Whom have I for such embassy?

GRANIA.
>Eila! why not?
>Men like to see her, and to hear her words.

FIONN.	Eila! my daughter! for those cruel men!
	A wife should be a stay unto her husband. Thou
	Would'st give my daughter, prisoner, to the foe.
GRANIA (*aside*).	
	Ransom or kingdom! Now shall this day prove
	If I or that proud minx be stronger! (*To* FIONN)
	Fionn,
	Thou lovest Eila better than thy wife!

(*Throws herself down at his knees and caresses him.*)

        Let Eila, as thine envoy, go with gifts.
        So she can serve thee best, and, all unhurt,
        She shall return, or wed some Norseman Yarl.
        Oh, listen to the counsel of thy wife—
        Thou saidst my love would be supreme with thee.

FIONN.   Have patience, Grania, for my friends will come!

(*Messengers arrive.*)

1ST MESSENGER.
        Thy friends would come, O King—they bid us say—
        Were not their men afar. They counsel thee
        Make peace with Eragon. (*Messengers retire.*)

GRANIA.   'Tis even as I said! (*Rising.*)

FIONN.   Alas! what hope is there? My false allies
        Have sent this answer to my urgent call!
        Suspicion dogs the old; and Grania's eyes (*aside*)
        Follow Diarmid! Would that he might fall!
        Soon I will send him forth to rally those
        Who hide behind the hills, refusing aid:
        Yet I will wait, for still the danger grows!
        What if his carcase clog the Norseman's blade?

GRANIA.   Let Eila go—so shalt thou reign in peace.
        I will not live, but as a queen, a wife,
        And reign supreme—I say let Eila go!

FIONN.   Grania, have patience—oh my daughter dear!
        Grania, smile on me!—now shall Eila go!

(*Quick Curtain. The Orchestra is heard while the Curtain remains down.*)

(*Attacca* Sc. II)

SCENE II

(Afternoon. A group of Scots firs on mound on a moor. NORSE WARRIORS *and* VIKINGS *gathering for battle, and carrying the Raven Standard, which they plant and display as the* KING *enters.*)

NORSE WARRIORS.
    Our King has come, with ladies fair
    Among his host, these lands to share;
    Old Fionn hides in mountain lair,
    And from their forts no Feinne dare!

    (*Enter* KING ERAGON.)

ERAGON. Up with the Raven Standard here!
    Good day unto you all—good cheer!

WARRIORS. Good day, our King! The foe is dumb,
    And from their forts no Feinne come!
    They could not stand; and fled before our King!

(*Looking off.*)
    Lo! here some messengers their tidings bring!
    A lady with them. Who is she?—
    With step so light, and air so free?

    (*Enter* EILA, *with Attendants and Messengers carrying hawks and rich gifts, some of the latter carried in pieces of netting.*)

MESSENGERS
    King Eragon! we bring, as Envoy, this fair maid,
    The daughter of our Monarch, Fionn. She will speak.

ERAGON (*to a Viking*).
    Go, Sigurd, ask her what she may desire.

EILA. I speak to none but to the King. O King,
    Our countrymen have angered thee; but they
    Are ever hasty, and their anger flies
    As sudden squalls across clear waters pass.
    Thine should be brief as theirs, to make amends,
    And spare the lives dear both to thee and us.
    My father sends these gifts—thou lovest hawks?
    Thou likest hunting?

ERAGON. Now, by the gods, she questions us! Sigurd!
        Tell her, though fair she be, she speaks in vain.

    (SIGURD *approaches* EILA. *She continues to address the King.*)

EILA (*to Attendants*).
        Bring hither now the gifts. (*To the King, showing the gifts*). This for thy Queen—
        A girdle, with the stones like shallow sea,
        That flows in purple over bannered rocks.
        A goblet, with the stone like amber clear!
        (*Shows this as she has shown the girdle.*)
        And amber beads are here, and here, O King,
        A belt of pearl!—thou hast a queen? They said
        That she had come. (*To the* VIKINGS) Your wives are here?

WARRIORS *and* VIKINGS.
        King, she insults thee!
        Thine are these treasures!
        All, in these islands—
        Gold, and the women,
        Grain, herds, and silver—
        All are thy spoil!

EILA. He speaks not! (*Aside*) But King Eragon! I'll give
        My message. (*To the King*) All the gifts within these nets
        Are thine—Oh listen! else my folk will think
        I have not spoken as I should. (*She weeps.*)

    (*Murmurs among Norse.*)

ERAGON. Ha! let her tell her father, that old fox,
        His goods our ours; for Norsemen have been slain,
        And each Norwegian life is worth his crown.
        Let him come here, and kneel, and mercy crave!

    (*Viking goes to* EILA, *who turns furiously.*)

EILA. Never! Now make your vaunting good by fight;
        No host brought here shall make my father kneel!
        His curse and mine be on you! Loathly men!

    (*She turns to depart.* ERAGON'S *men try to stop her.*

    Her guards resist. These guards are overpowered and brought back. EILA *is surrounded.*)

ERAGON. Nay, let her go, nor cage a hooded hawk!
    Soon shall she answer to a Norseman's lure.

EILA. The hawk shall not return; but eagles, loosed,
    Shall scatter all your raven's croaking host!
          (*Exit with her guards.*)

ERAGON. A whelp from old fox Fionn! Come, let our men
    Challenge, and meet and overthrow his host.

  (*Norse war-trumpets sound behind the scenes. Distant sounds of fight.*)

 (*Enter a fugitive Norseman breathless and wounded.*)

FUGITIVE. Attack with all your force—you need it all!
    There is one there whose sword like lightning slays!

  (*Staggers out—consternation among Norse.*)

DIARMID'S *voice* (*without*).
    We fight with equal force! Seven seven score,
    O Eragon, if thou hast heart for fight.
    They who are borne for seven score paces back
    Shall own themselves defeated, and shall yield.

ERAGON. Let seven score advance, and challenge give!

  (*Norse war-trumpets again sound behind the stage. Nearer sounds of fighting.*)

WAR CHORUS OF SCOTS (*without*).
    Suassa! Suassa! Lochlanner's death-cry
    Sounds in their onset. Erin-go-bragh!
    Erinners onward! On with the sunburst
    Banner of victory! Erin-go-bragh!

SOME VIKINGS *and* WARRIORS (*looking forth at the combat*).
    See how the Scottish hero's tread
    Tramples on bodies of our dead.
    King! they who flee are Norsemen—they are thine!
    Thine are the vanquished, pressed back to the line!

  (*Enter some Norse with a Prisoner.*)

ERAGON. Burn him! in hell his soul shall find its place!

PRISONER (*to* ERAGON).
    I see thy shroud! 'Tis high about thy face!
        (*Prisoner is hurried away.*)

DIARMID'S *voice* (*without*).
    Eragon, sendest thou more to the slaughter?
    Or tak'st thou the terms of Fionn's sweet daughter?

ERAGON. Down on them! Now for an onset worthy of Norsemen!

VIKINGS AND WARRIORS.
    All go! The best leap down and press forward—
      The captains of ships, the best in the sword-play!
    Diarmid strikes—they fall—he makes onward
      Like fire through the pines, in the hot summer day!

(*All Vikings and Warriors on stage crowd round* KING ERAGON.)

ALL. The lines are passed! Our bravest fall! Defend the King!

DIARMID *rushes on the stage, followed by the Scots bearing aloft the "Dheo-Greine"* (*Sunbrightness*), *the Banner of the Feinne.*)

SCOTS. Food for the worm, and the fish of the ocean!
    Ha! see the wreckage cast up by the sea!
  Spear them! and scatter them! Laughter, in winter,
    Greets their death-story at hearths of the free!

DIARMID. Name yet a champion. Him will I vanquish!
Sparing the others—this yet for peace' sake!

ERAGON. Sigurd! I trust thee. Teach him thy sword-play!

VIKINGS (*to* KING).
    Let us avenge thee,
    King! We will slay him!
    Curse on him! Vengeance!
        Ah

Scots.   Suassa! Suassa! Lochlanner's death-cry, etc., etc.

(SIGURD *and* DIARMID *fight;* SIGURD *falls. Others attack* DIARMID, *when others of the Feinne, resuming their fierce war-cries, come to assist him.* DIARMID *springs at* ERAGON, *and kills him. Sounds of fight and pursuit are heard as all leave stage; sounds getting fainter.* DIARMID *alone remains, standing leaning on sword, and looking at dead bodies of* SIGURD *and* ERAGON.)

(CURTAIN FALLS QUICKLY)

END OF ACT II

ACT III

SCENE I

(*A Celtic circle of standing stones, with rude shelter, formed by one great stone fallen against another. Under shelter,* DIARMID *lies asleep at slow fire. Night. Moonlight.*)

CHORUS AND BALLET OF GNOMES, HOBGOBLINS, AND FAIRIES

(*Enter Gnomes, gambolling and playing.*)

CHORUS OF GNOMES.
    Ho! ho! ho! now dance the Gnomes!
    Out we go from our hidden homes.
    Ho! ho! ho! for all our tribe
    Ever at man must laugh and jibe!
    See how vain his oaths and deeds!
    Few are faithful—most are weeds:
    Ho! ho! ho! the human heart
    Thumps this tune, ere life depart.
      Devil do, as Devil must:
      Ho! ho! ho! the dust is dust!

Man or maid; 'tis ever so—
Chance it and dance—Ho! ho! ho!
(Hobgoblins enter and dance a grotesque measure.)

*   *   *   *   *

(Some Fairies enter, others are seen flitting across the stage. The fairy lights are seen. Dance of Fairies, Sprites, Hobgoblins, and Gnomes.)

CHORUS OF FAIRIES (*behind the scenes*).
>The lights are seen of the fairy dance
>On circles of green their hosts advance,
>And the lightsome steps of the fairies' feet
>To music soft a measure beat;
>And never a care have they to bear,
>For peace they bring, and in peace they meet.

GNOMES (*on stage*). Ho! ho! ho! etc.

FAIRIES.
>Oh, hush! beware lest they hear and go,
>For the tides of luck with the fairies flow!
>They hurt not a blossom of frosty rime,
>Nor bells that are blue in the summer-time,
>When their dances sweep through the land of sleep
>With silent wing, in a peaceful clime.

GNOMES (*on stage*). Ho! ho! ho! ect.

(Pas seul, etc.)

(Dance of Fairies, Hobgoblins, etc.)

(All Fairies, Gnomes, Sprites, and Hobgoblins dance in wild whirling circles. When the dance is at its height they suddenly vanish.)

(Short pause—Attacca SCENE II.*)*

SCENE II

(The same. Grey of morning coming on. Light increasing gradually. Flush of early dawn towards end of Scene.)

INTRODUCTION

*(*GRANIA *enters, agitated and torn by conflicting emotions. As she approaches the shelter of* DIARMID *she looks towards it many times, with passionate yearning.)*

GRANIA.	I hear the heron cry—first sign of morn !
	Diarmid sleeps, kissed only by the mist.
	Oh ! Fionn's curse is o'er my head—but Love
	Bears armour proof to fury or to scorn !
	No favouring star has looked on my desire—
	Can love like mine be thought a baleful fire ?
	If he be there, he shall not fly the spell
	That bids me, wandering, follow where he goes !
	Ah me ! my track through dewy grass may tell
	A queen's humility—a woman's woes !
	Grey time, when Love's dreams reign, be kind, and weave
	Thoughts day and night are fain to dusk to leave !

(*She slowly approaches the threshold of the shelter* DIARMID *starts up in alarm.*)

DIARMID.	Avoid the lair of the hunter ; a shaft
	May ask if the shadows are silent at morn !
GRANIA.	Diarmid ! Come ! I follow thee—
	Well lost be all for thy dear love !
DIARMID.	'Tis Grania ! Nay—I know thee—have no fear !

    *   *   *   *   *

	By oath I am bound to follow the shout
	Or horn of the King, to war and to chase :
	I go not with thee, nor will look in thy face,
	If standing, or lying, or sitting thou art,
	By day or by night, in the house or without,
	On horse or on foot—O Grania, depart !

GRANIA (*crouching close to threshold of shelter.*)

	Now wilt thou go with me. Morn has not come—
	Not on foot or in saddle, in field or in home,
	Am I who so love thee—Oh, come, be my King !
DIARMID.	No King to thee ; my oath and sword
	Are for my land—sole Love and Lord. Begone !
GRANIA.	Yea, King to me, thy love, and slave !
	Here take my hand—be kind, be brave !
DIARMID.	No waves of love this stony heart have won !
GRANIA.	Yet rocks I know by frost and sun undone !

    Oh! woman, when conquered by love is the
     stronger!
     Her power is more potent than sun or than wave!
    Resistance but makes it endure ever longer,
     And fiercer the bliss of the love she may crave!

DIARMID. Shall love, then, ever come
    And make my heart his home—
     No stony place,
    But fair, and nurtured well,
    Wood-shaded, where may dwell
     Man's happy race?

GRANIA. What dost thou ask? I know
     Of nought on earth
    Love's fire cannot bestow,
     Or thence have birth.
    See, now, my hands in thine! *(takes both hands)*
     Let me cast out
    From thy blue eyes the sign
     That tells of doubt.

DIARMID. I thought of three evils:
     The one to be slave,
    The other, be lonely;
     And last—of the grave!

GRANIA. My arm around thee thrown *(throwing arm round*
     Shall bring thy thought   *his neck)*
    Where heart is never lone,
     And suffers nought!
    For comradeship lives on
     When lovers meet,
    With love to shine upon
     And guide their feet!
    If lonely pride descend
     From barren height,
    And down to Love can bend
     His searching sight,
    Both shall arise, to soar
     To hills joy-crowned,
    Because from peak to shore
     By Love long found!

DIARMID. I swore in haste! and now
 The spell must fade!
 Vows must unloose a vow
 In error made!

GRANIA. And heart with heart beat! (*embracing him*)
 So that Will
 And Love, with bliss so sweet,
 Be comrades still!

DIARMID. Grania! Grania! see, thy name
 Means "Light of Light"; is Sun and Flame.

DIARMID *and* GRANIA.
 As the light from sky to stream,
 As the day-thought to the dream,
 As the call to echo thrown,
 Thy spell I feel, thy love I own!
 Come! come! come away!

BOTH. Throw thy rosy mist around us,
 Love, who hidest care!
 Thou hast sought, and, following, found us!
 Stay our joy to share.
 How to make thee tarry, tell us—
 Thou alone canst know!
 Be not hasty, be not jealous,
 Stay through weal and woe.
 How can all thy bliss enfold us—
 Melt our souls in one!
 Ah, we feel thy spells now hold us—
 Love, our cause is won!
 Come, if e'en by all forsaken,
 Fear has lost its powers!
 Heart to heart, to sleep and waken,
 Love, true love, is ours!

(*They go, looking often behind them, pausing at shelter for* DIARMID *to get his spears, sword, and shield—then exeunt swiftly.*)

(QUICK CURTAIN)

END OF ACT III

ACT IV

(SCENE.—*Cliff, over which cascade falls. Cavern behind. Half-way up cliff, large, full-foliaged rowan-tree grows out of rock ledge, hanging over sward that slopes to pool, out of which water flows by side of stage. Split in cliff behind rowan-tree. Beyond, plateau drops towards distant sea. Bright sunlight.*)

ORCHESTRAL INTRODUCTION

Scena.—DIARMID *and* GRANIA

DIARMID. How sweet to rest from toil of war!
The first frost comes, like foam, that cools
Hot sands of seas afar!
Grania! Grania!

(GRANIA *appears at mouth of cavern, and goes to the water's edge, looking back laughingly at* DIARMID.)

GRANIA. How beauteous is the water's sheen!
Thy frame of strength reflected there!
Like torrent thou wert: now, changed thy mien,
Love thou dost breathe on the radiant air!

DIARMID. Who drinks not with delight the dew,
Where blushing heaths are bowed?
Who does not love the lights of blue
'Twixt white and rosy cloud?
The head that lies on happy hills
Well knows that youth is sweet;
And joys in sunlit dusk that fills
The glens where torrents beat.

DIARMID *and* GRANIA.
O hill and moor, O wild ravine,
Your magic all to know,
With beating hearts, unheard, unseen,
With love for Lord we go!

Who drinks not with delight the dew,
Where blushing heaths are bowed? etc.

Diarmid

DUET.—"The Cherry and Rowan."

GRANIA.
    The cherry and rowan
      In colour are chief
    Of all in the forest
      At fall of the leaf.

    The fruit of the autumn
      In crimson is hung,
    That joy-notes of summer
      By birds may be sung.

DIARMID *and* GRANIA (*together*).
    Then hey for the cherry,
      The rowan, and all
    The trees that make merry
      The woods in the fall!

DIARMID.
    Sweet, Sunbeam thy name is,
      The trees thou dost burn
    To Rose, and Love's flame is
      Where'er thou dost turn.

    No winter shall sever
      The gold from our bough,
    Our love shall last ever
      As ardent as now!

DIARMID *and* GRANIA (*together*).
    Then hey for the cherry, etc

GRANIA.
    To cold winter's hunger
      Bright seasons I'll give!
    Our love shall be younger
      The longer we live.

    Your spring I will beckon
      To summer's full bloom;
    Our love shall not reckon
      Time's changes and gloom.

DIARMID AND GRANIA (*together*).
    Then hey for the cherry, etc.

FINALE

(*Distant sounds of hunting horns and hunting chorus.*)

CHORUS (*in the distance*).
  The boar follows fast where the roe-deer has led—
   Y-orla! Be-orla!
  The hind stands at gaze where the hart has his bed!
   Lua-luar! Fionn-morar!
  The hunter has drawn the long shaft to its head!
  The boar is afoot, and the arrow has sped!
   S'assa-ro! Ho-iero!

(*Both* DIARMID *and* GRANIA *stand on cliff-ledge to listen.*)

DIARMID. Old Fionn's horn! I must away!

  (*Horns sound nearer.*)

GRANIA (*in terror*).
  Oh leave her not, who for thee bears
   All love! all pride!
  Who only in thy presence cares
   What may betide!
  What woman, lone and loveless, dares
   The world so wide?

BOTH.
  O cruel fate, that sunders those
   Whose lives are one!
  We know, if parted, these will close
   Distraught—undone;
  That over them a darkness grows—
   Slow sinks their sun!

(*Horns and hunting chorus much nearer.*)

CHORUS.
  Ha! Death to the boar, and long life to the man!
   Y-orla! Be-orla!
  Whose life with his hounds and his hunting began!
   Dur-dana! Dur-dana!
  'Tis sport makes a hero, and warfare a clan!
  In peace or in fight let us be in the van!
   S'assa-ro! Ho-iero!

(*They climb back, and conceal themselves in tree.*

Diarmid

(FIONN *and his hunting train (armed with spears, bows, etc.), followed by people (men and women variously armed with scythe-blades on poles, sickles, clubs, etc.) rush on the stage tumultuously.* GRANIA *escapes up cliff-pass.* DIARMID *comes down as though to defend pass and prevent pursuit of* GRANIA, *thus facing* KING FIONN.)

FIONN (*aside*)
    Diarmid the traitor! Ah! now for vengance! curse him!

(*To* DIARMID.)
    Diarmid, see there below the boar at bay;
    Take off thy foot-gear to make climbing sure,
    And kill him!

DIARMID. King, I hear, and will obey!

(*Takes off foot-gear and goes over cliff at side of stage.* FIONN *remains at stage front. Some of the men crowd to the cliff edge looking downwards towards the fight.*)

CHORUS (*tutti*).
    "Ha! death to the boar and long life to the man,"
        Y-orla! Be-orla! etc., etc.

MEN (*at the cliff top*).
    The boar dies!

FIONN. Nay, tell him, if the boar be dead,
    To measure it with naked feet;
    Then come and tell me how the fight has sped.

MEN (*at the cliff top*).
    He maketh measurement!

(DIARMID'S *voice gives a cry of pain.*)

(*Men let down a rope, helping him; he appears at cliff-top, and is supported, wounded and sinking, to stage front, where* FIONN *has seated himself.*)

PEOPLE.   The poison bristle draws a crimson tide!
           Oh, what can aid him? What can heal such wound?

DIARMID (*to* FIONN).
           Thou hast the golden cup that heals all wounds;
           One drop suffices to quench thirst—to live!

PEOPLE, ETC.
           Give him the golden cup of healing; it hath stood
           'Twixt many a man and death. Drink from the cup!

FIONN (*rising and going to* DIARMID).
           Here is the cup, Diarmid. Yes, one drop
           Would save thee— see it flung away!
                              (*Throws cup away.*)

PEOPLE (*with horror*).
           Ah!

DIARMID.   My life ebbs so fast—give me drink from the spring;
           Remember my deeds, and thank me thou art King!

FIONN.   What good is thy life? can its fair deeds o'erpower
           The guilt of one act, and the curse of an hour?

DIARMID.   Water!—Grania!—Darkness!—Thirst!
           Without thy love I die—accurst!   (*dies.*)

PEOPLE, ETC. (*all except* FIONN).
           Woe! woe!

                    (QUICK CURTAIN)

              END OF THE OPERA

Opera in English

It is not very many years ago since German Opera was neglected in England. Indeed, music-lovers who had heard Wagner's Operas in Germany said that the stage effects were fine, but that the music was too rough and it took too long a time to listen to one of his works. Italian composers held the love of London. But in Germany native talent was encouraged. Although people there had also been educated in the belief that nothing really good was to be found save in Italian works, their national pride rebelled against such doctrine; and musicians were encouraged to set German themes to German music. As yet there has been little in Britain to encourage her musicians to attempt like feats. No trial is willingly given by the supporters of our leading Opera Houses to British works. Instead of giving a variety including such native music, the rage has been entirely to harp on the strings of selections taken entirely from the German and the Italian. Sullivan made an attempt with *Ivanhoe*, but committed the mistake of giving nothing else, and after a time the friends of English Opera found that variety was wanted, and *Ivanhoe* has not been given again. So it has been with the fine music of Stanford, and with the charming music of Hamish MacCunn. I wrote for him a "book" on

Diarmid's Celtic story, and it could only be given in the off season, and with the aid of the Moody Manners Company, who pluckily have with fair success produced Opera in English.

The excellent voice of Miss Kirby Lunn interpreted his music admirably, and the Opera was performed with success at Covent Garden, in Manchester, and in Liverpool. But there has since been no revival, and the leaders of the Opera world have wholly neglected any effort to place among their productions on the stage the things in English which have had success. No doubt the day of English Opera, in combination with German, French, and Italian, will come. It only awaits the accident of a sympathetic supporter or patrons to have a chance. The shameful robbery of any tunes written by composers and filched from them by "pirates" of music has now been stopped by Act of Parliament, and good results are sure to follow from this tardy act of justice to our own countrymen. Fashion is a capricious mistress, and will not always favour the foreigner to the exclusion of her own folk.

THE END

INDEX

Abbala, Lake, 581
Abeken, Dr., 241, 268, 360
Abercorn, Duke of, 369
Aberdeen, Lord, 228
Abyssinia, 334, 579
Acton, Sir John, 45
Adalbert, Prince, 244
Adamnan, 535, 540
Admiralty rights, 569
Agates, 452, 455, 464, 565
Airlie Gardens, 201
Airolo, 105
Albania, 259, 282
"Alberite," 429
Albert, Prince, 469
Alberta, 506, 510, 511
Algonquins, 226
Alice, Princess, 237, 248
Allan, Sir Hugh, 409
Alma, The battle of the, 15
Alps, Crossing the, 106
Amand, 309
America and the Ballot, 354
— Criticisms of, 125
— Visit to, 1866, 230 et seq.
American aboriginals, 124
— letters, 207
Amethysts, 452, 457
Andrassy, Minister, 277, 281
Anne, Queen, 200
Antigonish, 456
Anton, Prince, 249

Antonelli, 315
Apaches, 505
Apple cultivation, 427
Appleton, 233
Apponyi, Count, 277, 310
Apsley House, 199
Aray, River, 133
Archibald, Duke of Argyll, 133, 134, 194, 195
Archibald, Mr., 409
Ardencaple, 185, 190, 192
Arezzo, 328
Argyll, 134, 137, 140, 196, 199, 202, 372
— Eldest brother of, 187
— Field-Marshal, The Duke of, 6, 187
— Former Dukes of, 196, 570
Armada wrecks, 570
Arndt, German song-writer, 47 et seq.
— The spirit of, 50
Artillery, 238, 287, 359
Aschaffenburg, 237
Ascot Races in 1863, 44
Ashantee, 442
Ashburton Treaty, 447
Askaris, 586
Assiniboins, 473
Augusta, Queen, 243
Augustenburg, 359
Australian Federation, 519

Austria, 237, 238, 252
— Emperor of, 275, 280
— The Empress of, 281
Austrian costume, 277, 278
— defeat at Königgrätz, 239 et seq.
— diplomatic secrets, 255
— war with Prussia, 255
Austrians, 115, 219, 255
Awe, Loch, 132
Aytoun, 58

Baa Loch, 542, 553
Babelsberg, 246
Baden, 237, 274, 275
Baden, Grand-Duke of, 270 et seq.
Badgers, 126
Bagot, 443, 458, 463
Bahr-el-Ghazel, 579
Bailey, 231
Bailie, Mrs., 43
Bakewell, Mr., 582, 585
Balkan States, 268
Ballot, The, 353
Balmoral, 189
Bamboo, 151
Banana-bird, 152
Bancroft, 275, 492
Bank of Egypt, The Agricultural, 34
Banking, Canadian systems, 436
Bannockburn, 140
Barrett, Trial of, 383
Barry, Mr., architect of Trentham, 29
Bastiat, 424
Bath, Jamaica, 151
Batson, Mr., 435
Battleford, 468, 513
Bavaria, 237, 256, 268
Bear-trap, 453

Beaver, 452, 483, 494
Bedford, Duchess of, 200
Beech avenues, 132
Bellenden, Mary, 65
Bellerophon, H.M.S., 432
Bellinzona, 105
Belvidere, 287
Benedek, 255
Benedetti, 244, 257, 262
Bengal Government, 345
Ben More, 544, 554
Benmore, 536, 546, 558
Ben Tallagh, 543
Ben Verâgy, 527, 531
Berlin, 236, 241, 268, 357, 359
— French Embassy in, 242
— the Palace, 260
— Social life of, 242
— University of, 242
Bernstoff, 255
Beust, Count, 277, 280, 269
Bierstadt, Mr., 444
Big Mud Creek, 513
Bill, curious carpenter's, 104
Birch Creek, 514
Bird-life, California, 504
— Canada, 465, 469, 473, 482
Bird-shooting, 234
Birds in London, 201
Birtle, 513
Bishops, Austrian, 289
Bismarck, 241, 250, 251, 257, 258, 260, 273, 266, 296
— and Rome, 253
Bismarck's dogs, 252
Bistritz, 239
Blachford family, 545
Blackfeet, The, 473, 474, 479
Blackfoot Crossing, 513 et seq.
Blaine, Mr., 459, 492
Blake, Mr., 417, 437

Blake, Miss Jex-, denied admission to lectures, 79
Blidah, 162
Blockade-running from English ports, Prevention of, 45
Blomfield, Lord, 255, 276
Boar, Wild, 249
Boguslav, Prince, 249, 360
Bohemia, 238
Bokhara, 347
Bologna, 292
Bomba, 108
Bombs, Orsini, 308, 313
Bonin, General, 258
Bonomi, 187
Bow River, 516
Bowmore, 464
Bracelet, Quaint, 148
Bradford, 589
Brandenburger Thor, 242, 245
Breadalbane, Lord, 197
Bread-fruit, 151
Breech-loader, needle, 238, 240
Bright, John, 190, 344, 354, 446, 459
British Columbia, 482, 485
British East Africa, 575 *et seq.*, 580, 584, 589
Brougham, Lord, 59 *et seq.*, 218
Browning, 55 *et seq.*
Bruce, Robert the, 192, 193
Bruce, Sir F., 169
Brühl, Gräfin, 270
Brunswick, 237
Brussels Conference, 597
Buchanan, Isaac, 495
Bucovina, 268
Buffalo, 471
Bunsen, 202, 212, 228, 257, 263, 361, 363
— letters from, 218

Buol, 219
Burke, Mr., 373
Burns, 137
Bury, Lord, 347
Butrinto, Off, 285
Buzzards, 130
"Byng, Poodle," 62

Caballino, Duke of, 111
Cabinet meeting, A, 346
Cactus, Crimson, 153
Cairoli, 317
Calgary, 470, 510 *et seq*
Cambridge, 95 *et seq.*
— custom of attire, 100
— clubs, 103
— discontent with, 102
Cambridge, Duke of, 200
Camden Place, 388
Cameron, 139
Camp, In, 451
Campbell, Captain D., 545
— Clan, 133, 138, 193
— Craignish, 397
— Lady Charlotte, personal charms of, 63
— — — troubles with creditors, 66
— Lord John, 2
— Major, of Inverawe, legend of, 142
— Sir Alex., 495
— Sir Colin (afterwards Lord Clyde), 12
— — — sent to the Indian Mutiny, 16
— Thomas, the poet, 64
Campbell of Sonachan, 6
Campbeltown, 561
Canada, 170, 199
— animal life in, 473, 484
— Bismarck's interest in, 254
Canada's population, 523

Canadian Academy, 442, 447, 460
— formalities, 412 *et seq.*
— Liberals, 446
— Mounted Police, 425, 471, 513, 515, 516
— M.P.'s, 414
— Municipal representation, 503
— representatives, 441
— Royal Society, 460, 473
— Tariff, 424
Cannes, 218
Cannon, Old French, 135
Canterbury, Archbishop of, 401
Cape Breton, 454
— Blomidon, 457
Capitol, The (Washington), 171, 241, 492
Caprera, 295, 327
Capri, 109
Cardigan, Lord, 17
Cardross, 192
Cardwell, 344
Carl, Prince, 267
Carlisle, Lord, 38, 370
Carlton Terrace, 200, 227
Carlyle, elected Rector of Edinburgh, 46
Carnarvon, Lord, 349
— Lord and Lady, 497
Carpenters' shop, 191
Carriages, Early Victorian, 57
Cartwright, Mr., M.P., 338
Cascapedia River, 96, 450, 474, 492
Cashaw, 154
Castel Uovo, 111
Castle Giubeleo, 318, 325
— Howard, 385
Catholic supremacy, Roman, 256

Catholics in Austria, 256
— Powers, 256
Catholics, Roman, 342, 364, 456
Cavagnac, 212
Cavaliers, 194
Cavendish, Lord Frederick, 373
Cavour, 107 *et seq.*, 111
Celtic customs, 568
Celts, 139
Cenis, Mont, 106
Central Asia, 345
Chamois hunt, 87 *et seq.*
Champlain, 424
Chancellorsville, Forces at, 168
Chandière Rocks, 414
Charette, General, 331
Charles II., 195
Charlotte, Princess, 261
Charlottetown, 457
Charters, Captain, 368
Charters, Old family, 195
Chase, Chief Justice, 181
Chatham, Town of, 455
Chatsworth, 111
Chelsea Hospital, 227
Chindi, 582
Chinese, 486, 487, 490
Chiswick House, 74, 121, 122
Chlum, 239, 262
Church Street, 200
Churches, Attitude of the, 203
Cialdini, 259, 293, 296 *et seq.*, 303
Cities, Continental, 241
Civil War, American, 229, 368
Civita Vecchia, 292, 305, 316
Clarendon, Lord, 122
Clanwilliam's account of chamois hunt, 87 *et seq.*
Clark, Dr., 408 *et seq.*
Clerical incomes, 401, 403

Cliff dwellings, 445, 505
Clubs, 184
Clyde, The river, 190, 191, 196
Coach and Six, The (Comedy), 603
Cobden, 424
Cockburn, Chief Justice, 346
Cocoa, 151
Colorado beetle, 420
Coloredo, 317
Colfax, 178
Collingwood, 463, 464
Colquhoun, Sir James, 191
Columba, 534, 540
Columba's hymn, 540
Comitato, 322, 324
"Commoners, Fellow," Cambridge, 100
Commons, House of, 190
Comte de Paris, 368
Comus, H.M.S., 476
Concordat, 289
Confederate Grey, 165
Congo, 578
Convent trial, 346, 348, 351
Convention, September, 293, 291
Coriante, 141
Correse, 319, 321, 326
Corsica, 296, 316
Cotton-tree, 151
Courtenay, 346
Courts, Bourbon, "Tedeschi," 115
"Courts of Justice,"Negro, 155
Coventry, Lady, mobbed in the Park, 65
Cowal, 195
Crealock, Colonel, 287
Crees, 445, 473
Crispi, 300, 327, 329
Cromwell, 195
— and Jamaica, 154

Crown Prince, The, 239, 243, 254, 255, 260, 269, 358
— Princess, 243, 246, 266, 360
Crystal Palace, 76
Cuckoo Weir, Bathing in, 73
Culloden, 197
— Battle of, 134
Cul-ri-Alban, 554
Cul-ri-Erin, 554
Cumberland, Duke of, 134
Cumming, Dr., 229
Curling, 420, 422
Cutface Bank, 514
Cyphers, 194

Dagoreti, 586
Dalchenna, The village of, 19, 584
Dalhousie, Lord, 346
Dana, 232
Danish War on question of Schleswig-Holstein, 46, 270
Dante, 231, 234
Danube, 277, 289
Davis, Jefferson, 170
Dawson, Principal, 460
Deak, 203
Death Duties, 40, 42, 135
Debating Society, the Cambridge Union, 98
De Boucherville, 421
Deer, Red, 141
Deputies, Italian, 112
Derivation of names, 138, 139, 186, 507, 530
Dettingen, Grandfather's recollection of, 6
Devonshire, The old Duke, 75, 108, 384
— — interest in Sir Joseph Paxton, 76
Diarmid, 137

Diarmid (Opera), 652
Dickens, 226
Disraeli, 202, 251, 261, 373, 390, 394, 432, 459, 461, 496
Diving-bell, 137
Divining-rod, 572
"Doctored," Cambridge, 95
Dogs at Rosneath, 195
Domville, Major, 431
Douglas Forest, The, 484
Douglas, Margaret, 194
Down, Bishop of, 370
Downshire, Lord, 380
Dress of the Regency period, 60
Drummond's Bank, 242
Dublin, 368
Duc de Blacas, 503
Duckopolis, 499
Duck-shooting, 500
Dudley, Lord, 156
Dufferin, Lady, 531
— Lord, 71, 380, 390, 395, 416, 428
Dumont, Gabriel, 514
Dun of Dunaverty, 561
Dunadd, 561
Dunbarton, 192
Dunlop, 43
Dunoon, 141
Dunrobin, 198, 525
Dunsmuir, Mr., 485
Dunstaffnage, 196, 561
Durando, General, 303
Dyde, Col., 459

Earl Robert Fort, 530, 532
Earthquakes, 157, 158, 162
Eber, General, 267
Ecclesiastical Commissioners, 404
Edge of Salt Plain, 513
Edinburgh, 195

Edinburgh Academy Dinner, 351
— Duke of, 409
Edward I., 192
Egyptian calendar, 264
Ehrenbreitstein, 366
Elcho, 347
Election expenses, 351 *et seq.*
Eley, Lady, 390
Elizabeth, Letters of Queen, 7
Elk, Irish, 368
Ellesmere, Lord (also Egerton), 542
Ellice, 513, 514
Emerson, 213
Emmanuel, King Victor, 113
Endowments, Church, 202
Englishmen in Confederate Army, 168
Eorsa Island, 544
Erdödyi, Countess, 278
Esquimaux, 434
— dogs, 457
Eton, My arrival at, 68
Eugenie, Empress, 385
European Conference, 1832, 219
Evangeline, 455
Evans, Dr., 388
Evarts, 425, 435, 437, 496
Everett, 202, 212

Faido, 105
Fairfield, 139
Falcons, 130
Falkirk, 134
Family, Argyll, 199
Famine, Potato, 198
Father, My, 203
"Fatherland, The," 365
Fawcett, 351
Fenians, 363, 370, 374
Fergusson, Sir J., 395

Ferns, Tropical, 152
Fion, King, 138
Fisher dogs, 441
Fishing, 132, 546
Fishmongers' dinner, 348
Fitzgerald Family, 368
Flanders, the Count, 261
Fleet, French, Lord Hardwicke's opinion of, 101
Flodden, 193, 194
Florence, 105, 112, 291, 294, 321, 333
Florencia, The, 136
Forbes, Principal, 80
Forkenbeck, 263
Fort Carlton, 513, 514
— McLeod, 470
— Shaw, 472
— Shaw (Montana), 513 *et seq.*
Foot Point, 582
Fowler, Sir John, 582
Fox hounds, Run with, 84
France and Prussia, 270, 274
Franchi, 253
Franchise in Canada, 423, 459
Francis, Emperor of Austria, 219
Franklin's expedition, 434
Fraser River, 478, 482, 486
Frederick Charles, Prince, 244, 255
Frederick, Emperor, 246
Fredericktown, P. E. Island, 432
Free Trade, 35
Freitag, 241, 268
French Ambassador, 138
— Canadians, 421
— demands, 257
— in Mexico, 177
— intervention in Italy, 303
— soldiers, 386
— Volunteers, 294, 305

Frosinone, 316
Frosts, 511
Fry, Mrs., 198
Ftelia, Off, 283
Fuligno, 302, 322
Fundy, Bay of, 454, 457
Funeral of Emperor Frederick, 246
— Duke of Wellington, 227
Fürst of Hohenzollern-Sigmaringen, 267
Fyne, Loch, 18, 128, 132

Gabriel Dumont's Crossing, 513
Gaelic, 376, 433, 456
Gaels, 555
Galt, Sir Alexander, 447, 519
Game packing, 427
Gare, The (Gareloch), 186
Garibaldi, 114, 120, 121, 259, 267, 293, 294 *et seq.*, 297, 300, 302, 315, 323, 324, 328, 329
— Arrest of, 329
Garibaldians, 300, 308, 310, 317, 318, 319, 327
Garibaldi's visit to Stafford House, 117
Garnier, 218
Garonne, 186
Garotte robberies in London, 80
Garscube, 188
Geese, Brent, 455
Generals, American, 179 *et seq.*
Genoa, Duke of, 113
George IV., 187
Georgian Bay, 465
German Bill introduced by king, 257
— Bund, the great, 269, 272

German Chamber, 258
— Confederation, 273, 282
— education, 364
— education of Officers, and, 366
— feeling, 358
— ideals, 245
— ideas of rank, 243
— Liberal element, 269
— navy, 244
— North States, 274, 269
— Socialism, 246, 254
— South States, 256, 275, 268, 271, 360
— sovereigns, 237, 242
— titles, 243
— Trade Unionism, 263
Ghosts, 81, 83, 557
— Tennyson and, 54
Gilmore, 138
Girardin's Article, 270
Girls' education, 402
Gladstone, Mr., 43, 45, 108, 118, 122, 170, 190, 202, 337, 342, 343, 346, 348, 354, 426, 446, 476, 590
Glasgow, 192, 186
Glasgow's connection with Jamaica, 150
Glen Clachig, 554, 558
Glenmore, 558
Glenshira, 146
Gloucester, Duchess of, 200
— Duke of, 201
Glover, Sir John and Lady, 441
Gneist, 240
Goldfinches, 446
Golf at St. Andrews, 86
Golspie, 422
Gordon, Mr., 543
Gorringe's house, 536
Gortschakoff, 251

Government House, British Columbia, 485
— of blacks, 151
— of Ireland, 375 *et seq.*
Gower family, The, 27, 39, 530
— Lord, 250
Graburne, Corporal, 471
Grainia, Queen, 138
Grande Pré, 455
Grant, Colonel, 145
— Dr., 422
— General, 177, 492
Granville, Lord, 348, 350
Grape, cultivation, 427
Grasselini, Cardinal, 310
Graves, Ancient, 551
Greece, 344
Greek, Dislike for, 96
Gregory XVI., 219
Gribun, 547, 551
Grosbeak, 442
Grosvenor, Lord, 201
Grouse, 453
Grunewald, 249
Guelph, 495
Guelphs, The, 530
Guillotine, Scottish, 194
Guizot, 212
Gulf Stream, 526
Gunning family, 372
Gzowski, Colonel, 426, 458

Halifax, 409, 463
Hall, Captain, 434
— Sydney, Mr., 417, 463
Halt, 513
Hamilton, 495
— Duke of, 192
— Place, 199, 200
Hamish, Dr., 463, 469
Hammond, 349

Hanover, 237
— King of, 272, 274
— Separatist and Particularist feeling, 253
Hanoverian Society, 360
Harbord, 418, 443
Harcourt, Vernon, 590, 594
Hardinge, Lord, 349
Hardman, 318
Hardwicke, Lord, Visit to, 101
Hares, 132
Hart, Sir R., 145
Hartington, 168, 446
Hawks, The, 72, 131
Hay, Lord Wm., 347
Heathcote, Sir William, 349
Hebrides, 539, 456
Herat, 349
Herchmer, Captain, 513
Hereditary Justice of Scotland, 140
Herrenhausen, 274
Herring, 129
Herons, 453
Hesse Darmstadt, 237
High Commissioners (Colonial), 519
High River, 514
High Street, Eton, 73
Highclere, 349
Highland Brigade in Crimea, 13
— dress, 113
— Prophecy, 147
— stories, 556
Highlander, The, 127, 131, 197, 198, 401, 433, 455, 456, 463, 497, 555
Highlands, 530
Hill, Sir Clement, 598
Hinterland, The, 591
Hodgkinson, Captain, 581
Hohenlohe, 268

Hohenthal, Gräfinn, 261
Hohenzollern, 269
Holland Park, 200
Holmes, Oliver Wendell, 54, 232
— Richard, 335
Holyrood Palace, Lady Charlotte's "sanctuary" in, 67
Home Rule, 375, 378
— Rule Bill, 203
Homer, 231
Hood, 180
Horner, Captain, 345
Hosmer, Miss, 310
Hotel de l'Europe, 307
— Dieu, 462
Houghton, Lord, 57
Howard, General, 182, 475
Hudson Bay Company, 468
Hudson, Sir James, 291
Hudson Straits, 460
Humbert, King, 333
— Funeral of, 335
Humboldt, 513
Humming-bird, 152
Hungarian constitution, 289
— uniforms, 279
Hungary, 259, 275, 287

Illustrated London News, 385
"Imperial" beard, 388
Imperial Defence, 502
— Federation, 518 *et seq.*
"Impressions of America," 225
Inchkenneth, 548
India Office, 344, 346, 357
Indian Council, 466
Indians, 445
Inglefield, Admiral Sir E., 411, 434
Insurrection in Jamaica, 150

684 Index

Inveraray, 123, 130, 134, 142, 261, 441, 457, 479, 602
Iona, 533, 536 *et seq.*, 548
Ireland 341, 361, 364, 368, 372, 383, 459, 461
Irish Bill, 366
— Church, 140, 354, 356, 538
— land question, 378 *et seq.*
— wit, 380 *et seq.*, 383
Irrigations, 344
Irvine, Colonel, 516
Islay, 463, 497
Italian Alliance with Prussia, 259
— Central Committee, 301, 303
— emigration, 334
— Question, 219
— troops, 294, 322
Italy, King of, 293, 332
— — and Garibaldi, 301

Jacobites, 134, 196
Jahde, 358
Jamaica, 149 *et seq.*
Japanese, 96
Jasper, 452
Jefferson City, 506
Jenkyns, M.P., 202
Jenner, Sir William, 189
Jesuit, Ultramontane party, 256
Joass, Mr., 525
Johnson, Dr., 548
— Joe, 179
— Judge, 460
— Mr., 164, 169
Joly, Mr., 421
Juba River, 334, 577, 581, 582

Kaffa, 581
Kaiser, The, 255
Kamloops, 481
Kampalla, 580
Kansas, 506
Kanzler, 315, 325
Karl, Prince Frederick, 239
Karolyi, Madame, 277
Kearsarge, The, 435
Keepers, Highland, 127
Kelp-weed, 486
Kelvin, 591
Kemball, Sir Arnold, 597
Kenia, 577
Kenmore, 124
Kensington High Street, 207
Kent, Colonel, 516
Kent, Duchess of, ball given by, 69
Kestrel, 130
Khartoum, 579
Kiel, 561
Kildare, Lord, 368
Kilkea, 369
Kilindini, 601
Kimberley, 350
Kingsley, 98
Kingston, 497
Kingston, Jamaica, 149
— earthquake, 158
Kintyre, 196, 560
Kismayu, 581, 582, 596
Kites, 130
Kleinsky, 267
Knock House, 544, 553, 558
Königgrätz, 239, 258, 262
Kossuth's brother, 278
Kriegschule, 366

Lacaita, Italian Deputy, 108, 112
Lake Superior, 463
Land legislation, 361
— tenure in Ireland, 370
Landlord's compensation, 379

Index

Landseer, 20 et seq.
— facsimile of letter from, 23
Langensalza, 237
Lang's, Andrew, connection with St. Andrews, 81
Lansdowne, Lord, Regency dress of, 61
La Marmora, General, 112
Lamartine, 212
Lamont, M.P., 347
Lateran, 319
Lathe, 189
Lawrence, Sir John, 355
"Lays of Ancient Rome," The, 201
Lee, General, 164 et seq.
— General Curtis, 164
— — Hugh, 164
Leeds, 440
Legion of Antibes, 305, 315, 320
Lennox (Leven-ax), The country of, 192
— Duke of, 193
Leopold, Prince, 450
Lepsius, 240, 264
Leslie, 195
Letellier, Lieut.-Governor, 416, 420
Letter to Duchess of Argyll, 218, 224
Letters, Mother's, 202
Lexington, 162
Lincoln, Mrs., 235
Lincoln, Son of, 492
Lismore, 509
Littleton, Colonel, 410
Livings in gift of Argyll, 203
Loch Awe, 138
Loch, Lord, 36
— — Grandfather of, 529
Loftus, Lord Augustus, 244, 255, 359, 360

Logan, 181
Lombardy, 107, 219
Londonderry, Lord, 380
Londonderry Mine, 457
Longfellow, 230
— and the beggars, 234
— his gift to Tennyson, 51, 232; letter to Duchess of Argyll, 224
Long, Loch, 186
Long Point, 498
— Thatch, 152
Longmore, John, 575
Lord Steward, The, 187
Lords, House of, 197
Lorne, The Pass of, 138, 194, 196
Lorne's, Lord, pamphlet, 197
Los Angeles, 478, 490
Louis, Prince of Hesse, 237
Louisburg, 455
Louise, Princess, 390
Lowe, 202, 349, 350, 426, 446
Lowell, 233
Lowlander, The, 128
Lowther, Mr. William, 244, 283
Lucca, 264
Lugard, Sir Edward, 577, 587, 599

Mabinogion books, 230
Macaulay, 154, 201
MacCunn, Hamish, 673
MacDonald, Sir J., 410, 413, 416, 447, 458, 459, 461, 495
Macdonald, 586
Macdonalds, 134, 136
MacDougal, Sir Patrick, 502
Macgregor, Dr., 157, 462, 468, 472
Machakos, 586
Machrihanish, 561

Mackay family, 528
Mackenzie, Mr. G., 590, 596
Mackinnon, Sir William, 580, 600
Mackinnon's Cave, 549
Macleod, 513, 516
MacLeod, Dr. Norman, 399
MacNab, Sir A., 495
MacNivan, 143
Magazine, the University, 81
Magdalen Island, 460
Maggiore, 106
Maguire, 357
Malakoff, French success in taking the, 14
Malcolm, Mr., 156
Mamore (Big Pass), 196
Mandeville, 160
Mango, 151
Mangroves, 149
Manteufel, General, 258
Marlborough Club, 356
Marmora, General La, 259, 298
Marriage, 390
Mars-la-Tour, 236, 397
Marten in Highlands, 126
Masai, 577, 601
Masella, 253
Massari, 112
Masson, M., 421
Mathilda, Archduchess, 278
Mau Plateau, 579
Maximilian, Emperor, 275
Maxwell, 380
Mayo, Lord, 65, 347, 349, 363, 372; assassination of, 373
McClellan, 492
McDonalds, The, 194
McDowell, General, 476
McKellar, 495
McNair, 441
McNeill, 445
Medici, 291

Menabrea, 259, 299, 324
Menotti Garibaldi, 324, 331
Mentana, fight at, 326
Merlin, 131
Merrivale, 346
Mexican horsemanship, 491
Mexico, New, 505
Meyer, Carl, 264
Mhor, Colin, 138
Middleton, General, 515
Miev, 158
Milbank, Jamaica, 151
Millais' love of sport, 18
Milman, Dean, 15
Milne, Professor, 158
Mina, 253
Minie, Rifle used in the Crimea, 15
Minto, Lord, 349
Mirage at Inveraray, 145
Mirimichi, 454
Missionaries, 539
Mitchell, Mr., 154
"Moabite," 248
Modane, Stay at, 106
Moil, 56
Moltke, 241, 247, 257, 258, 260
Mombasa, 576, 580, 595
Moncton, 430
Monmouth, 195
Monoliths, 564
Montana, 516
Monte Cassino, 338
— Cittorio, 112
— Rotondo, 315, 322, 326
Monterey, 488
Montezuma, 505
Montreal, 450
Moose, 417, 443, 496
Moreland, Jamaica, 154
Moreton, 410
Mormons, 508 *et seq.*

Morris, Sir D., 158
— William, 57
Mother, My, 197
Mother's sisters, My, 201
Motley, Mr., 276
Mount Baker, 457
Musk-rat, 466
Mwanga, 577, 587, 594

Nachod, 238, 255
Names, Negro, 157, 166, 170
Nanaimo, 487
Napier of Magdala, 335
Naples, Court of, 110
Napoleon I., 459
— Louis, The Emperor, 257, 293, 295, 385
— speech of, 262
Naworth Castle, 42
Neale, Countess, 359
Negroes, 166, 170
Nerola, 509
Nevada, 476
New Brunswick, 421, 429
— Palace, The, 246
Newab Nazim of Moorshedabad, 357
Nicholsburg, 262
Niger, 578
Night-blowing Cereus, 153
Nile, 578, 580
Nomenclature in Jamaica, 154
Nordenei, 237, 360
Norfolk, Duke of, 342
Norman settlers in Ireland, 372
North American Indians, 131, 178, 448, 459, 464, 468, 470, 478, 486, 514
Nyanza, 583

Oban, 196

O'Brian, Mr., 447
O'Donoghue, 357
O'Duin, 138
O'Farrell, 356
Ofen, 277
Okanagan, 484
Omaha, 475
O'Neal, Miss, afterwards Lady Becher, 62
Ontario, 467
— self-government, 459
Opah, 128
Opera, English, 673
Orange, William of, 134
Orbitello, 305
Oriola, Gräfinn, 260
Orte, 294
Ottawa, 437, 470, 473, 497, 503, 515
— Parliament Buildings, 414
Otter chase, 122
Ottway, 144
Oubril, 244, 250
Owen, Professor, lectures attended by Prince Consort, 61
Owls, 442

Pacific Railway, 446, 458, 479, 497
Paddle steamer, 106
Pagania, Off, 283
Paget, 287, 304
Pahlen, Count, 38
Pains and Penalties Bill, 357
Palfrey, 230
Palmerston, Lord, Reception at Edinburgh of, 86
Papal States, 107, 120, 294, 297, 321, 331
—— subscriptions for, 292
— troops, 294, 311 *et seq.*, 315, 325

Papalini, The, 303, 318, 326
Pardubitz, 240
Parioli Hills, 317
Paris, Captain, 368
Park Lane, 199, 200
Parliament buildings, Ottawa, 414
Parliament, Italian, 107, 112
Parrots, 152
Partridge, 453
Passaglia, 111
Paton, Herr, 361, 363
Paul, 138
Paxton, Sir Joseph, 76
Pelissier, General, 386
Pentland, Mr., 310
Pepper plant, 153
Peregrine, 130
Pereira, 134, 351, 571
Persian army, 349
Pesth, 275
Petersburg, Retreat from, 167
Peton River, 514
Philippe, Louis, 212
Piazza de Popolo, 319
Piccadilly, 199
Pictou, 432, 456
Pierpont, 492
Pimento, 151
Pincian gate, 319
Pio IX., 219, 289, 300, 305
Pitti Palace, 333
Poerio, 111
Pole-cats, 126
Poles, 359, 363
Politicians, English and American, 439
Politics, American, 170, 165 et seq., 176 et seq., 181, 202, 207
— Italian, 218, 296
Ponderosa Forest, The, 485
Pope, The, 120, 339, 457

Porcupines, 454
Porridge, Virtues of, 189
Portal 589, 592
Port Ella, 513
— Florence, 601
— Royal, 150
— Sudan, 578
Porter, Admiral, 492
Potato famine, 528
Potentates, The, 73
Potsdam, 248, 269, 360
"Pound-maker," 515
Prague Treaty, 271, 274
Prairie, 507, 512
Prater, The, 287
Presbyterian Church, The, 202, 355, 398
Prim, 327
Prince Albert, 469
— Adalbert, 244
— Anton, 249
— Boguslav, 249
— Carl, 267
— Consort, 397
— Crown, 239, 243, 247, 260, 269, 358
— Frederick Charles, 244
— Gortschakoff, 251
— Henry, 246
— of Wales (1871), 374
— — Festivities for marriage of, 85
— Solkofski, 359
— Wilhelm, 249, 263, 270, 360
Princess Alice, 237, 248
— Charlotte, 261
— Crown, 243, 246, 360
— Royal, 246, 247, 260
Pringle, Capt., 595
Protection, 377, 523
Protestant Church, The, 203
Provost of Eton, Burial of the, 70

Index

Prussia, The King and Queen of, 39, 248, 261
Prussian Army, 236, 275
— society, 237
Ptarmigan, 132

Qu'appelle, 513, 514
— River, 465, 467, 513
Quebec, 450, 496
Queen and Prince Albert: dance at Frogmore, 69
Queen Anne's Bounty, 405
— Victoria, 187, 262, 342
— — and Canada, 396
— — and Emperor Louis Napoleon, 385
— — and Scotland, 367
— — and Sir John Lawrence, 355
— — Fund, 401
— Visit to, from Eton, 68
Queen Victoria's letter to Mrs. Lincoln, 235
— — visit to Inveraray, 2

Radical Party, 366
— — (America), 165,
Radziwill, 249, 359, 360, 364
Railway, British East Africa, 583
— Cape to Cairo, 577
Ranger, Deputy, of Hyde Park, 61
Ranke, 240, 266
Rapids City, 513
Ratazzi, 292, 293, 296, 298, 324
Raumer, 273
Rawlinson, 347
Reception Hall, 169
Reconstruction Committee, 165, 167
Red Deer River, 515

Red merganser, 452
— Prince, The, 238, 244
Reeves, H., 345
Reform Bill, 199, 219, 261
— — riots, 199
Regency period, 59
Reichstag, 359
Rent Banks, 363
Rents, Payment of old, 141
Repression of Crime Bill, 350
Republicans, French, 385
Revolution, French, 212
Reynaud, 218
Reynolds, Sir Joshua, the fading of his carmines, 20
Rhine Provinces, 362, 366
Rhodes, Cecil, 577, 593
Ricciotti Garibaldi, 324, 328, 331
Richmond, Sir W., 338
Richmond, U.S.A., 181
Rifle shooting, 99, 102
Rimont, 219
Rio Grande, Jamaica, 151
Ritchie, Mr., 537
Rob Roy's house, 142
Roman vacillation, 314
Rome, 219, 294, 296, 305, 311, 336
— Arrival of French in, 319
— Confiscation of arms, 308
— Fighting in, 303, 307
Roon, 257, 258, 260
Rosetta-stone, 264
Rosneath, 191, 192, 193, 195, 196, 437, 440, 495
— Castle, 187 et seq.
— The climate of, 8, 185
Ross of Mull, 457, 539
Rosslyn, 347
Roumania, 280
Roumanian dishonesty, 267
Roundheads, 194

Rudini, Marquis, 112
Ruger, General, 472
Russell, Dr., 276
— Lord John, 122, 170
— Odo, 309
Russia, 252, 349
— German Alliance with, 251
— Necessity of war with, 228, 386
Russian unscrupulousness in diplomacy, 255
Ryan, Mr., 459

Sadowa, 287
"Sagas" of Longfellow, 230
St. Andrews, 78
— Departure from, 86
— Life at, 84
— Arnaud, General, 386
— Gothard, 105
— Hilaire, R. de, 218
— Hubert's Day, 249
— John's, New Brunswick, 432
— Louis, 145
Salisbury, 251, 254, 349, 440, 588
Salmon, 478, 482
Salt duties, 344
— Lake City, 508
Sanda, 561
Sandpiper, 452
San Francisco, 476, 490
Sans Souci, 246, 358
Santa Barbara, 488
— Fé, 505
Sardinia, 386
— King of, 219
Sarolta, 264
Sarrelouis, Cession of, 257
— conferences, 267
Saskatchewan, 468, 513 *et seq.*, 576

Savoy, House of, 112, 114, 334
Saxon primogeniture, 362
Saxony, 258
Schleinitz, 254, 361
Schloss Engers, 365
— Coburg, 396
Schluster, 309, 314
Schofield, 180
Scholastica, Sister, 349 (also Miss Sawin), 351
Scholfield, General, 488
Schuvaloff, 251
Scone, 561
Scotch education 364
— Education Bill, 350, 355
Scotland, Church of, 401
Scott's novels, 250
Seals, 544 *et seq.*
Sea-serpent, 525
Sechenyi, Count, 277
Seckendorff, 360
Seely, 115
Selborne, Lord, 401
Sepoy army, 345
"Serotine," 233
Sersistori Barracks, 317
Servant, Mulatto, 157
Severn, Mr., 309
Seward, 168, 170
— Murderous attack on, 172 *et seq.*
— Frederick, 170
Shadiac, 432, 435
Shaftesbury, Lord, 119, 198
Shairp, Professor, 393
— — Visit with, to Magus Muir, 84
Shairp's, Professor, Ghost story, 83
Shambas, 589
Sharks, 153
Sharpsburg, Forces at, 167

Index

Shaw Lefevre, 590
Shea, 308
Sheep, 141
Shells, 489
Shere Ali, 345
Sheridan, 179
Sheriffmuir, Battle of, 196
Sherman, General, 179, 183, 491
Shira, River, 133
Shoal Lake, 513
Shuswap Lakes, 482 et seq.
Sicily, 291
Simmons, Sir Lintorn, 339
Simplon, 106
Sioux, 473
Sirius, H.M.S., 408
Sitting Bull, 424 et seq., 448
Skalitz, 238
Skating at Trentham, 35
Skeena River, 481
Skinner, Mr., 422
Slave-running, 584, 599
Sleeping fever, 599
Sligo, 370
Small holdings, 361
Smith, Alexander, 231
— Sir Harry, 11
Smithsonian Institute, 473
Snakes, 443
Soapstone, 565
Socialism, 246, 254
Soldiers, American, 184
Solkofski, Prince, 359
Sonachan, Mr. Campbell of, 6
Soult at Stafford House, 10
Sounding Lake, 514
South, Sir James, 201
Southend, 561
Southern States, 181
Soyer, The cook, 386
Spain, 502
Spanish Armada, 135

Spanish Town, 157
Spencer, Lord, 372
Sport, 132, 282, 285, 474, 487, 482, 492, 500, 553, 560
Staffa, 550
Stafford House, 121, 227
—— Garibaldi's visit to, 116
—— Social life at, 10, 43, 113, 199, 200
Stanley, 597
— Dean, 393
— Lord, 309
State trial, Last, 140
Steele, Colonel, 513
Stephenson, Mr., and the Regency dress, 60
— Mrs., 459
Stevens, Thadeus, 167
Stewart, 140
— Sir Donald, 583
Stockmar, 241, 264
Stone of Destiny, 561
Stones, carved, 545
Stonor, Mgr., 310, 315, 351
Storks, Sir Henry, 151
Story, Mr., 310, 492
Stranraer, 526
Strathcona, Lord, 519
Stuart party, 133, 194, 196
Stumm, Lieut., 304, 315
Sugar-cane, 154
Sugar plantations, 150
Sumner, 168, 170, 176, 202, 224, 235
Surrender of Church patronage, 203
Sutherland, Countess of, 528
Sutherland, Harriett, Duchess of, 39 et seq., 116, 528
— The Duke of, 10, 42, 199, 200, 325
— Emigration from, 529

Swinburne, 55, 231
Sydney, Cape Breton, 456

Tabley, Lord de, 346
Talbot, Gerald, 365
Taylor, Fred, water-colour painter, 22
Taylor's play, 356
Taymouth, 197
Tennyson, 50 et seq., 86, 231
Thiergarten, 249
Thomas, 180
Thompson River, 480 et seq.
Thornton, Sir Edward, 419, 429
Thunder Island, 463
Ticonderoga, 144
Tilley, Sir Leonard, 436
Tinto, Jacque, 306
Tivoli, 325
Tobermory, 571
Tocquevill, 218
Tories, 118, 197, 346
Toronto, 436, 496
— Club, 495
Tosti, Padre, 337
Town, submerged, 150
Trastavere, 307
Trawl-netting, Loch Fyne, 129
Treaty of Washington, 435
Trench, Dean, Verses of, 15
Trent, The river, Pollution of, 35
Trentham, Childhood at, 28
— Christmas at, 37
— Offered to County Council, 35
— Old customs at, 33
Trevelyan, 366
Tribal organisation, 139

Trinity cup, Won the (rifle-shooting), 99
Trinity Hall, Cambridge, 96
Trout, 452
Troutbeck, Canon, 401
Tucker, Bishop, 598, 599
Tuileries, 387
Tupper, Mr., 410
— Sir C., 519
Turin, 107, 300, 304, 323
Turks, 283
Tutor's fees at Eton, 69
Twining, 595
Tyree, 457, 463, 539

Uganda, 579, 588, 592, 595, 598
— financial difficulties, 588, 590
— railway, 598
Ulva, 544
Union, The, 166
United States, 207
Ure, boat accident, 345
Usedom, 301, 304

Vancouver, 477, 485
Van Luppen, 444
Varignano, 331
Vatican, 339
Vere district, Jamaica, 154, 161
Versailles, 247
Viceregal Lodge, 374
Victor Emmanuel, 333
Victoria, British Columbia, 482
Vienna, 240, 259, 276, 287
Villetri, 316
Vintimiglia, 111
Viterbo, 316
Volunteer artillery uniform, 260

Volunteer corps, Cambridge, 102
— force, 347
Volunteers, French, 294, 305
— Garibaldi's, 116
— Government encouragement, 324
— Italian, 297, 298, 326, 330
von Bunsen, George, 228, 257, 263, 361, 363
von Paton, 361
von Roon, 257, 258, 260
von Wright, General, 236
Vulture, 153

Wagner's operas, 673
Walcheren, 189
Walker, 360
Wallace, the patriot, 192
Walpole, Horace, 65
Walrus tusks, 460
War between France and Germany, 249, 270
Washington, 241
— College, 164
— Visit to, 168 *et seq.*, 491
Water, Dr., 158
Water-snakes, 150
Way-wa-sa-ka-po, 467
Weald of Kent, 455
Welby, Sir Reginald, 586
Wellington, The Duke of, 9, 199, 227
— meets Soult, 10

Wenzel, The converted musket, 287
Werndel rifle, 288
West Indies, Resolve to visit, 98
Westminster, Duke of, 201
Whales, 128
Whately, Archbishop, 370
Whigs, 196, 197, 386
White House, 169, 491
Whittier, 234
Wickham, General, 164
Wilhelm, Prince, 249, 263, 270, 360
Wilhelmstrasse, 241, 249
William, Emperor of Germany, 246, 251, 268
Willow Creek, 514
Wilson, Professor, 436
Windhorst, 360, 361
Winnipeg, 472
Winton, Colonel de, 373
— Sir Francis de, 589
Wolfe, 456
Wordsworth, Visit to, 49
Wright, General, 236

York, Duke of, 137
Young, Brigham, 509
Yuccas, 154

Zambesi, 581
Zanzibar, 590
— Sultan of, 596

Lightning Source UK Ltd.
Milton Keynes UK
UKHW05f2120190918
329193UK00003B/42/P